CONTEMPORARY ART

FROM CRESCENT MOON PUBLISHING

The Art of Andy Goldsworthy
by William Malpas

The Art of Andy Goldsworthy
by William Malpas

Andy Goldsworthy: Touching Nature
by William Malpas

The Art of Richard Long
by William Malpas

Constantin Brancusi: Sculpting the Essence of Things
by James Pearson

Alison Wilding: The Embrace of Sculpture
by Susan Quinnell

Eric Gill: Nuptials of God
by Anthony Hoyland

The Erotic Object: Sexuality in Sculpture From Prehistory to the Present Day
by Susan Quinnell

Minimal Art and Artists in the 1960s and After
by Laura Garrard

Land Art: A Complete Guide to Landscape, Environmental, Earthworks, Nature, Sculpture and Installation Art
by William Malpas

Andy Goldsworthy In Close-Up
by William Malpas

Land Art In Close-Up
by William Malpas

Colorfield Painting: Minimal, Cool, Hard Edge, Serial and Post-Painterly Abstract Art From the Sixties to the Present
by Laura Garrard

Mark Rothko: The Art of Transcendence
by Julia Davis

Jasper Johns
by L.M. Poole

Brice Marden
by Laura Garrard

Frank Stella: American Abstract Artist
by James Pearson

Sacred Gardens: The Garden in Myth, Religion and Art
by Jeremy Robinson

Sex in Art: Pornography and Pleasure in Painting and Sculpture
by Cassidy Hughes

Richard Long

Pocket Guide

William Malpas

Crescent Moon Publishing

CRESCENT MOON PUBLISHING
P.O. Box 393,
Maidstone,
Kent, ME14 5XU,
United Kingdom

First published 2008. Second edition 2011.
© William Malpas 2008, 2011.

Printed and bound in the U.S.A.
Set in Helvetica Neue Condensed 9 on 11pt, Helvetica,
and Gill Sans.
Designed by Radiance Graphics.

The right of William Malpas to be identified as the author of
Richard Long has been asserted generally in accordance with
sections 77 and 78 of the Copyright, Designs and Patents Act
1988.

All rights reserved. No part of this book may be reprinted or
reproduced, stored in a retrieval system, or transmitted, in any
form or by any means, electronic, mechanical, photocopying,
recording or otherwise, without permission from the publisher.

British Library Cataloguing in Publication data

Malpas, William
Richard Long: Pocket Guide (Sculptors Series)
1. Long, Richard, 1945- – Criticism and interpretation
2. Sculpture, Modern – 20th century
3. Sculpture, Modern – 20th century – Great Britain
I. Title

709.2

ISBN 9781861713308

Contents

Acknowledgements 6
Abbreviations 7
Illustrations 9
Introduction 11

1 Sculpture in the Contemporary Era   14
2 Sculpture and Gender   21
3 Spirit and Matter: Aspects of Land Art   24
4 Richard Long and Other Land Artists   55
5 Richard Long and Hamish Fulton   63
6 Richard Long: The Art of Walking   69
7 Circles, Lines, Rows, Splashes and Other Forms in Richard Long's Art   119
8 Idea/ Text/ Desire: Textworks   149
9 From Photography to Installations   177
10 'A Place of Regeneration': Dartmoor   187
11 Walking As Ecstasy   195

Illustrations 205
Notes 227
Bibliography 236

Acknowledgements

Thanks to Anthony d'Offay Gallery, London; Sperone Westwater, New York; Verlag der Buch-handlung Walther König, Köln; Thames & Hudson, London; Coracle Press, London; Karsten Schubert, London; Konrad Fischer Galerie, Düsseldorf; Hayward Gallery, London; MW Press, Noordwijk, Holland; Musée d'Art Moderne de la Ville de Paris; Center for Contemporary Arts, Santa Fe, New Mexico; Phaidon Press, London; Tate Gallery, London; Tate Publishing.

Photographs by Jeremy Robinson.

Poetry quotations: University of California Press, Berkeley. Routledge, London. Methuen, London. Faber & Faber, London.

Abbreviations

RICHARD LONG

IC 1/2	*Richard Long: In Conversation*, Parts 1 & 2
FS	*Five, Six, Pick Up Sticks*
OW	*Old World New World*
WC	*Walking in Circles*
MW	*Mountains and Water*
SF	*An Interview with Richard Long*, 1994
RC	*An Interview with Richard Long*, by R. Cork
RL	*Richard Long*, text by R. Fuchs, 1986
WAF	*Words After the Fact*
FC	*Fragments of a Conversation I-VI*
GL	Interview with G. Lobacheff
1994b	*No Where*, interview, 1994
1995a	"Question For Richard Long", 1995
WL	*Richard Long: Walking the Line*
SS	interview, *Stepping Stones*
2003a	"I am just passing through the world", interview, 2003
2004b	"Still walking, after all these years", interview, 2004

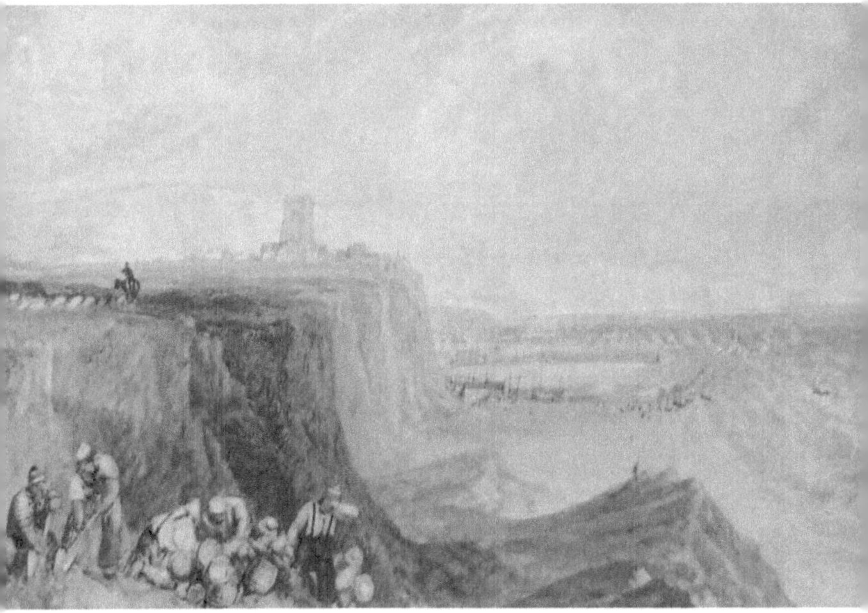

This page and over: examples of the landscape painting tradition.
J.M.W. Turner, watercolours of Folkestone (above) and Bridport (below).

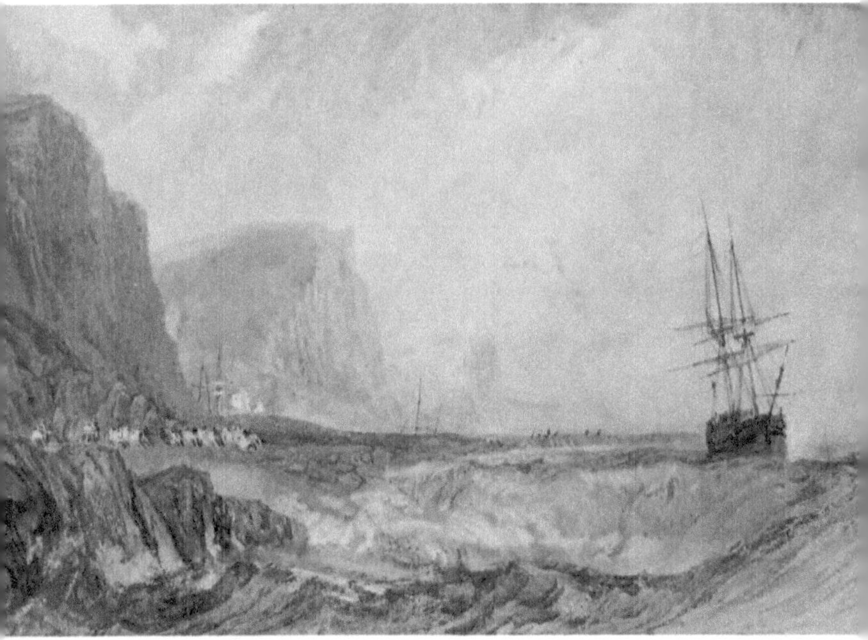

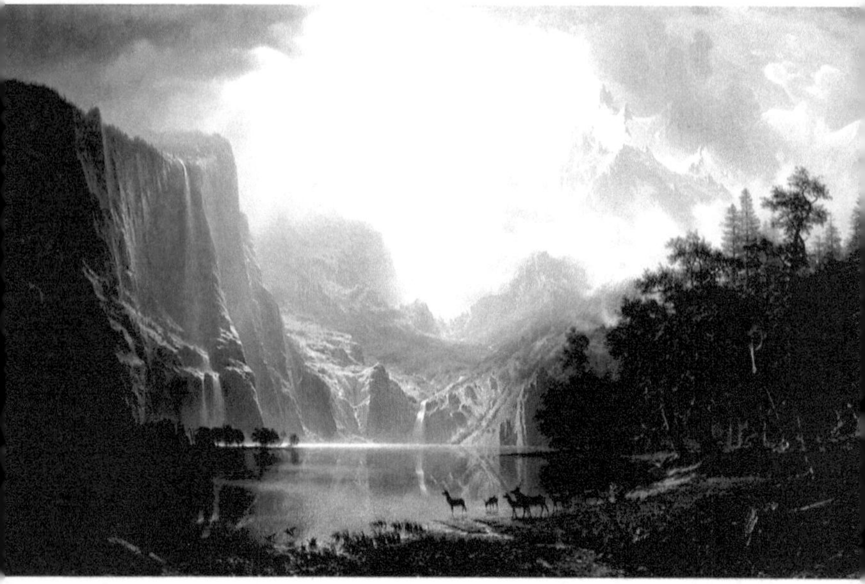

Albert Bierstadt, Among the Sierra Nevada, California, 1868 (above).
Thomas Cole, Indian Sacrifice, 1826 (below).

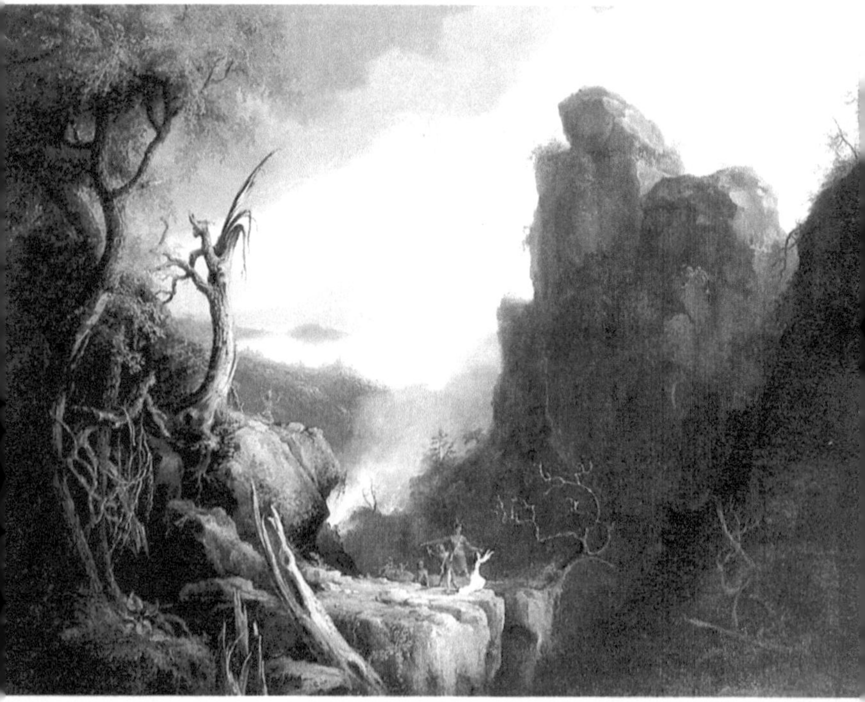

Introduction

This study looks at a living, contemporary artist, Richard Long. It uses some of the material in an earlier monograph on Richard Long (1995 and 1998), and my companion books on Andy Goldsworthy (1995, 1998, 2004) and land and environmental art (1996, 1998 and 2004).[1]

Before the chapters on Richard Long I consider topics such as contemporary and postwar art and sculpture; Long's contemporaries, including fellow British sculptors; and land art. Throughout the study I make comparisons between Long and land artists such as Andy Goldsworthy, Hamish Fulton and David Nash, similar artists, and I discuss their differences as well as their similarities. The artist closest to Long in many respects, is Fulton.

Richard Long is sometimes termed a 'Romantic' sculptor, and part of this book relates his art to British Romanticism, as found in the literature of William Wordsworth, Percy Bysshe Shelley, John Keats and others, and the British landscape tradition, as in J.M.W. Turner, John Constable, Thomas Girtin and other landscape painters. Aspects of British Romantic culture in 20th century and 21st century art also considered (such as the 'New Ruralists', 'New Romantics', 'New Arcadians' and 'Neo-Romantics'). I also explore some of the aspects of Romantic culture in Europe as well as Britain.

In the course of this book I make references to Richard Long's contemporary British sculptors (Tony Cragg, Bill Woodrow, David Nash, Barry Flanagan, Alison Wilding,

Shirazeh Houshiary, Richard Wentworth, Boyd Webb, Hamish Fulton, Stephen Cox, Philip King, Anthony Caro, Tim Head, William Tucker, Anish Kapoor, Anthony Gormley, David Mach, Peter Randall-Page, Nicholas Pope and Gilbert & George). I realize that much more could, and should, be said about these artists and their relation to Richard Long's art. Of those artists, I discuss mainly the ones that have most affinities with Long's art, such as Hamish Fulton, first and foremost, and David Nash, Chris Drury, Andy Goldsworthy, Tony Cragg and Alison Wilding).

Further chapters include: one on women, feminist, body art and performance sculptors, as a comparison with Long's art, which has a strong component of performance (even if it's nearly always private). Also, a consideration of gendered sculpture and art. In the chapter on Minimal, Conceptual, Process and other 1960s and post-1960s art and artists, I'm interested in the artists (primarily European and American) who have most in common with Richard Long's art: the great Minimal and land artists, such as Donald Judd, Robert Morris, Carl Andre, Sol LeWitt, Dennis Oppenheim, James Turrell and Robert Ryman, and the important Conceptual artists, such as Hans Haacke, Bruce Nauman, Yves Klein and Lawrence Weiner.

The 'new British sculpture' and 'New Generation' of the 1960s are also discussed (Long was part of this culture, although he soon moved out into the international scene in the 1970s). The 'Young British Artists', 'Brit-art', *Sensation* and *Freeze* crowd of the Nineties and after are only noted in passing: Tracey Emin, Damien Hirst, Mark Wallinger, Sarah Lucas, the Chapmans, etc. Long's art is diametrically opposed to the kind of art of the YBAs and Brit-artists, not least in its determined attention-seeking, its cultivation of celebrity and stars, its love of camp, ironic, playful, insincere poses, and its emphasis on the immediate and the easily digested.

The chapter on the most celebrated works of land artists (mainly in the US and Europe) is probably the most pertinent to an exploration of Long's art. No book on Richard Long's *œuvre* would be complete without references to Robert Smithson (still probably the most revered of all land artists), Walter de Maria, Michael Heizer, Alice Aycock, Mary Miss, Nancy Holt, Dennis Oppenheim, Christo and James Turrell. Among British land artists – Goldsworthy, Nash, Fulton, Drury, Harris, Cooper, Martin – Long is among the most famous and perhaps the most important (at least in the international frame).

When it comes to performance art – an area Richard Log's art is related to – the field is vast. Performance, live art, happenings and action art has many links with land, environmental, nature and installation art. There isn't space here to consider them all (there are plenty of other studies). By comparison with most of the performance, political, Conceptual, body, action, happening and installation artists in the era from the Fifties onwards, Richard Long is distinctly mellow and calm and unobtrusive. But his art remains inspiring, and some of the reasons for its enduring spirit are explored in this book.

William Malpas. London, England

1

Sculpture in the Contemporary Era

Richard Long is a land artist and sculptor (sometimes he's also called an earth artist, earthworks artist, nature artist, landscape artist or environmental artist. I should note that the term 'land art' is used here as a shorthand to refer to many kinds of art, including landscape art, earth art, earthworks, nature art, art and nature art, green or ecological art, and installations. In a way, almost all major contemporary art made nowadays is some kind of 'installation art').

Richard Long works with and in the natural world, but also with and within the highly sophisticated, artificial and human-made world of art and culture. 'I too wanted to make nature the subject of my work,' Long explained of his early work, 'but in new ways. I started working outside using natural materials like grass and water, and this evolved into the idea of making a sculpture by walking'. Long's sculpture developed out of late modernism, High Modernism, Minimal art, Process art, Conceptual art and, in particular, the culture of 1960s art, the era of late Henry Moore, Robert Morris, Robert Smithson, Yves Klein, Lawrence Weiner, Anthony Caro, William Tucker, Tony Smith and Carl Andre. It was the 1960s-70s era of what Rosalind Krauss called 'expanded field' sculpture, the High Renaissance of land art.[1] Krauss's 'expanded field' sculptors included Robert Irwin, Michael Heizer, Richard Serra, Walter de Maria, Sol LeWitt, Bruce Nauman, Alice Aycock, Mary Miss,

Dennis Oppenheim, Nancy Holt, George Trakis, Hamish Fulton, Christo, Joel Shapiro and Long. It is worth going back a little to look at postwar and contemporary sculpture for a while, to see where Long's art fits in.

THE SCULPTURE OF ARROGANCE: BIG, BIG, BIG

The awareness of scale is a function of the comparison made between that constant, one's body size, and the object. Space between the subject and the object is implied in such a comparison.

Robert Morris (1966, 21)

However exciting a painting by, say, Julian Schnabel, Robert Longo, or David Salle may be, sculptures by artists such as Tony Smith, Nancy Graves, Rebecca Horn, Mark di Suvero, Eva Hesse, Louise Nevelson, Tony Cragg and Richard Long have the edge over the painters. While Renaissance painting may represent the apotheosis of 'high art', and ancient Greek sculpture may be the height of 'high sculpture', contemporary sculpture really is some of the most startling in the history of art (and Richard Long's art is close to the core of contemporary sculpture).

Richard Long's sculpture is not 'monolithic' in scale, usually – but his works can stretch over many miles, far longer than even the Christos' fences, valley curtains or wrapped coasts.

Richard Long's art, like many land artists' works, is clearly part of the art installation culture: it's an art of environments, where even the relatively small addition of a stack of stones forming a stone ring can set alive the surrounding landscape. One sees the landscape in a new way: context is all-important.

LESS IS MORE: ARTE POVERA

Richard Long's art has affinities with the Italian Arte Povera ('poor art') movement, with its insistence on simple, organic materials (soil, grass, fire, wood, wax) and a simple, direct method of art-making. (The Arte Povera connection has been emphasized by Long himself in interviews). The Arte Povera artists (Jannis Kounellis, Mario Merz, Michelangelo Pistoletto, Luciano Fabro and Giovanni Anselmo) brought unadorned (though not unmanipulated) 'natural' materials into the gallery, which produced a different sort of æsthetic shock: fluffy, unworked cotton packed into a Donald Judd-like steel enclosure; an igloo made from broken glass, slate, clay, wax and branches; a piece of lettuce bound to a chunk of granite. Like Walter de Maria filling a gallery with soil, Jannis Kounellis brought nature – some horses – into a gallery in Rome. The horses stabled in the white, modern gallery provided a striking contrast between nature and culture, the animal and the humanmade worlds. Of his Italian horse piece, Kounellis said the aim was to increase awareness of the 'basic nature of a gallery, of its bourgeois origin', its economic and ideological aspects.[1] Long made similar statements about the dichotomies of indoors/ outdoors, culture/ nature, artificial/ natural when he brought River Avon mud and blocks of slate into the art gallery (though Long has always tended to avoid economic, political or ideological discourses in his art).

CONSTANTIN BRANCUSI AND LAND ART

The influence of Constantin Brancusi is apparent in Minimal, Arte Povera and Postminimal sculpture. Robert Morris, Donald Judd, Carl Andre, Dan Flavin, Barbara Hepworth, Scott Burton, Chris Drury and Andy Goldsworthy have acknowledged Brancusi's art, in particular his *Endless Column* (1918). Andre's early work *Last Ladder* (1959, London) is something like

Brancusi's *Endless Column* (putting Brancusi along the ground, as Andre remarked). And Andre wasn't the only postwar sculptor to have his/ her Brancusi phase.

SAMUEL BECKETT

Contemporary with Jasper Johns' paintings in the 1960s was Samuel Beckett's exploration of self-referential fiction. Richard Long doesn't feel an affinity with many travel writers, but has cited Beckett as a literary parallel. Like the art of Le Witt and Johns, Long's art is also an art of numbers, of sequences, systems and series, of counting. Long said he sometimes produced walkworks specifically to illustrate or embody a simple idea, which could involve adding up or subtracting numbers (or hours, or stones, or days). Don't forget that pretty much all of Long's works contain numbers as well as letters and words (even if it's the date or the year of making the work).

> I have read a few bits and pieces of [Samuel] Beckett's work [related Long]… he does use things like country lanes and bicycles and stones and doing nothing… like an incredible minimal view of life, which is very attractive and powerful. So I think there are some similarities, in the same way there are similarities with Zen Buddhism. It is just a sort of coincidental, human… we all live in the same world. It would be maybe very surprising if you could not find parallels with the work of other artists or other religions. (IC 2, 7)

THE WORLD OF MINIMAL AND POSTMINIMAL ART

Sixties Minimal and Postminimal sculpture in the late Sixties and into the Seventies was marked by its extremely hard edges, creating angular and linear forms: lines, rows, corners, rectangles, triangles, octagons, polyhedra, pyramids. It was a blocky, rectilinear art movement, characterized by white, black and grey smooth planes of plastic, glass, aluminium, wood and steel. The cube and box was one of the most highly favoured forms. Suzi Gablik wrote of the Minimal artists: '[c]onjugating the cube to infinity, they conveyed an impression of perfect equilibrium, and produced a visual symmetry that never deviates from its own rigidly plotted field'.[1] Symmetrical, unadorned, industrial.

Minimal sculptures are not set on pedestals or daises, like Renaissance or Greek sculpture; they sit on the floor, or lean against walls (as in Robert Morris's *Floor Piece*, or Carl Andre's *Cedar Piece*). Minimal sculptures exist in the same space, on the same plane (the floor) as the viewer. They are, as Morris said, in an in-between cultural space, somewhere between being monuments and being ornaments, between being architecture and jewellery.[2] Long's sculptures are wholly within this Minimal/ Postminimal tradition of dispensing with the pedestal.

But – whether the 'system' is serial or modular, whether there is progression or simply repetition – the notion of Donald Judd's of 'doing the next thing', 'one thing after another' – explains so much of Minimal art. It explains so much of Judd's work, for instance, those 'ladders' or 'stacks' of forms ascending to the ceiling in bronze or plastic, and those long lines of crenellations set on a wall. It also describes how artists simply go on making work, as variations, or repetitions, or progressions, like Mark Rothko with his many canvases that explore different combinations of purple or yellow clouds floating on oceans of red or blue, or Ad Reinhardt's seemingly repetitious but actually methodical explorations of five foot square black abstract canvases. Or

Richard Long making one stone circle after another, or walking across the same stretch of Dartmoor in Devon time after time. Minimal ethics can produce some extremes of mathematics and seriality.

By limiting himself to white, Robert Ryman freed himself up for an exploration of different media, because he painted in white on many kinds of material: canvas, linen, cotton, wood, paper, steel, copper, aluminium, mylar, fibreglass, Plexiglas, cardboard, etc, and with various sorts of media: oil, baked enamel, paper, glue, shellac, vinyl acetate emulsion and so on. As Ryman said, typically of so many late 20th century artists: '[t]here is never a question of what to paint, but only how to paint'.[3] In the same way, Long took up the Minimal and Postminimal use of simple geometric forms — circles, rows, lines, columns — which would give his pieces a structure upon which he could explore other things.

By contrast with the Minimal artists, Richard Long has not excised as much from his art as Minimal painters such as Marden, Ryman, Martin, Baer, Mangold and Kelly did in the 1960s: Long has held onto things like landscapes, the movement of objects in the sky, and the sensuality of walking. He has not gone the whole way into abstraction, and produced radically emptied works such as the canvases of Stella, Marden or Ryman.

Like the Minimal artists, Richard Long was much concerned with seriality, processes, mapping, permutations and variations. Long was very fond of numbers and number systems, and of measuring his walks: he walked so many miles for so many hours on such and such a day, for instance. His walkworks record the everyday events of a walk, as well as the number systems and measurements. Long made walks based on number systems. Many of his walks are repetitions of the same basic idea, just as the Minimalists would take one format and reproduce it many different ways. In fact, as a walker, Long was in love with repetition, because a walk is basically one step then another... then another. The walk's basic unit is the step. Similarly, Minimal artists like Carl Andre constructed larger works from simple, small units (in Andre's case, the metal tile).

THE ART OF SPACE AND LIGHT

Numerous sculptors, installation artists and land artists have worked with light and lighting: James Turrell with his 'skyspaces', Robert Irwin's reworked gallery spaces, Dan Flavin and his fluorescent tubes, Bruce Nauman, who made very narrow corridors lit by green fluorescents, Maria Nordman's extensions to studio exteriors, Nancy Holt's *Sun Tunnels,* Eric Orr's sound and light environments, and DeWain Valentine's acrylic tubes hanging alone from gallery ceilings. (Others include Douglas Wheeler, Hap Tivey, Susan Kaiser Vogel, Stephen Antonakos, Keith Sonnier and Larry Bell).

Some artists made the reconstituted gallery interior one of their trademarks. Richard Long has used lighting effects in his works, though not in the manner of many of the light artists noted above. For instance, there are many Long walks based around sunrises and sunsets, or full moons, or eclipses. Many of the indoor sculptures of Long – the stone circles, the mud and wall installations – require fairly standard gallery lighting. Long does not create special indoor environments like Robert Irwin or James Turrell in which the lighting plays a major role.

2

Sculpture and Gender

Sculpture is a three dimensional projection of primitive feeling: touch, texture, size and scale, hardness and warmth, evocation and compulsion to move, live and love.

Barbara Hepworth[1]

Richard Long's art is not the most obviously 'feminine' among 20th and 21st century artists. His art doesn't appear to address issues that preoccupy feminists or female artists (for instance, identity, the body, equal rights, labour, pregnancy, healthcare, exploitation of women, and so on. But Long also isn't particularly interested in addressing political issues in general, whether gendered or not). Yet the forms of Long's art – the circles, ovals and stones – can be seen as 'feminine' forms, while his intuitive, poetic approach, though not without its 'masculine', mathematical and logical elements, can be seen as a 'feminized' æsthetic methodology.

The eroticism of Richard Long's sculpture is of a different order (though related) from traditional, figurative sculpture, the sculpture of Michelangelo and Bernini. The sensuality of Long's art is 'non-human'; there are no 'human' figures in his work, but the sense of humanity is always stressed. Due to the 'abstract' (or at least non-figurative) nature of Long's sculpture, his work generally escapes obvious manifestations of sexism. However, there is a striking emphasis on touch, the body and the hand in Long's *œuvre*: the mud wall drawings are made by smearing mud on a wall by the hand of the artist, while the stone ellipses, circles and rows are built by hand by the artist on the gallery floor (the stone is not carved by the sculptor, but used as it comes from the local quarry). The mud splashes and hand, foot and finger prints Long makes on gallery and museum walls are his personal stamp: only the artist can make them (but the stone rows and circles can be built by others – Long leaves instructions on how to put them together so that museums and galleries can display the work without him needing to install it).

One can see the body written into, say, Richard Long's smeared Avon mud circles, or Constantin Brancusi's extraordinary egg shapes, but not, perhaps, in the giganticism of Michael Heizer's *Double Negative* (1969-70). Yet, even here, the human body is present – if only by the way it is violently dwarfed by the scale of Heizer's earthwork (but the best way to see *Double Negative* is to experience it firsthand, by walking around it). The body, in short, can never be totally erased. Much of land art is vast.

The body features occasionally in the art of Richard Long. One sees the grass rubbed flat or stones kicked by Long's feet. Handprints smear mud on walls. And Long very occasionally appears in photographs, beside his work. But there is nothing in Long's work that is as ferocious as feminist and women's body art and performance art and happenings.

One could see Richard Long's circles or Robert Smithson's spirals and circles as a kind of Goddess art, because circles so clearly evoke Goddess themes such as time, cycles, (Moon) phases, dance, transformation, ritual, initiation, astronomy, and so on. The circle is also a profound shape for alchemists; as the mediæval alchemical tract *Rosarium Philosophorum* has it: 'make a round circle and you will have the stone of the philosophers'.[2] Long created, in his favourite stamping ground of Ireland, an ancient maze form out of small stones set on grass (*Connemara Sculpture*, 1971), and returned to similar forms in *North South East West Circles* (Switzerland, 2000). Robert Morris has also made a labyrinth (*Labyrinth*, 1974). The shape of Long's and Morris's labyrinths directly recall the Cretan labyrinth of initiation and ritual, and the spirals at the entrance to Newgrange in Co. Meath, a huge passage grave some 4,500 years old.

3

Spirit and Matter: Aspects of Land Art

SPIRIT OF PLACE

The whole planet is potentially an artist's studio for the land artist (perhaps even the whole cosmos: if art can be anything, there can be no limits either). The land artist ranges over the whole globe. A desert, a beach, a field, a piece of waste ground can become a studio (and has been, countless times). A forest becomes a place of creative activity. The landscape itself is crucial in land art: everything about a landscape, every detail, the very texture and colour and shape and dampness and springiness and strength and size of grass, for instance. Or a crevice in a rock formation. Pine cones, closed-up. Fallen apples. A small dewpond on an empty hillside. Flowers turning sunward in the late afternoon. The history of a place, its social uses, the layers of human interaction. These are the things land artists deal with in making art. These are the actualities that artists employ when they create artworks. To fully appreciate land art, then, one has to look really closely, to grasp the details, as well as the overall conception. This is true of Richard Long's sculptures, as well as the larger American earthworks of Alice Aycock, Mary Miss and Robert Smithson.

For David Nash, land art is about getting as near as possible to nature: the land artist does not paint nature, from way off, with a paintbrush or watercolour block in front of her/ him. The sketchpad or easel is a wall between artist and world. The land artist, rather, dives in, 'gets right in there', as Nash says. The land artist does not use oil or pastel or ink to 'represent' nature. Rather, s/he works directly with nature, getting her/ his fingers dirty with mud, snow, sheep shit, stone, ferns, wood.

The rise in popularity of Richard Long's art has parallels perhaps with the developments and trends in gardening and garden art in Britain and elsewhere. The popularity of Richard Long's art is in tune in the UK with the rise in gardening shows on TV (and those shows' links with programmes on houses, food, vacations, tourism and interior design); the spread of out-of-town household stores, and rural gardening centres; more and more gardens are open to the public (including many more private gardens in the *Yellow Book* scheme); the increasing interest in ecological and environmental politics (for instance, Friends of the Earth, Greenpeace, World Wildlife Fund, saving rainforests, whales, dolphins, elephants, rhinos, tigers, endangered species and habitats); anti-pollution and recycling drives; anxiety about ozone, global warming, car owning and pollution; and the increase of New Age and mind/ body/ spirit pursuits (such as *feng shui*). Some of the things that fuel this revived (or new) interest in gardens, art and the environment include an increase in leisure time, more money for entertainment and travel, low-cost tourism, a bigger ageing population (which also lives longer), new technologies, and new distribution and consumption networks.

ART AND LIFE

Land artists, like nature poets and nature mystics, are inspired by particular places. Richard Long said 'places gives me the energy for ideas' (FC VI, 6). Nature poets, like religious mystics or land artists (or all artists), can be described as 'following their bliss' (Joseph Campbell's term). When you follow your bliss 'you come to bliss'.[1] Campbell used the model or metaphor of following the 'pollen path' of the Navaho Indians. As Campbell defined it:

> The Navaho have that wonderful image of what they call the pollen path. Pollen is the life source. The pollen path is the path to the centre. The Navaho say, "Oh, beauty before me, beauty behind me, beauty to the right of me, beauty to the left of me, beauty above me, beauty below me, I'm on the pollen path".[2]

This is one way of imagining the creative journey – towards the centre, the life source. Paradise, the Golden Age, Eden, was not back there then, but it is now. 'Eden *is*…this is it, this is Eden' Campbell stressed (ib.). It's *now*, and can only be 'now'. There is no other time it could possibly be. The journey, whether physical (as in Richard Long's case) or psychic, spiritual or imaginary, is along the *feng shui*, the 'dragon lines', or along the 'lines of song' or 'dream tracks' of the Australian aborigines, the primrose paths, the 'fairy paths' of Celtic mythology, or the 'pollen paths' of the Navaho Indians.[3] Long has been walking the pollen path for most of his artistic career. In *Heaven and Earth* (2001) Long talks of the 'the walk as a true path' (WL, 180). There are millions of paths, but each one is individual, as well as being identical with all the others. When Long's walked one path, he's walked them all.

Like Chris Drury, Hamish Fulton and Long, British author Bruce Chatwin spoke lovingly of walking, of wandering, of nomads and wildernesses. In *The Songlines*, Chatwin made notes upon Australian dreamtime and 'songlines', the lines that crisscross the landscape. Britain has its own version of this *feng shui* or earth magic: ley lines ('discovered' by Alfred Watkins).[4] Richard Long's maps often look like those of a New Age ley line hunter, crisscrossed with ink lines. Oppenheim, Fulton and Long produced their own versions of 'songlines', whether in powdered snow, drips of water, or words. As in the work of Bruce Chatwin, Paul Theroux, Jonathan Raban, Iain Sinclair, Colin Thubron and other travel writers, there is a deep sense of motion and travelling in the art of Fulton, Drury and Long. Theirs is an art born out of travels, even if the journeys are nothing more than morning walks out from the studio. These journeys don't have to be weeks long, crossing the Sahara on foot or over the Poles by sled; they can be made on an afternoon stroll (although Long has travelled the globe far more than many land artists).

Land art gains much of its power from particular places. Many land artists, for instance, work away from built-up, urban areas (though they choose *urban* zones far more than *sub*urban realms if they have to – partly because the art galleries and museums who fund or exhibit their work tend to be based in cities rather than the suburbs). The 'glamour' of the locations enhances the sculptures. Some land art is overpowered by the Romantic settings. Some of Richard Long's stone circles, for instance, look feeble in their desert or snowscape locations.

In a key text, the essay "Landscape and Character", Lawrence Durrell spoke of being a 'residence writer', that is, someone who lives in a place not as a tourist or visitor.[5] This is the opposite of Richard Long's desire, which is to pass through the world 'invisibly', to create ephemeral artworks, and not make a lasting mark on the world, but Long does also get to know an environment over many years (such as Scotland, Somerset and Dartmoor).

THE ALCHEMY OF MATTER

The 'Land Art Sublime' (*pace* Robert Rosenblum's coining of the term 'Abstract Sublime' to describe Barnett Newman's and Mark Rothko's paintings) might include the snow and stone circles made in the wildernesses of Scotland, Nepal and Peru of Richard Long; Dennis Oppenheim borderland snow circles, the stone circles of Nancy Holt; Christo's islands surrounded with pink polypropylene; and of course Robert Smithson's *Spiral Jetty*.

The nature poet uses the same emotional/ cultural stuff as the land artist: the human relationship with the natural world. Whatever the poet writes about or the land artist sculpts, it is the *feeling* for nature that is important, the relation between self and nature, that is employed by both poet and land artist. As Clement Greenberg, the foremost critic of postwar art in America, wrote: '[a]rt is a matter strictly of experience, not of principles', a statement which chimes with the views of Long, Drury, Turrell and other land artists, for whom experience is primary.[1] For Long, subjectivity is primary: his art must please himself first, before anyone else. 'I just make art in the way that gives meaning, purpose and pleasure for myself. If it is any good I think it will naturally resonate in all manner of ways for other people.'[2] The Arte Povera artist, said Germano Celant, has 'chosen to live within direct experience, no longer the representative... he aspires to live, not to see' (1969).

'TRUE CAPITALIST ART'?: THE ECONOMICS OF LAND ART

Not all but much of land art is very expensive. That is, it is expensive moving tons of earth around or building enormous structures. Taking a motorbike out into the desert and drawing lines with it is one thing (as Michael Heizer had done in *Circular Surface Displacement* [1968], North of Las Vegas), but making a 40 mile 18 foot high fence (Christo) is another.

Much of land art requires patrons, sponsors, co-ordination with galleries, lawyers, public administrators, helpers and industry. (The costliness of land art may help to explain why much of it is American).[1] Land art requires investment with no immediate return. Patrons are crucial to land art. In American earthworks the key patrons were the Dia Art Foundation, Robert C. Scull and Virginia Dwan, director of the Dwan Gallery between 1966 and 1971.

Richard Long voiced a common view (perhaps) among many British sculptors when he wrote of his aversion to American earthwork art:

> In the sixties there was a feeling that art need not be a production line of more objects to fill the world. My interest was in a more thoughtful view of art and nature, making art both visible and invisible, using ideas, walking, stones, tracks, water, time, etc, in a flexible way... It was the antithesis of so-called American "Land Art," where an artist needed money to be an artist, to buy real estate to claim possession of the land, and to wield machinery. True capitalist art.[2]

Although Richard Long (and other Brits) may despise the amounts of money spent by the American earthwork artists, aren't they also part of the system of 'true capitalist art'? Don't they also (partly or wholly) live off their art? Doesn't Long just wander around the planet on his sacred 'walks', putting a few stones into a pile, and taking a photo of his efforts? Aren't Richard Long, David Nash, Shirazeh Houshiary, Rachel Whiteread, Richard Wentworth, Bill Woodrow, Helen Chadwick, Alison Wilding, Hamish Fulton and Richard Deacon (among British artists) also a part of the 'capitalist' art world? Don't their artworks sell for lots of money, a lot more money than the materials plus a little profit cost? Aren't (British) artists being hypocritical when they criticize the bombastic aspects of American land art when they benefit from the hugely over-priced art gallery system, where even mundane art it seems (such as artists' prints) are sold for 'silly prices'?[3]

Long himself produces artists' books, postcards, and posters (many of these items are limited editions, sold on websites, via catalogues, or tele sales, or bookstores, by publishers, distributors, museums).

THE OBJECT IN LAND ART

With the development of Minimal, 'Process, Arte Povera and Conceptual art in the 1960s, sculpture became all 'object'.[1] Sculpture was (just) an object, in amongst millions of other objects. 'Objecthood' (Michael Fried's term) became crucial, the 'thing-in-itself', as Existential philosophers such as Jean-Paul Sartre and Edmund Husserl put it.[2] Inner and outer space became one, objects were simply what they are/ were, without referring to anything outside themselves.

The all-overness or instantaneity of modern art certainly applies to Richard Long's stone circles: one sees them all at once, without frames, without being 'led', illusionistically, into the work (although there are plenty of pictorial elements in some of Long's works: Long uses Renaissance illusion, artificial three dimensionality, Renaissance perspective, frontality, figure-ground relations, framing, negative space, selective viewpoint, *chiaroscuro*, silhouettes, outlines, and Classical proportions). All of Long's art is founded, like most of Western art, on familiar Renaissance principles about visual representation and visual perception. Although elements of Long's art are postmodern and conceptual and part of the contemporary art world, most of it is grounded in Classical and Renaissance art.

LAND ART AND CONCEPTUAL ART

Land art is related to, or a part of, Conceptual art.[1] For much land art exists only in photographs, memories, words, various texts which are not the land art itself. Works that can be seen and those that are hidden or 'invisible' have the same importance for the artist. 'Seen and unseen works have equal importance' said Richard Long (IC 1, 5). That's an insightful observation. One of the hallmarks of the 'ideal Conceptual work', as Mel Bochner opined, is 'an exact linguistic correlative, that is, it could be described and experienced in its data and it could be infinitely repeatable'.[2] Land art is often Conceptual art (although Long will, if one commissions him, come round and smear mud on your living room wall for you: how long it would last, though is another matter, open to dispute).

While much Richard Long's output could be collected into a small space – the slides, the cans of film, the textworks which could be summarized in notebooks, and the Avon river mud in a bag – plenty of it is pretty big and hefty (the circles and ellipses and rows of stone, bone, slate and wood).

Land art is meta-art, art about art, art that relies on other art to 'exist'. Land art exists for a brief moment, then becomes myth, gossip, photography and words (and most often criticism and journalism). Many of Richard Long's works are simply collections of words, printed in capitals, in Eric Gill's font, Gill Sans, on large pieces of paper. Part of the text of one of Long's works can be printed here – *Walking To a Solar Eclipse* (1999) – and this text here will approximate to a Richard Long artwork in itself (although he likes them printed larger). Thus:

STARTING FROM STONEHENGE
A WALK OF 235 MILES
ENDING ON A CORNISH HILLTOP
AT A TOTAL ECLIPSE OF THE SUN

Well, that's part of a Richard Long artwork. Is that it? Yes. Here's another one:

GRANITE LINE

SCATTERED ALONG A STRAIGHT 9 MILE LINE
223 STONES PLACED ON DARTMOOR

ENGLAND 1980

It seems as if Richard Long has nothing much to 'say'. Well, he is a sculptor, so he wouldn't have to be so good at writing or speaking. Wrong. He's a land artist and Conceptual artist (though he dislikes the term 'land art'), and land and Conceptual artists are always much concerned with writing and written texts. A Richard Long exhibition, for instance, features written texts on display, and photographs, as well as installation works and sculptures (like most land artists, Long won't let go of real objects. He likes to include sculpted objects in his exhibitions, not only Conceptual photoworks or textworks).

The texts of land and Conceptual artists also draw on poetry, on what's sometimes called concrete or 'visual poetry' or typewriter art. Long, for instance, prints his laconic texts in circles (*Full Moon Circle of Ground*, Dartmoor, 1983), in concentric circles (*Three Moors, Three Circles,* Liskeard to Porlock, 1982), in vertical lines, as in trendy style magazines (*The Isle of Wight as Six Walks*, 1982), and in curved swathes of text (*A Moved Line in Japan*, 1983). *A Moved Line In Japan* was a textwork with short phrases printed in a gentle curve ('shell to crab / crab to feather / feather to fish', and so on.

Sixties Conceptual artist Lawrence Weiner produced text works, capital letters on a wall or in a book (Barbara Kruger, the Art & Language group and Michael Craig-Martin and Long have also made post-Conceptualist wall works of words). Weiner's solution to making sculpture was that a sculpture on a plinth has to be 'translated' into language, so that people can understand it. Sculpture is language, and words are language, therefore, Weiner reckons, words can be sculpture:

> when you see a piece of wood lying on the ground with a piece of stone on top of it, you must translate that in your own head into language. What I try to do is present language itself as a key to what sculpture is about... It is a presentation of a piece of sculpture in language.[3]

Like John Baldessari and Sophie Calle, and like Richard Long's own text pieces, Weiner produces capital letters in short phrases which are about a viewer's relationship with an object. The words are a means or the expression of a relationship with something. Richard Long commented that '[t]he discovery [Weiner] made that art does not necessarily have to be made, that was a great breakthrough'.[4] Weiner is right, of course: words alone can be sculpture, for poets have long known that language is an *experience*, not simply abstractions or concepts.

MAPS

Richard Long's walks are often based on maps: one of Long's biggest debts must be to the mapmakers and publishers of the world (in the UK, that's Ordnance Survey, based in Southampton. Their Outdoor Leisure maps, Explorer maps and Landranger maps must have been used by Long countless times. The Outdoor Leisure series includes many areas favoured by Long for his walks: Dartmoor, Snowdonia and the Cairngorms. Britain may not have quite the deserts, mountains and wildernesses of the Magreb, Andes or Central Asia, but it does have beautiful cartography. 'One reason I make mapworks in Britain is because you can get good maps' said Long [1985, 2, 15]).

Some of Richard Long's artworks are just maps, sometimes maps with a photograph added (as in the Cerne Abbas work), sometimes with text explaining the work, which is usually a walk. The mapworks are usually 'completely planned beforehand' Long remarked.[1] The text that accompanies the Cerne Abbas walk (1975) anchors the meaning of the work firmly (RL, 85).

A SIX DAY WALK OVER ALL ROADS, LANES AND DOUBLE TRACKS INSIDE A SIX MILE WIDE CIRCLE CENTRED ON THE GIANT OF CERNE ABBAS

The Cerne Abbas walk is a mass of its black lines drawn on the map, the postcard image of the prominently ithyphallic Cerne Giant, and the intricacy and delicacy of the Ordnance Survey cartography. It's a work rich in allusions. For walkers, Ordnance Survey maps themselves are treasured items, with their familiar green blocks of colour indicating woods, the red A roads (highways), the brown B roads (country roads), the black railway lines (so familiar to me from so many train journeys across this part of the UK – through stations such as Maiden Newton, Dorchester South, Upwey and Wool). Maps, for walkers and geographers, have their own special poetry, a graphic style that is cherished.

The idea with the early map walkworks, Richard Long said, was to create 'a new art which was also a new way of walking: walking as art' (WL, 68). In 1994 Long described maps as important aids to making walking art, walking as art: maps were layers of information and history (personal and social), they showed the time and space of a walk, the distances traversed, the campsites, the route, the time taken, and were useful aides in planning a walkwork. A map is an 'artistic and poetic combination of image and language' (WL, 84).

Richard Long's maps, then, are pictorial records/ representations/ descriptions of his walks. The maps are 'inner landscapes'.[2] Long writes that a 'map of inner landscape is an important step towards understanding and self-knowledge.'[3] In black pen he traces his routes along the riverbeds on Dartmoor, across the summits of the Scottish Highlands, in

Chinese mountains, in County Mayo, Ireland, etc. *A Dartmoor Walk* (1987) is a large piece of paper with the squiggly lines of Long's movements across the granite tableland set above the usual piece of Long's text which describes some of the aspects of the walk:

DEEP BREATHING TO GRIMPSOUND TO BENNETT'S
CROSS TO MIDGES TO A NEW BORN CALF
TO GREAT KNEESET TO A LARK ON A BOULDER TO
COTTON GRASS TO THINKING TO A FOX SMELL
(OW, 44)

The work is that curious collection of elements, of graphics and text, which constitute, Richard Long asserted, a record of an 8 day Dartmoor walk:

> It was about the experience of being alone in a place of nature, the topography, the weather, the naming of places, real time, autobiography, imagination. Each new walk carries with it memories of all the others. For me Dartmoor is a place of regeneration, knowledge, history and continuity.[4]

Mapping relates again to Minimal art, for the dominant structure in modern painting is the grid,[5] which is found everywhere (in Agnes Martin's pencilled grids, in Sol LeWitt, Stella, Noland, Marden, Mangold, Andre, etc). Laid over Richard Long's walks is the grid of the map. Minimal and Conceptual art created a 'museum of language', a gallery space made up of... words, ideas, concepts, intangible notions. It is an imaginary space, this new museum of art, for it requires the imagination to make it work. It is something like Jorge Luis Borges' infinite library, existing in the imagination, wholly reliant on the imagination to make it come alive.

Just about every land artist used maps in their work. Not just in the obvious sense of mapping (and finding) future sites for artworks, but as key elements in the artworks themselves. Richard Long said he planned out his walks using maps, examining maps very closely to look out for possible routes, and potential obstacles. Maps are used to ensure there aren't any cliffs, bogs, rivers or other snags along the route. For the mapworks, Long tended to draw the lines first, and follow the route when he made the walk. The idea comes first, then the map and the lines, then the walk (1995b).

LAND ART AND PHOTOGRAPHY

In land art photographs, the viewer is not offered a *range* of viewpoints of a work, although land artists clearly take more than one shot of each work they make. No artist takes just *one* photo out of a 36 exposure 35mm film, or one frame out of a twelve shot 120mm format film, or one digital shot out of hundreds. No, an artist, like an photographer, takes a range of shots, at different, bracketed exposures, from different viewpoints (much as the trendy advertizing film director of today shoots twelve hours of footage for just one thirty second advert).[1]

Very likely Richard Long would try out a number of viewpoints, and would shoot a number of photos of the work, to give him more possibilities later (although it's apparent that Long has sometimes selected the viewpoint for his photograph *before* he builds his outdoor sculptures. The sculptures are made *for* or *because of* the viewpoint: an interesting range of hills as a background, for example). Due to the size of many of Long's indoor and outdoor stone circles and lines, and the scale of the landscapes he makes work in, most of Long's photographs are taken standing back, using standard or wide angle lenses. To include the whole artwork and the surrounding landscape, Long needs to be positioned some way back. Long also liked to include the background scenery. His sculptures are often constructed for one particular viewpoint, and that's the one that gets into the photograph. Some of Long's work is about visual alignments – between the viewer, the sculpture, the landscape and the horizon (WL, 147). Thus, Long uses far fewer close-up shots of his land art than some land artists. In *Evolution Circle* (1995), made in the High Sierra, the open circle is framed against the distant hills, rocks and a lake. *Cotopaxi Circle* (1998) follows the same principle, with a snowy mountain as the backdrop to the open stone circle (the photograph recalls countless images of Mount Fuji in Japanese art).

In terms of framing and viewpoint Richard Long favours, for the indoor floor works, a high angle, looking down the work. Often Long shoots his floor sculptures from ordinary head height, but also sometimes from higher up. The wall drawings are usually shot head-on, from a right angle to the centre of the artwork. Long also likes to frame two works in the same photo – typically a mud wall drawing and a floor stone circle. Very occasionally, Long plays visual tricks, such as shooting the indoor sculpture *Atlantic Lava Line* (1995) end-on, so the loops of stones on the floor looked like a solid block of stones. But most of the photography is simple and straightforward, using traditional notions of Renaissance space, perspective, proportion and illusion. For the outdoor works, Long prefers Classical proportions to his compositions, usually with the landscape taking up the lower two-thirds of the frame. Again, Long is often tilting his camera down slightly from head height, to include the whole of the sculpture and its surroundings.

Jan Dibbets said that documenting the work wasn't important: 'I've done lots of works without taking photographs'.[2] But most land artists record their activities (e.g.: 'walk this morning; made a snow sculpture; it wasn't successful; back home for lunch'). Ultimately, *any* activity can be land art. Going to the stores can be a piece of art. One might drop a stone on the path as one goes, or perhaps not. Either way, you've just made a work of art. Is, then, walking to Gilmor's corner store for a pint of milk and a pack of cigarettes a fully accomplished and thoroughly authentic work of art, like Richard Long's *A Straight Northward Walk Across Dartmoor*?

Where does authenticity end and artifice begin? Or, rather, where does life end and art begin? Clearly, they are a continuum in land art.

Richard Long told me that '[n]ot all walking is art'; that is, a walk becomes art when it is conceived as art. The conception of the walk, made before the walk, is crucial, even if there is no 'reason' at all for the walk. 'A walk, and place, can be chosen for any reason'.[3] Long also said, though, that '[a]nything an artist makes, is art', but adds '[n]ot everyone is an artist.'[4]

The relation between outdoor and indoor works, between stone circles in some remote zone and a stone circle in a Western gallery, is resolved simply in much of land art by being regarded by the artist as a continuum. One can see how for Richard Long both inside and outside works are one, i.e., part of the same thing. (For Long, all of the forms his art takes are part of the same thing. 'The photos, the walks, the sculptures, the text works, they're all just formal variations, just different ways of sort of doing the same thing all the time' (SS, 309).) But the viewer might see them as separate, because the viewer (usually) can't see Long's outdoor pieces (Long likes to keep his locations secret and anonymous).[5] The artist is also focussed on her/ his work, it's part of her/ his life, it's what s/he does. But the spectator is doing all sorts of other things in her/ his life, not just consuming art.

The viewer only knows Richard Long's outdoor pieces from his photos, textworks and documentation. So it's always an odd relationship with Long's work for the viewer. For the artist, it's great, because the big photos and writings relate to his own experiences, of working outdoors. He knows the work inside out: *he lived it*. The viewer, though, gets a different experience: s/he sees odd phrases, titles, dates, measurements. Odd snippets of info. Or photos. Or a zigzag line. Or fingerprints or footprints on the floor. So people love Long's work (and land art) not because they love the photographs, or his writing. They love it, perhaps, because of *what it suggests*. Long's work, and land art in general, persuades people to look outwards, away from cities, towards the landscape, towards stones and water and all the rest of it. Perhaps that's why people love it, and other land art, and nature poetry, and all things to do with nature, from gardening to walking the dog to vacations in wildernesses. As Hamish Fulton put it, 'I walk on the land to be woven into nature' (1995). For Chris Drury, there is no indoor—outdoor divide, because the artist, like all people, is part of nature.

The outdoor work itself, the *walk itself*, isn't present in Richard Long's text pieces or photos. The work isn't 'in' the gallery. No, the work is *elsewhere*, and it is to that *elsewhere place* that people want to go (and the indoor art points to those places). Land art creates *desire* in people, as the work of J.M.W. Turner or Aleksandr Blok creates desire – for travel, for other places. Long spoke in the Santa Fe interview of feeling refreshed and renewed after a good walk: that's the experience, perhaps, that viewers wish to gain from land art, from all art.

One can see how, for Richard Long, Patricia Johanson, James Pierce, Michelle Stuart and other land artists, it's much more interesting to use a stone as a stone rather than as a representation of something else. Stones in Long's art are always stones, perhaps only ever stones, perhaps never more than stones. 'I am interested in showing real sculpture in galleries and museums as well as just photographs' Long said (1994b). Robert Smithson's definition of an earthwork is pertinent here: 'instead of putting a work of art on some land, some land is put into a work of art'.[6] Smithson's ethic can be applied directly to Long's art.

INTERIOR AND EXTERIOR ART

Sometimes it's odd to see land art in a gallery, because the mound of soil, the cairn of stones, the slate circle, the living tree, demands the viewer to look outwards, to nature, to the wildernesses, to the supposed origins of this kind of art. The viewer is always aware of the place of origin of land artworks (sometimes also the time and season of origin), and how uncanny and disruptive they can look indoors.[1] The leaves and stalks and mud smears and slate slabs are tiny parts of the natural world, bits extracted, rearranged, as all art is nature chopped up and reformed according to the artist's æsthetics. Land art creates an ambiguous continuity with the world of nature that exists outside the gallery (but also inside, and inside the spectator, too). Sometimes this ambiguity works against the art on show in the gallery space.

Land art sites, in the first wave of land art (late 1960s/ early 1970s – by common agreement land art's 'golden age' – tended to be wildernesses, deserts, post-industrial spaces, waste grounds, quarries and dumps. One of the reasons for going far from the gallery, the city and pretty countryside spots was because land artists wanted to avoid the 'pastoral' and the 'picturesque' at all costs.[2] It didn't want beauty for the sake of beauty. Land artists, asserted Dennis Oppenheim, wished to go beyond the picturesque (while British land artists, such as Richard Long, had some relationship with the picturesque, Oppenheim added [ibid.]).

Ephemeral, land art aims for an eternity in one place: the soul. As Lawrence Weiner, the Conceptual/ Process artist who exhibited 'statements' (texts on a wall), said: '[o]nce you know about a work of mine, you own it. There's no way I can climb into somebody's head and remove it.'[3] Thus, much of land art exists in that socio-cultural space which is actually inside people's heads (the 'cultural imaginary' as postmodernists like to call it). Thus, anyone can 'own' land art – simply by thinking about it. Once thought about, land art, Conceptual art or Process art is 'possessed' by the viewer, in Weiner's system. Indeed, some Conceptual art requires the existence of the viewer to make the work work at all. The viewer brings the piece alive. (Richard Long, though, requires a physical manifestation of a work, a realization, if it is going to work fully. 'My work is not conceptual in the sense it can be an idea only' [IC 1, 7]).

LAND ART AND CHANGE

Crucial in land art is the concept and reality of change, time and decay, for these works in wood, snow, ice, leaves, water, slate, grass, and so on, do not stay around. They are not 'permanent', in the way that, say, bronze, marble, steel or stone can be (the *concept* of change is as significant as the reality). (Long says he 'stands the stones down' after making a stone sculpture outdoors).

Richard Long has made many sculptures using water only: he has poured water in a line over stony ground, so the water darkens the stones. Typical Long water-sculptures include *Water Lines in Ladakh* (1984), where, near a river and crossing point, Long poured water from his flask in a line then photographed the result. Similar waterlines occur in *Sea Level Waterline* (Death Valley, 1982) and *Footpath Waterline* (197, Mexico). A waterline was made on a wooden bridge in the Piemonte Alps in 1989. In *Water Walk* (1999) Long poured water from one river (in England and Wales) into the next one (i.e., from the River Teme into the River Severn, from the River Severn into the River Arrow, and so on). In *Continuum Walk* (1998) Long carried water from the mouth to the source of the River Dart. Often he throws water at a wall (in Nepal), or over the ground (in Lappland and Spain), or over rocks, as in Switzerland (in 1991), which makes dark stains. These 'sculptures' do not last very long. They have a 'natural' lifespan, which is in keeping with the Conceptual artists' emphasis on simplicity and not interfering too much with the natural order of things (or letting the material dictate the work). Water, Long acknowledged in 1997, was a 'very important theme and idea in my work' (WL, 147). Long said he used water on its own outside, but in a gallery it was better to use mud, because water disappeared when it dried. Talking about water recalls that wonderful Taoist phrase, 'the sound of water says what I think'. In the *Tao Te Ching*, Lao-tzu states 'highest good is like water' (VIII).

Richard Long has also made waterline sculptures in the gallery: *Waterline* (1989), installed in Long's New York dealer (Sperone Westwater), was a long line of white splashes on a black backing. *Footprint Line* (1989, Turin) was a long floor-piece comprising Long's footprints in white paint on black cloth. *Muddy Feet Line* (1990) was a wide line of white footprints, made with paint, on the floor of the Musée d'Art Contemporain de Bordeaux, snaking through the gallery space in square zigzags. To make the splashes and trails of liquid show up, Long uses white paint or mud against a black background, in either floor or wall pieces.

Artists with a large vision of life know that nothing on Earth will be truly 'permanent'. After all, 'civilized' humanity is only 10,000 years old, or 40,000, or two or three million (depending on how one views 'civilized'). And the planet itself will not last forever: millions more years (maybe), but not forever. As Richard Long said in an interview:

> The planet is full of unbelievably permanent things, like rock strata and tides, and yet full of impermanences like butterflies or the seaweed on the beach, which is in a new pattern every day for thousands of years. I would like to think that my work reflects that beautiful complexity and reality.[1]

LAND ART AS RELIGION

It's no surprise that the American form of earth art and the British land art of Richard Long and Hamish Fulton should be sympathetic to Oriental mysticism: Zen and Taoist religion were in the air (like pot smoke or tear gas) and particularly prevalent in 1960s culture (in the Beats, the 'dharma bums' and the West Coast hippies, for example). It was an inevitable cultural development, it seems, from Parisian Existentialism to Californian Zen Buddhism, from the Old World philosophies based on Classical ideals to the New World's appropriation of the even older Oriental philosophies. Many of the chief precepts of Taoism, Confucianism, Hinduism, Shinto and Zen Buddhism chime with those of land art, not only the American earthworks, but also the British form of land art of Long, Drury, Fulton, Nash and others. Matsuo Basho, an important Oriental poet, wrote:

> Go to the pine if you want to learn about the pine, or to the bamboo if you want to learn about the bamboo. And in doing so, you must leave your subjective preoccupation with yourself.[1]

That's straight out of an art school manual. Makoto Ueda explained Basho's tenet thus: '[f]or learn means to enter into the object, perceive its delicate life and feel its feelings.'[2] These notions of searching for the 'essence' are absolutely in tune with the æsthetics of Richard Long, Brancusi, Andre, and Judd. Minimal art pursued the oft-used maxim that 'less is more', a radical reductionism and simplification.

In the paradoxical bliss of Oriental mysticism, emptiness is also fullness, and to 'have' nothing is to 'have' everything. Zen Buddhist, Hindu and Taoist philosophy thrive on paradox, on the 'not-this-not-that' dialectic of philosophy, as a way of getting at the unsayableness of the essence. As Anne Seymour says of Richard Long, his 'approach also corresponds with the Zen view, which recognises human nature as one with objective nature, in the sense that nature inhabits us and we nature' (OW, 54).

Like many land artists, Richard Long is ecologically-friendly, and is careful to make sure his artworks do not scar the landscape. There is no litter in the land artists' photographs of their artworks. Long speaks of wanting to 'pass through life without leaving a trace'.[3] They are ecologically and societally conscientious artists. Long said that his art is about finding a harmony between the human and the natural world, between the abstractions of humanity and the reality of nature. As Long put it, his work is 'a balance between the patterns of nature and the formalism of human abstract ideas like lines and circles.'[4] 'Above all,' wrote Irving Sandler, 'Long's art has been a countercultural dialogue with the earth, bringing humankind close to untamed nature, glorifying it, and pointing up ecological concerns' (1996, 64). (I think the eco-friendly aspect of Long's art has been overdone by critics: there are many more things that Long is concerned with in making his art before you get down to green issues).

Richard Long and other land artists always affirm the 'livingness' of their art, that they *live* their art. Their art, they claim, is not intellectually dissected (or dessicated) or made at a critical distance. Rather, the artist is right in the middle of her/ his art, living it. There is no separation of art and life. Land art is a way of mythicizing one's sense of being-in-the-world, a way of making presence visible, tactile, *there*. 'Presentness is grace' wrote Michael Fried in his influential essay "Art and Objecthood".[5]

In Richard Long's art, the act of establishment and installation is clear to see. A good deal of Long's walking art is precisely about mapping and measuring territories, traversing terrain, orientating oneself to the horizon and the cardinal points (N, S, E and W), having the right relationship with the natural world (in the American Indian sense of harmony, but also in the Buddhist sense of 'right action'). And it's about creating individual structures (stone circles and rows) or performing ritual acts (pouring water, carrying stones) which celebrate finding the centre (the spiritual centre can be anywhere: it is wherever the artist is – it is wherever you are). In Long's art the process of reconnection with the sacred is made visible. The textworks break it down into stages and strategies. The sacred is something wholly other; it might be called, at various times, the walk, the landscape, nature, the self, the moon, a sunrise, a mountain, or time itself. But it's all fundamentally about the same thing.

For the land artist, most, if not all, of the world is not just potential art material, but beautiful. Land artists, declining to admit to being romantic or emotional, nevertheless create art that is Earth-loving, nature-loving, ecologically-friendly; that is, in short, full of emotion. The walks of Richard Long can be regarded then as a means of re-establishing a connection with 'the real', with what is meaningful or valuable for the artist. As Eliade wrote, 'the sacred is always the revelation of the real, an encounter with that which saves us by giving meaning to our existence' (1984, 162).

Aspects of Richard Long's sculpture can be related to a primal (ancient) animistic response to the natural. Animism, the 'belief in spiritual beings', as anthropologists and psycho-analysts emphasize, is the origin of all religion. There is an affinity, then, between Long's (and any contemporary artist's or viewer's) response to rocks and sculptures and the so-called 'primitive' or ancient people's response to certain stones, or hilltops, or rivers, and statues, icons, totem poles, standing stones, and so on. For ancient peoples, rivers became goddesses and trees were spirits. Long's stone circles and linear paths made by boots are not much different from the primæval response to the 'energies' in nature of ancient religions and cults. The spiritual aspect of Long's art is not too far from the responses of ancient communities calling a river a Goddess, or regarding the buffalo as holy, or speaking of the Earth-Goddess Demeter and her daughter Persephone who was taken by Pluto into the Underworld for half the year and relating it to the seasonal cycle of agriculture and crops.

Uncomfortable as they are with notions of 'spirituality' or 'mysticism', land artists such as David Nash, Chris Drury and Robert Smithson are religious artists, sensitive to the emanations of particular places. Richard Long, for instance, concedes that 'art is magical', as of course it is (IC 2, 17). Art has been deeply associated with magic and religion for at least 40,000 years, and probably millennia more. Land art, like all art, is full of deep emotions. These emotions collect in clusters around certain places. It is understandable, then, that critics and the public see these emotions as potentially religious.

> Well, sacred I suppose has particular religious meanings and my work is not about religion [Long said]. Probably a special place would be a better word. I suppose, sacred really means a place of intense feelings. If you think of religion as being about intense feelings and emotions, art can be close to religion. (IC 2, 17)

STONE CIRCLES: LAND ART AND PREHISTORIC ART

The circle motif, one of the primæval symbols of eternity, cycles, time, rebirth, and so on, is employed throughout the work of much of land art. Circles in land art are made from slate, timber, snow, flowers or by walking in a circle; they seem to be gentler, more eco-friendly kinds of sculpture. The circle shape itself speaks of organic forms, and, in some religions, evokes the 'feminine', the maternal realm and the Goddess. Not a few sculptors and land artists have made the circle crucial to their works: Alison Wilding, Richard Deacon, Stephen Cox, Mary Miss, Anish Kapoor, Peter Randall-Page, Robert Morris and Dennis Oppenheim. And Richard Long.

Some land artists work in megalith-rich landscapes (such as Richard Long in the South-West of Britain). There are over nine hundred stone circles in the British Isles, a fact which surprised Long when I told him ('900...? That's an amazing fact I did not know').[1] Long too makes connections with prehistoric art in terms of manufacture: the cave paintings at Lascaux, Long said, were made by people's hands on the rock. 'And my work is just the same as that. It is very positive, very exciting that I am part of the continuation of... Art itself can be a circle' (IC 2, 24).

Richard Long has made references to some of the key sacred/ religious/ prehistoric sites of Britain: to Silbury Hill, apparently the largest humanmade mound in Europe, so the textbooks say; to the ithyphallic Cerne Giant in Dorset; to Glastonbury Tor, mecca for hippies, occultists and 'New Age' travellers (like Avebury and Silbury Hill); to Windmill Hill, and so on. (Interestingly, although Long has referred to Silbury Hill, Stonehenge and Glastonbury Tor often, he rarely includes Avebury stone circle in his works. Long seems to prefer Stonehenge, even though Avebury is a superior site in many respects).

In Rome, Richard Long made a reference to mythology in his *Romulus Circle and Remus Circle* (1994). Long even put a picture of himself with a rucksack in Africa right next to one of the famous ancient hill figures of England, the so-called 'Long Man of Wilmington', 231 foot tall, in Sussex. This is one of those prehistoric sites that some see as being an alien, or St Paul, or King Harold, or a Roman soldier (some reckon is much more recent than prehistoric). Richard Long ironically compares himself here with another 'Long' Man.[2]

Locations such as Silbury Hill, Stonehenge and Glastonbury have long been revered by the faithful as holy sites, 'places of power' as they are called. Land artists capitalize on the mystery of such places. One of Richard Long's works is a walk between two prime magical centres of Britain, Stonehenge and Glastonbury, both deeply associated with prehistoric astronomy, ancient priesthoods, Arthurian legend, Merlin the Magician, the Age of Aquarius, ley lines, Druids, geomancy, and a million other Outta Sight Ideas:

ON MIDSUMMER'S DAY
A WESTWARD WALK
FROM STONEHENGE AT SUNRISE
TO GLASTONBURY BY SUNSET
FORTY FIVE MILES FOLLOWING THE DAY[3]

The photograph that Richard Long puts with this textwork is the sort of picture postcard view one finds in newsagents and heritage centres around the UK: Glastonbury Tor in a dreamy sunset. Like St Paul's, the Tower of London, Big Ben, Buckingham Palace, Beefeaters, the changing of the guard, red buses and red telephone boxes, this is one of the archetypal images of tourist Britain. And, typically, it is Glastonbury Tor that Long chooses to photograph, not the stores nearby, the electricity pylons, the junk yard behind the highways, the rows of garages, the housing estates.

Note that Richard Long walked from Stonehenge to Glastonbury, very New Age. To mark the solar eclipse in Britain in 1999 (which was a big event in popular culture in the UK), Long walked from Stonehenge (where else?) to Cornwall, like some latter-day shaman or a high priest of some obscure cult (the Cult of the Art-Walk, perhaps, or a long-lost sect called the Ecstatic Taoist Walkers of Dartmoor).

Land artists' stone circles – including Richard Long's – often recall prehistoric stone circles. While they may deny it verbally, Nancy Holt's *Stone Enclosure*, Robert Morris's *Observatory* and Long's circle sculptures evoke the great circles of Britain: the Rollright Stones in Oxfordshire, Boscawen-Ûn and the Merry Maidens in West Penwith, Cornwall, Castlerigg in Cumberland, Stanton Drew in Somerset (a huge and little-known set of circles, and the nearest large ancient circle to Long's home in Failand, Bristol), and of course the mother of all stone circles, Avebury in Wiltshire (also not far from Bristol). Another link to circles are the 'fairy rings' of folklore and Celtic mythology. And the many rituals of dancing in circles, of course (with Matisse's famous *Dance* painting as one of the best renditions of this ecstatic theme, though Emil Nolde also made some memorable images of wild dancers).

There are many circles in Richard Long's repertoire: *Touchstones*, made in Iceland in 1982, which features long stones, some two feet high, arranged upright in a circle, *Circle of Standing Sandstones* (Düsseldorf, 1983), *Elterwater Stone Ring* (Kendal, 1985), *Stones and Suilven* (Scotland, 1981), *Stones In Switzerland* (1974), *Summit Stones* (the Swiss Alps, 2000), *Stones in Iceland* (1974), *Stones On Inishmore* (1975), *Stones in Nepal* (1975) and *Stones In Ladakh* (India, 1984). Obviously, Long has to work with what's there, at the location. If there's only long, thin slabs of stone, then that's what he has to use, if he's going to make a sculpture (he could import stones, but that's not his methodology for outdoor art made on walks). Arranged flat, these slabs of stone might not stand out against the rocky ground underneath them. Long does often employ flat slabs of stone, but often in indoor sculptures, such as the *White Marble Circle* (Ottawa) or *Helsinki Circle* (both 1983). Standing upright, the stones make more of a mark, as the builders of stone circles knew well. In *Orcadian Circle* (Cambridge, 1992), irregular slabs of stone are piled against each other, raising the circle a couple of feet off the ground in Jesus College's quad. In *Muir Pass Stones* (1995), the stones are chosen so they stand easily upright, their pointed ends skyward.

Some land artists, such as Richard Long, maintain that their stone rings are subjective, private, individual works, quite different from the public, social art of the prehistoric stones circles. The ancient stone rings were made by a group of people, a society constructed, perhaps, according to the architectural plans devised by a priestly élite (but they might have been made by workers for an exclusive few in a community, like a millionaire commissioning a fashionable new garden design for one of her/ his homes). Land art circles are (nearly always) the work of one person, but a major contemporary artist is no less a member of the cultural, æsthetic élite.

Prehistoric stone circles may have been built for religious rituals, perhaps connected with the position of celestial bodies. The circles in stone, snow, dandelions, trees and concrete of contemporary land art are made for private consumption, for the artist alone, or for an onlooker who wanders into a gallery or a space then out again, back into the chaos of the city. Yet the ancient sacred sites and land art/ Postminimal/ Arte Povera/ earthworks have much in common, because art and religion join at so many points. (And contemporary artists have their own rituals: for instance, to make *Footprint Circle* [1989, Italy], Long trudged around in a small circle, turning snow into sludge and forming a small open circle.)

LAND ART AND CONTEMPORARY SCULPTURE IN BRITAIN

Sculptors in the UK, whether of Richard Long's *alma mater* St Martin's School of Art, the 'New Generation', the 'New British Sculptors' and others, benefited from the influence of openness and freedom of American sculpture (at least in the 1960s and 1970s). 'America made me see that there are no barriers and no regulations' wrote Anthony Caro, the influential British sculptor and teacher at St Martin's when Long was there (although Long was part of the other group).[1] Caro had visited the US and been impressed by the new art (such as Kenneth Noland's paintings). According to William Tucker, postwar or 'modern', post-Cubist sculpture 'could be made from anything, about anything.'[2] (Tucker, though, in a TV documentary on 1960s sculpture, didn't regard Long's walks as sculpture).

1960s British sculpture was connected with the art schools (St Martin's, Chelsea, Slade, RCA); with teachers and modernists such as Anthony Caro, Philip King, Hans Haacke, Lawrence Weiner, Joseph Beuys and Henry Moore; with American Minimalism and Conceptual Art; with New Realism;

and with Italian Arte Povera. Long was on the Vocational (Advanced) Sculpture Course at St Martin's School of Art, and was part of the more loose, experimental, Conceptual group (which included teachers such as Peter Atkins and Frank Martin). The other group was headed by Anthony Caro (and included William Tucker), and was associated with welded, modernist New Generation sculpture.

Famously, Long and Fulton were among those art students who organized group walks as artistic statements: one in 1967 involved the students meeting in central London on the corner of Greek Street and Old Compton Street and walking to St Martin's entrance on Charing Cross Road, while roped together. In another walk work, students walked from St Martin's into the countryside.

Richard Long said he thought in the late Sixties that art could be more than constructing sculptures from metal: even the 'new sculpture' (the reference was probably to Caro) was traditional:

> I had a very strong feeling that art could embrace so many more things than it was at the time, that it could be about things like grass and clouds and water, natural phenomena, rather than just the slightly sterile academic, almost mannerism of welding bits of metal together, or using plaster, or the general kind of studio work at that time. (1994b)

The 'new' British sculpture was loved and loathed passionately. Amazingly, art critic David Sylvester reckoned that Richard Long 'has too many admirers'. What did Sylvester mean? That people uncritically adore Richard Long's works? Or that there is too much criticism written about him? Can an artist become too popular?

Kate Blacker discussed Richard Long and Tony Cragg:

> When Cragg made *New Stones, Newton's Tones* in 1978 he was responding directly to Long. The absence you detect in Long is there to the same extent in Cragg but it is caused by the distance between the status of his material as rubbish

and as 'art'. Unlike Long, Cragg is not seeking to present spiritual experience.[3]

Postmodern and post-Conceptual art ignites many important questions, such as: how does one gauge the 'authenticity' or 'originality' of something when it is mediated by the mass media? How does one know something is 'the real thing', when all that's known of it is through images and sounds on radio, television and the press? Does it matter if the 'original' artwork is fake when the mediated product has such 'truth', such apparent presence? Is an artwork that consists of photographs that refer to an idea or object or experience that exists elsewhere (like Richard Long's *Thirty Seven Campfires* [1987], or *A Trail of Water Circles* [2000], or Lawrence Weiner's printed words 'wall statement' *Sometimes Found*) as 'authentic' as a bronze sculpture by Degas or Donatello? Is an artwork that is an 'idea' as sensual or compelling as one made out of marble or oil? The 'new' British sculpture, with its scavenged objects and seemingly 'ordinary' objects displayed on the floor, disrupts modernist/ traditional notions of 'beauty', 'purity', 'tradition', 'objecthood', 'presence', 'value' and 'meaning'.

THE BRITISH LANDSCAPE TRADITION

I actually believe in Modernism, in the excitement of new ideas. Art is anyway beautiful if the idea is beautiful, if it has clarity and truth. A lot of the history of landscape art has been to reveal the beauty of nature, a sort of religious celebration. All that beauty is still there and can be overwhelming, but I was always interested to develop landscape art in new ways.

Richard Long (interview, April, 1985)[1]

American/ New York/ Abstract Expressionist/ Minimal/ Arte Povera influences constitute a number of influences in contemporary sculpture in the UK, but another is the 'British' art tradition, and yet another is the British landscape itself. Landscape art in the UK is bound up with notions of Romanticism. The works of Fulton, Drury, Nash, Long et al, are part of this Romantic tradition, as expressed in British landscape art. (Associated with land art were the groups of British artists variously dubbed the New Romantics/ Neo-Romantics/ New Ruralists/ New Arcadians.)

The influence of the landscape in the UK on British sculpture is apparent in many, but by no means all, of British sculptors. Specifically *British* landscape, as opposed to other kinds of landscape, occur in David Nash, Hamish Fulton, David Tremlett, Chris Drury, Roger Ackling and Long, as one might expect. It was Carl Andre who noted, quite rightly, that the British landscape is 'one vast earthwork'.[2] Long has spent much of his life walking all over this giant earthwork, mapping it, measuring it, photographing it, writing about it and building sculptures with it. (*The Sierra Madre*, a 5 day walk in Mexico in 1979, was about 'walking on rock', 'lighting fires on rock', 'sleeping on stones', 'throwing stones' and 'placing stones').

Richard Long, Fulton, Nash, Drury and Goldsworthy, in particular, evoke the British landscape tradition in art, the tradition of the pastoral, the sublime, the Arcadian. Long, Fulton, Goldsworthy, Drury and Nash are Romantic, in the sense of British Romantic poetry (Blake, Wordsworth, Keats, Shelley, Coleridge); in the sense of the British Romantic painters (Turner, Constable, Girtin, Cotman, Wilson); and in the sense of the Romantic attitudes and aspirations of infinity, nostalgia, mythology, soul, magic, nature and the Gothic. In sculptors such as Tony Cragg, Nash, Fulton, Shirazeh Houshiary, Anish Kapoor, Richard Wentworth, Bill Woodrow, Barry Flanagan, Ian Hamilton Finlay, Anthony Caro and William Tucker, one can see the elements of British Romantic literature (as well as the Neo-Romanticism of the 1930s and 1940s): the anarchic idealism of Shelley, the luscious sensuality of Keats, the epic nature poetry of Wordsworth, the angelic visions of Blake and the synæsthetic poesie of

Coleridge. Romantic culture in other countries should be cited here too: German Romanticism for example (Novalis, Friedrich Hölderlin, Casper David Friedrich, Philipp Otto Runge, Friedrich Schiller, Ludwig Tieck, Heinrich Heine, the Schlegel brothers, and Johann Wolfgang von Goethe). The Romantic ethics of taking things to extremes, of going to the infinite and the eternal, of solitude, of the individual's experience, of the sacred, are very much to the fore in land art, which is an art which quite definitely sustains Romantic myths and tenets.[3] For Stephen Bann, the precursor of Long's formalism is not the Romantic mimesis of J.M.W. Turner, but the cut and paste techniques of the Cubists.

Some of Richard Long's photographs and textworks are reminiscent of a poetic kind of eidetic imagery. In a way, what poets are talking about is the sense of heightened awareness which Long aims for on his walks (something like the enhanced perception which mountaineers sometimes experience). There are many ways of achieving it (drugs, sex, music, yoga, meditation, sleep deprivation), but for Richard Long, it's walking.

4

Richard Long and Other Land Artists

ROBERT SMITHSON was the chief mouthpiece of American land art/ earth/ site æsthetics, and is probably the most important theoretician among all land artists (he is also the premier land artist by common consent among critics and fans of land art). Robert Smithson's theoretical statements were published in three important essays. In "The Crystal Land" Smithson recounted a trip he made to a quarry with Donald Judd, the key Minimal artist (this sort of trip was a favourite Smithson activity). Smithson evoked the decayed nature of the quarry in his article, those aspects of entropy which would feature in his own work ('cracked broken shattered earth, of fragmentation, corrosion, decomposition, disintegration, rock crisis, debris slides, mud flow avalanche' [1979, 20]). In the second essay, "Entropy and the New Monuments" (1966), Smithson discussed the important Minimal show *Primary Structures* at the Jewish Museum.

CARL ANDRE is an important figure in a discussion of the art of Richard Long. Apart from the fact that they are good friends, and have had exhibitions together, Andre's ideas on art, and the kind of art he produces, have many affinities with Long's view of art and the work he creates. Andre, like Smithson and Morris, has been among the most lucid of Sixties theorists among artists.[1] Andre has many pertinent things to say about sculpture. His mid-1960s summary of the history of sculpture applies directly to land art:

The course of development
> Sculpture as form
> Sculpture as structure
> Sculpture as place.[2]

One of Carl Andre's most intriguing theoretical statements is this: 'my ideal piece of sculpture is a road'.[3] This applies not only to Andre's lines of bricks or hay bales, but to Long's lines of stones and walks along roads, to Christo's *Running Fence*, to other land artworks. Andre's notion of the ultimate earthwork as a road has a parallel with the famous anecdote of US artist Tony Smith who, when driving along the New Jersey turnpike, was impressed by the 'dark pavements moving through the landscape of the flats, rimmed in the distance, but punctuated by stacks, towers, fumes, and coloured lights'.[4] Something in such a long stretch of empty roads, as with airstrips (and, more dubiously, a drill ground at Nuremberg) impressed Tony Smith, who wrote '[i]t seemed that there had been a reality there that had not had any expression in art' (ib., 131). Roads are not 'art', not wholly functional either – they have an aura or mystery which Smith tried to explain. Richard Long emphasizes the functional or workaday aspect of his walks. He sees his walks as hard work; roads, in the Tony Smith view, are also for and about labour and functionality. The road, for the Minimal, serial or Process artist, in the Carl Andre manner, embodies materially the sense of a sequence or process. One unit (the foot or brick or slab of tarmac or concrete) is placed next to another, forming a road. Artists such as Carl Andre (and LeWitt and Judd) did exactly the same, putting one unit next to another, creating a line or sequence of units.

The road also may have no obvious end: endlessness was crucial to Minimal, Process and Conceptual art, as it is to land art. Many land artists emphasize art that goes on and on. Christo's fence, for example, goes on and on for 26 miles. One imagines that Christo would love a fence that could run across a whole country, or, even better, a whole continent. Similarly, Long's walks could extend far beyond their limits (his art could be regarded as one very long walk), and the modular art of Judd, Morris, Bladen and LeWitt could expand indefinitely, once the basic pattern had been established. The seriality or endless process of art was identified by Judd as the idea of 'one thing after another'.[5] Andre's concept of the road as the ideal artwork fits in with this urge towards endless process and seriality. The road motif also fits in well with stereotypical American culture, with its love of the 'open road', photography (Robert Frank), road movies (*Easy Rider, Duel, Natural Born Killers, Bonnie & Clyde*), the frontier spirit (in the Western literary and movie genre), the drifter, wanderer or nomad character, and in hippy and beatnik culture (Jack Kerouac's *On the Road*, Allen Ginsberg and the hippies).

DENNIS OPPENHEIM. Many aspects of Dennis Oppenheim's art chime with those of Richard Long's: the dematerialization of the art object; the emphasis on location (though Long doesn't make works to be visited outdoors); the emphasis on concepts; enlarging simple geometric patterns and projecting them onto the real landscape; forms such as circles, shoe prints and mazes; borderlands; and the photo, map and text pieces.

MICHAEL HEIZER. There are irreconcilable differences between Richard Long and Michael Heizer, which Long has drawn attention to (including economics, funding, scale, æsthetics). They do share, though, a love of deserts and wildernesses (in particular the South-West United States, where they have both made works). And they both love to work with stones and dirt.

JAMES TURRELL. Richard Long's æsthetics are not the same as James Turrell's: Long takes experiences he's had on his walks and presents them to the viewer, in his photoworks and text pieces. Rather than Turrell's notion of leading the spectator towards their own experience of a particular place, Long takes what he regards as the significant aspects of the location and presents them, packaged as he wants them (edited, reworked, framed), to the viewer. The biggest difference between Turrell and Long of course is that Turrell invites viewers to visit his structures and experience them firsthand – they can visit *Roden Crater* or the other skyspaces around the world. Indeed, it's the only way to truly understand what Turrell is trying to do. By contrast, the spectator is never invited to see the places of Long's walks. When William Furlong asked Richard Long whether he thought of the sites in the wildernesses where he took photographs as places people should visit, in order to experience the work directly, Long replied 'definitely not': 'he ruled it out as being in no sense relevant to the experience. The photograph was the thing'.[1]

WALTER DE MARIA made a dramatic land art gesture when he cut a 4.5 mile-long 6 foot-wide drawing in the desert in Nevada with a bulldozer (*Las Vegas Piece*, 1969). It was a classic piece of land art in the Michael Heizer or Robert Smithson mode (de Maria embarked on art-making excursions with both). Detractors have spoken of this cut as a 'wound' or 'scar' on the Earth. The ultimate in macho, 'look at me!' male land art must be de Maria's *Vertical Earth Kilometer*. At a cost of $500,000, de Maria sunk a one kilometre brass rod into the planet. Nothing can be seen of it except a two inch brass disc on the ground. A kilometre-long piece of metal stuck into the ground with nothing of it showing except a tiny disc was, in Richard Long's words, '[t]rue capitalist art', an art of excessive cost, and maybe excessive waste (it took 79 days to bore the shaft).[1] Shown at Kassel Documenta 6 in 1977, de Maria's *Vertical Earth Kilometer* irritated British artist Stuart Brisley so much he made *Survival in Alien Circumstances*. This was a hole in the earth dug with his bare hands, which Brisley lived in for 2 weeks, intending to mock de Maria's overblown American earthwork (Long has often commented upon other artists, but I don't think he's undertaken a political protest like Brisley's about de Maria).

DAVID NASH. One of the most intriguing and sensual of

land artists working in the British Isles is David Nash (born in the same year as Richard Long, 1945), with whom Andy Goldsworthy worked early in his career. David Nash's æsthetics chime with those of Long, Goldsworthy and Nicholas Pope among British artists.[1] Critic Hugh Adams saw David Nash as a kind of 'fixed abode Richard Long', working from one place (North Wales), while Long travels the globe, regarding the whole world as his studio, as material for making art. Hugh Adams wrote:

> Nash is Long in microcosm: the sensibility is the same but, whereas Long travels the world, making, marking, and recording, in distant places, Nash is more sedentary, and content to do the same thing where he has made his home.[2]

ANTHONY GORMLEY. It's Anthony Gormley who has made the sculpture in Northern Britain that has bedded itself in the public consciousness since the late Nineties: the *Angel of the North*, a 65 foot tall steel figure at Gateshead (1998). For many, especially those who drive past *Angel of the North* regularly, Gormley will be a name known to them via this hard-to-miss work, while Richard Long will still be largely unknown. It's ironic, because Long has been on the international art scene much longer than Gormley. However, if Long accepted the kind of commission Gormley undertook for *Angel of the North*, what would he make? A giant stone circle or line perhaps?

ANDY GOLDSWORTHY has created land art in Grise Fiord, the North Pole, in Japan, upstate New York, California, Castres, Digne, La Rochelle and Sidobre in France, the Australian outback, and in Haarlem, Holland. Goldsworthy has wound up in many of the same spots as Richard Long: Japan, California, and Australia, all favourite countries among international land artists, and has also exhibited in some of the same museums.

Andy Goldsworthy has not created art everywhere. There are plenty of places Goldsworthy has not visited for making art (he is not nearly as well-travelled as Richard Long). Even in the British Isles, Goldsworthy has not made much art in

Cornwall or Devon or the South-West (Long's stamping ground), or the East (Norfolk, Suffolk, the fens), not much in the English Midlands, only a few works in Wales, and hardly any in Ireland. If Goldsworthy makes work in the UK, it's usually Scotland, Northern Britain (Cumbria and Yorkshire, but not so much the North-East), or London. By contrast, Long has made many pieces in Scotland, but not so many in the Northern counties of Britain. Southern Britain, though, is Richard Long Central.

Andy Goldsworthy works with the natural world, and within nature. He uses natural materials in (apparently) natural shapes and forms set in natural contexts. Goldsworthy takes his cue from nature: as Jan Dibbets put it in 1969: 'I realized that if you want to use nature, you have to derive the appropriate structure from nature too'.[1] Goldsworthy seems to be a particularly gentle, modest and sensitive artist, compared to many sculptors and land artists: he stitches together leaves to form lines (which're often placed in water, or over branches), or makes circular slabs of snow, or entwines twigs in an arc. He creates a delicate spiral of chestnut leaves, called *Autumn Horn* (1986); he pins bright yellow dandelions on willowherb stalks in a circle, on bluebells (1987); he makes lines and cairns of pebbles; a horizontal line of red sumach leaves was pinned to a willow (at Storm King in 1998); he rubs red stones to stain rockpools; he pins leaves to tree trunks; he makes hollow, circular structures, recalling igloos, from slate, leaves, driftwood and bracken; he makes long wavy ridges in Arizonan and Australian desert sand; he throws sand and sticks in the air and photographs the moment; he makes arches, globes, hollow spheres, slabs, spires, spirals and star-shapes out of snow and ice. Very impressive it all is.

Then there's the globe made from oak leaves in various states of autumnal decay, superb (Dumfriesshire, 1985). Or the globe of sticks made in Fairfax, California (1995), set next to a sheltering tree. Or the sand serpent in the British Museum (1994). Or the globe made out of snow, and perched amidst some young trees (1980), or the slabs of snow, set up in a line with slits cut in them (1988).

For Richard Long, Andy Goldsworthy is a 'second generation' artist, and is 'decorative (!)'.[2] That's a put-down, by the way. Many critics, though, have been extremely praiseworthy of Goldsworthy's art. Goldsworthy sculptures such as *Yellow elm leaves*, *Red maple leaves*, *Beech leaves*, *Red river rock pools* and other riverside works seem so simple, so easily put together. But Constantin Brancusi's eggs and fish and heads are also very 'simple' shapes and forms: he reduced and rationalized natural forms until he reduced them to an 'essence' (the 'essence' of a fish, of a head, of a bird in flight). Yet Brancusi does not get accusations of superficially and banality thrown at him (well, not so much nowadays). Indeed, his sculpture is really powerful precisely because he radically simplified it.

Andy Goldsworthy's art, and Long's, may hit home because it does *not* bombard people with telephones, computers, cars, factories, radios, TVs, microwaves, washing machines, hoovers, irons, faxes, and all those machines and devices that connote *labour*, that are the symbols and mechanisms of working life. In Goldsworthy's and Long's green world, all is natural, untechnological, with artifacts that evoke a return to basics: stone, wood, leaves, ice.

Andy Goldsworthy's installation work *Stone sky* in Brussels (1992) comprised flat pieces of slate covered the entire floor of the large space, with a whitish circle in the centre, made by scratching the slate. The circle recalled Richard Long's slate circles, but the title, *Stone sky*, referred directly to nature: the circle could be read as the sun, the moon, the sphere of the heavens, the orbits of planets, and so on. One or two of Andy Goldsworthy's works directly recall those of Richard Long: Goldsworthy's *Burnt sticks* (1995), for example, is reminiscent of some of Long's and Nash's installations which form circles from stone slabs on gallery floors. *Burnt sticks* consisted of sticks charred at one end, the blackened parts of the sticks were put together to form a circle on the gallery floor.

CHRIS DRURY. Born in 1948 (in Sri Lanka) and educated at Camberwell School of Art in London in the late Sixties, Chris Drury belongs to the generation of Michael Heizer, Alice Aycock, Mary Miss, David Nash, Hamish Fulton and Richard Long (all of whom were born between 1944 and 1946). Drury began to make land art in the mid-Seventies; he had started out, like Donald Judd and so many sculptors and land artists (i.e., just about everybody), with figurative sculpture. Among the artists that Drury admired were Roger Ackling and Constantin Brancusi (Drury said he found Joseph Beuys 'immensely irritating' and 'too self-obsessed' [2002, 91]).

Chris Drury's art shares some affinities with Richard Long's: spirituality; working directly with the hands; the same forms (circles and spirals, though Drury employs many more vortexes and spirals than Long, as well as baskets, globes, shelters and cairns); simple materials gathered from the Earth: stones, wood, snow, mud, clay (Drury, like Long, doesn't use complexly manufactured materials); and similar territories: Japan, Italy, the US and Scotland and Ireland (Eire was a favourite place for both Drury and Long). (Long has travelled too far more countries than Drury, than most land artists – few land artists are as well-travelled as Long).

5

Richard Long and Hamish Fulton

One British artist, more than any other, is closest to Richard Long and his walk-based art and art of walking, and that's Hamish Fulton. A fellow student at St Martin's art school on the vocational sculpture course, Fulton was a vital influence in the early development of Long's art. For Fulton, as for Long, the walk is central to the artwork. If there is no walk, there is no work: 'no walk, no work', as Fulton put it. 'First the walk second the artwork' Fulton asserted.[1] Most of his walks have been made alone, Fulton said (though Fulton has also walked in groups, which Long hasn't really done, such as with C.A.S.K. in Japan). But not every walk needed to be be made into a work of art. They were sufficient unto themselves.[2] On the other hand, Fulton said he had to walk to be able to make a work of art. The artwork came out of the work, and if he didn't walk, there couldn't be any art.

There's a social link between Hamish Fulton and Richard Long too: they are good friends, and have embarked on a number of walks together (eleven walks, between 1972 and 1990). Fulton called his walks with Long 'the walks of a lifetime' (2002). It's interesting to compare the different ways that the artists responded to the walks they made together. The walks became inspirations for some of the key works in the *œuvres* of both artists.

Of fellow walking artist Hamish Fulton, Long commented:

> We are very good friends, we have a great deal of respect for each other's work and get on well together. We are old friends and have the same sense of humour. In many ways we are very similar – we are both artists, both like walking and camping, but having said that, we are very different artists. When we are on a walk we are both making completely individual work along the way – the collaboration is the walking. (1994b)

Like Richard Long, Hamish Fulton has his favourite walks and territories, where he has made many walks: the Pilgrims' Way in England, the Cairngorms in Scotland, Japan, and the Himalayas. Both Fulton and Long feature celestial events, such as full moons and solstices, and Fulton, for instance, has a walk entitled *Starting On the Day of the June Full Moon, Ending On the Night of the Summer Solstice* (1995), which could easily be a Long walk and work. Both do coast-to-coast walks, and classic hiker walks. Both have walkworks which record the sounds heard on their walks. Both are nuts about the Orient – Tibet, Japan, China – and the poetry, customs and religion of those regions. Both tend to walk in wilderness or non-urban places (and only feature that type of terrain in their works). Both assert the primacy of The Walk above everything else, including all of the secondary material that comes afterwards, including art.

Both Richard Long and Hamish Fulton have conducted walkworks without sleeping, such as walking through a day and a night without sleep. Fulton, though, has gone much further than Long in this regard, and has tested himself by walking for long distances without sleep (such as his walk along the Pilgrims' Way in Southern England between December 21st and 23rd, in 1991, a 125 mile continuous walk without sleep. Or his *Seven Walk Without Sleep* (the *Winter Solstice Full Moon* walk of 1991 being one of them). Fulton likes to toy with the hallucinations and altered states that sleep deprivation brings (i.e., it can be a walk along a familiar route, but it's a completely different experience because the artist-walker's gone without sleep).)

Many of Hamish Fulton's artworks are very similar to Long's – text-works, photoworks, photographs of mountain tops or hillsides or country lanes or lakes or snowfields. And both Fulton and Long opt for irregular snaking lines on gallery walls to indicate the routes they undertook. And they both quote words in Japanese and Chinese ideograms. Like Long's textworks, Fulton photo-works and textworks recall concrete or visual poetry, word sculpture, *haiku,* diaries and journals, and Conceptual art.

Hamish Fulton's art differs from Richard Long's in terms of the appearance of the textworks and wall works. Fulton loves to set text in a variety of typefaces, so that his exhibitions and books look a little like a typographer has gone nuts. While Long usually sticks to trusty old Gill Sans, Fulton happily indulges in shadowed capitals, white out of black, vertical type, extra bold fonts. Fulton, like Barbara Kruger, also loves very large and very bold (and coloured) lettering (such as in *Sweet Grass Hills* [1999], and *Warm Dead Bird* [1999]). (Fulton did not, though, make the wall works in his exhibitions himself. Unlike Long with his handmade mud drawings, Fulton gave the job of putting up his texts and photoworks to others.)

Both Hamish Fulton and Richard Long employ short phrases which aim to capture some of the experience or remind the viewer of some-thing of their walks. In a seven day walk in Scotland, Fulton fills a work with lines and lines of descriptions of the walk which recall many of Long's works: 'sound of the small stream / pale grey pale blue yellow sky in the late afternoon / small herd of deer one rubbing a branch stop look turn and run'. In a 1987 walkwork made in Mexico, Fulton writes: 'shooting star – dark night – grey morning – snowflakes – snow covered ground' and so on. Short phrases which, like Long's, sometimes evoke a *haiku* approach to the evoking the experience of the walk (*less* may be *more*, but

Fulton certainly likes to fill some of his walkworks with hundreds of words). While Long counts hours or days or miles, Fulton has sometimes counted footsteps as a way of measuring a walk (as in *Counting 6234 Barefoot Paces* [1994-97], or the barefoot paces counted in Kent between 1999 and 2001).

Hamish Fulton had more a philosophical and ascetic view of walking-as-art than Richard Long.[3] Walking was not, Fulton asserted, for recreation or leisure or for studying nature, or for taking photographs or making sculptures along the way.

As well as the numerous similarities between the art of Hamish Fulton and Richard Long, there are plenty of key differences: no sculptures in Fulton's work, like Long's stone, bone, wood, slate and mud circles, rows, lines or ellipses, on the wall or the floor. No sculptures made out of doors on walks and photographed. No water splashes or waterlines. No lines made by kicking away stones or flattening grass. No marks made by sleeping places or tents. No fingerprint marks on pieces of wood or hand-made Korean paper. No walks within imaginary circles or along imaginary lines. No mapworks (or very few). No walks carrying stones (or throwing stones, or adding them to cairns).

As with Richard Long, Hamish Fulton rarely included images of people in his art, but his art 'should not be thought of as anti-people' (1995). Instead, Fulton's photographs are of wildernesses (mountains, lakes, forests, fields and country lanes). Fulton separated the walk from the artwork. 'The artwork cannot represent the experience of a walk', Fulton affirmed (1995). The walk was always elsewhere, always only for the walker-artist. 'The *location* of the walk is not in the gallery – and the walk itself is a past event'.[4]

The walk was the thing, always. 'I am an artist who walks, not a walker who makes art' Hamish Fulton said (1995); this is also Richard Long's stance. Although he walks to make art, Long definitely isn't a walker who also makes art. Fulton complained that he seemed to spend more time on organizing exhibitions, on admin and paperwork, than walking (1995).

And, like Long, Fulton said that his walks were not performances.

Hamish Fulton's artistic inspirations came from mountaineering and the exploits of mountaineers such as Reinhold Messner, Peter Boardman and Doug Scott (Fulton, like Richard Long, has travelled many times in mountain regions, but neither would call themselves professional climbers; Fulton has climbed some high peaks, but says he's an 'armchair mountaineer').

Another influence was American Indian culture (Hamish Fulton had visited the sites of Sioux, Cheyenne and Plains Indians in the late 1960s). Yet another was ecology and ecologists (Fulton voiced ecological concerns more often than Long, and is a more politicized artist). Fulton also drew on pilgrims and pilgrimages (he has walked a number of pilgrim routes, including Pilgrims' Way, near his home in Canterbury in Kent). Tibetan religious art, *haiku* poetry from Japan (Santoka Teneda and Basho), and 'the walking peoples of the world from all periods of history' were also cited by the artist (1995).

Among artists, Hamish Fulton has referred to Marina Abramovic, Nancy Wilson, Roger Ackling and Richard Long as influences. He also cited *Monsters From the Deep* (1997), a CD by Lawrence Weiner, Bruce Nauman's video *Good Boy Bad Boy* (1985), and native cultures as some of the art he admired (such as the Huichol of Mexico). The Marathon Monks of Mount Hiel (Tendai Buddhist monks in Japan) were also inspirations for Fulton (in particular their repeat walks, walking around a hill for seven years until they had travelled the same distance as the circumference of the Earth).

In "Old Muddy", Hamish Fulton ruminated on working and walking with Richard Long. In the course of the short piece (published in Walking *In Circles* for the 1991 retrospective), Fulton referenced Chuang-tzu, the *Tao Te Ching*, Shakespeare, Dostoievsky, Santoka Teneda (the Japanese *haiku* poet), Bob Dylan, and the Nazca Lines.

Hamish Fulton resisted being categorized as an artist

related to the British Romantic tradition or landscape tradition. He wanted to work, like Long, in an international mode, and not be tied down to the provincial British view of landscape art. He said he was not part of the outdoor sculpture tradition, either. He also preferred, like Long, to walk in landscapes wilder and more extreme than those found in dear old Blighty. Fulton said he respected and was a devotee of countryside walking, but he needed extreme conditions too, like the Himalayas or Alaska. Fulton was happy that his work had 'never been fashionable', that he had survived so long in the art world, and that he could continue to make a variety of work (2002, 107).

6

Richard Long:
The Art of Walking

A story current at the time [1967] told of Caro confronted by an arrangement of twigs in the exhibition hall of the St. Martin's sculpture department. A conversation ensued. Caro: "What's this?" Long: "It's one part of a two-part sculpture." Caro: "So show me the other half." Long: "It's on top of Ben Nevis." Caro: "So how can I assess it when I can't see all of it?"

Charles Harrison[1]

RICHARD LONG: ARTISTIC BIOGRAPHY

The central fact and act of Richard Long's art is walking. His work is founded on the art of walking, the act of walking, the actuality of walking, and on walking as art, as act, as experience. His walks become 'artwalks', artwalks which become artworks. He makes art-walk-works. For Richard Long, (art)walking is (art)working. As he walks he works. Art-walking and art-working become interchangeable. 'I have met with but one or two persons in the course of my life who understood the art of Walking, that is, of taking walks – who had a genius, so to speak, for *sauntering*' wrote Henry David Thoreau.[1] 'I like simple, emotional, quiet, vigorous art' said Long.[2]

Much of Richard Long's art consists of measuring walks, mapping walks, planning walks and executing walks. Memories of walks, dreams of walks... walks in the past, in history. Later and earlier walks in the same landscapes: Dartmoor, Somerset, Ireland, Scotland, Italy, Mexico, India. Real walks, but also artwalks. Walks along imaginary circles or lines. Walks between celestial occurrences such as sunrises or eclipses or solstices. Routes planned and mapped in the studio then carried out in the real world. Walks carrying stones, throwing stones, dropping stones, piling stones. Splashing water. Photographing campsites or mountaintops. Walks in forests and deserts and plains and villages and cities and leafy country lanes. Walks in which lots happens and walks in which nothing much happens. Walks in which hardly anyone is encountered. Walks executed mainly alone, but sometimes with others. Occasional walks with other artists, or critics, or friends. Walks which produce many sculptures along the way and walks which produce only a few words in a frame. Walks which don't produce any work at all. Favourite walks, favourite routes, favourite places, favourite terrain.

Walks that always work (there are no failed walks in Richard Long's art – Long has been walking for too many years to have a bad time walking... he doesn't seem bothered much by the harsh elements, and rarely mentions things that go wrong). But not all walks produce artworks: unseen walks are as important as the exhibited walks. However, not all artists exhibit their failures, and there could have been many failed walkworks (though this is unlikely).

Walks in all seasons and all weathers. Walks through the night. Continuous walks. Slow walks and rapid walks. Meandering walks. Short walks. Long walks.

Richard Long was born June 2, 1945, Bristol, UK. He's of the same generation of land artists such as Alan Sonfist, Charles Simonds, Michael Heizer, William Furlong, Alice Aycock, Mary Miss, Bruce McLean and David Nash, all born between 1944 and 1945. Long studied at the West of England

College of Art in Bristol (1962-65) and the famous St Martin's School of Art (1966-68). Long said he used to go on treks with his father – youth hostelling, hitchhiking and cycling (Long's father was a teacher; his parents had met at a rambling club [SS, 307]). Long still lives in Bristol, and is very active, travelling the world, making art, and having exhibitions.

In 1967 Richard Long made his first important walkwork, *A Line Made By Walking*. Long's first one-man show was in 1968 at Konrad Fischer in Düsseldorf, when he was 23 (success came quite early to the artist). Like most land artists, Long makes indoor (gallery) works and outdoor works (not intended for public consumption – at least when they are made). He also produces art books, which are not typical exhibition catalogues, but artworks in their own right, usually with text-works, photoworks, and sometimes map works (he publishes limited edition artists' books too).

Among the influences one can discern in Richard Long's art (*haiku* poetry, Zen Buddhism, Shinto, British Romantic culture, Lawrence Weiner, Yves Klein, Hamish Fulton, Constantin Brancusi, Carl Andre, Joseph Beuys), there is also Jackson Pollock. Long acknowledged the influence of Pollock in making his mud drawings: 'Jackson Pollock has always been an iconic and legendary modernist for my generation, and for me he is also authentically primitive in some ways' (1995a). Long cited John Cage as another inspiration (he had seen Cage give a lecture in central London while at St Martin's).

Richard Long has had one-man shows at most of the major Western galleries.[3] The biggest collections of Richard's Long's work available to the public are, as one would expect, in the United States and Europe (in Europe: mainly France, Germany, the Netherlands and the UK). There are examples too in Japan, Canada and Australia. Long has work permanently on display in many museums and institutions, including Donald Judd's Marfa site, Tokyo International Forum plaza, Jesus College in Cambridge, and museums in Bordeaux, Bristol, Edinburgh, Duisburg, Mannheim, Rivoli, San Francisco, Seattle and Beirut.

Richard Long hasn't nearly so many works in sculpture parks in the UK as many other sculptors (whether British or international). Many of the major British sculptors have works in the sculpture parks of Albion (Yorkshire Sculpture Park, Forest of Dean Sculpture Park, Sculpture at Goodwood, Grizedale Forest, and King's Wood, Challock), and around the world. Long has exhibited at Goodwood, and East Wintersloe, Roche Court, in the UK. Long prefers to donate or sell works to indoor museums and galleries, rather than outdoor sculpture parks. In the New World, Long's British contemporaries have many more works in sculpture parks and sculpture gardens than Long does (such as Andy Goldsworthy, David Nash, Anthony Caro, William Tucker and Barry Flanagan).

The three important, must-have Richard Long books are: *Richard Long* (1986), *Walking in Circles* (1992) and *Walking the Line* (2002). In the second rank of Longania would be books such as *A Walk Across England* (1997), *A Moving World*, (2002), *Mirage* (1998), *Spanish Stones* (1999), *Dialog with Jivya Soma Mashe* (2003), and Long's Anthony d'Offay books: *River Avon Book* (1979), *Five, Six, Pick Up Sticks* (1980), *Sixteen Works* (1984), *Old World New World* (1988), *Kicking Stones* (1990), *Mountains and Water* (1992) and *Walking, Mud, Stones* (1995).

In some of his more recent shows, Richard Long has taken to producing smaller works on plywood and paper (designed to be portable and sellable). At Sperone Westwater in 2004, for instance, Long installed mud drawings on wood, as well as his usual bigger sculpture (a stone floor-standing ellipse [*13th Street Ellipse*, 2004], and paths on the floor of pieces of wood set end-to-end, very much in the Carl Andre manner). The mud drawings, in the familiar Long forms, were smaller than usual: blocky spirals, open circles, but they also recalled paintings, in particular Minimal works of the 1960s, such as Robert Ryman and Brice Marden. For the 2003 *Hand Made* show at Galleria Lorcan O'Neill Roma, Long produced mud wall drawings (*Untitled*, 2003) on plywood.

Winning the Turner Prize in 1989 was probably the

highpoint for Richard Long in terms of media exposure in his homeland (although the premier arts prize in the UK has an even higher media profile now than it had in 1989). Long has been awarded a number of other prizes and awards (including a doctorate from the University of Bristol in 1995, the Chevalier dans l'Ordre des Arts et des Lettres in 1990, the Wilhelm Lehmbruck-Preis in 1996, and the Kunstpreis Aachen in 1988).

Richard Long also produces artists' books, signed editions and limited editions of his books. *Being in the Moment*, for example, comes in an edition of 60 (from PARC Editions, Holland), with screenprints and offset prints, signed by the artist, and retails at 4,000 Euros. The artist's book *Walking and Sleeping* is published by Ivory Press (London) in an edition of 58, with a price tag of £18,000. 16 copies feature hand paintings by the artist; price: £38,000. Long had produced artists' books from the start of his career: in 1970 he made *Along a River Bank*, a small book (4 by 8 inches) published an edition of 300 (by Art & Project).

Stones along the Way (1999) was a series of 12 etchings, each image comprising a thin line, roughly circular or elliptical, traced onto grey paper, with distances printed on each print: 572 miles, 846 miles (apparently records of walks). Richard Long publishes limited edition prints too. For instance: *Limestone Drawing One and Two* and *Slate Drawing One and Two* is a portfolio edition of four screenprints (in an edition of 40, published by Ridinghouse Editions, London), price: £3,500. A limited edition screenprint (200 copies), signed by the artist, was produced by Tate Gallery, St Ives, to coincide with its *A Moving World* show in 2002 (retail: £255, plus postage & packing). There are Richard Long postcards sets and posters, too. In terms of work sold in commercial galleries, a typical price for a Richard Long textwork in 2000 (being sold at Anthony d'Offay gallery in London) was £20,000.

Richard Long hasn't been as prominent a fixture on television or radio as many artists. Certainly, British artists like David Hockney, Richard Hamilton or Sean Scully are far more likely to crop up on a TV arts documentary than the much more reclusive Richard Long. The YBAs and Brit-art crowd are of course media-hungry: Damien Hirst, Tracey Emin, Sarah Lucas, Mark Wallinger, the Chapman brothers. They'd appear on TV even if it was to discuss the price of teabags. Long is the opposite of that kind of celebrity artist, art as celebrity, celebrity as art, the post-Warholian cult of celebrity.[4]

Richard Long is associated with the American land, Minimal, Process, Conceptual and postmodern artists (such as Lawrence Weiner, Michael Heizer, Walter de Maria, Dennis Oppenheim, Nancy Holt, Mary Miss, Alice Aycock, Judy Pfaff, Donald Judd, Robert Smithson, Eva Hesse, Richard Serra, Tony Smith, Robert Morris, Jackie Winsor, Sol LeWitt, and especially Carl Andre), and with European Arte Povera and Minimal/ Conceptual artists (Hans Haacke, Christo, Jannis Kounellis, Lucio Fontana, Alberto Burri, Piero Manzoni, Daniel Buren, Giovanni Anselmo, Mario Merz and Jan Dibbets). Other key names one might link with Richard Long include John Cage, Jackson Pollock, Joseph Beuys, Yves Klein, Constantin Brancusi, Isamu Noguchi, Mel Ramsden, Joseph Kosuth, Bruce Nauman, Barnett Newman, Anthony Caro and Henry Moore.

Contemporary students of Richard Long's at St Martin's art school included Gilbert & George, Bruce McLean, Barry Flanagan and fellow artist-walker, Hamish Fulton. Long is also associated, at various times, by various critics, with other British sculptors such as Tony Cragg, David Nash, Richard Deacon, Shirazeh Houshiary, Ian Hamilton Finlay, Michael Craig-Martin, Nicholas Pope, Peter Randall-Page, Stephen Cox, Bill Woodrow, Anish Kapoor, Hamish Fulton, Alison Wilding, Richard Wentworth, Boyd Webb and the Art & Language group. These sculptors are sometimes grouped together as the 'New British Sculptors' or 'the New Sculpture' (but every few years or season there's a *new* New Something or other). The 'Young British Artists' (Hirst, Emin, Wallinger, Lucas, Chapman), for instance, are well past their sell-by-date, and into their forties.

Richard Long employed Minimal forms throughout his artistic career: the circles, lines, rows, ellipses and arcs are very much Minimal forms. The materials Long used drew on Arte Povera (mud, stone, wood, bark, bones, grass). The art of the walk, which Long perfected to become the ultimate artist-as-walker (drifter, nomad, traveller), was based on Conceptual and Process lines: the *idea* of the walk was critical. Long walked in imaginary circles or straight lines (sometimes he meandered, or walked slow, but usually quite fast). He followed routes planned beforehand on maps. The walk itself was the sculpture, the artwork. The work could be as long as the walk. The emphasis was on making the walk itself, the experience of actually walking.

Richard Long appears as a late British Romantic landscape artist, someone who fuses Sixties Conceptualism with 1800s pantheism; he's something of a High Modernist and a postmodernist Conceptualist. He has been described a 'traveller, explorer, pilgrim, shaman, magician, peripatetic poet, hill-walker' as well as an artist.[5] He says it is not enough for him to have an idea or concept: he has to make it (RC, 23). That separates him from some of the more ascetic Conceptualists for whom art doesn't necessarily have to be made. The stone circles of Richard Long espouse the sensuality and beauty of the post-Romantic and modernist art object (as in sculpture by Rodin, Picasso, Maillol, Moore, Kollwitz), while his photographs, map-works and textworks exhibit the cool, philosophic distantiation and ideations of Process, serial, ABC, Conceptual and Minimal art. The mud and stone and terracotta works are real, sensual objects, which satisfy the modernist critics who exalt the art object (Long likes to provide real, physical sculptures at his exhibitions). The text and photographic pieces, hoever, 'feed the imagination', as Long told me;[6] 'they are the distillation of experience'. But they are only understandable (assimilable), like television shows or traffic signals, by a heavily enculturated imagination. The text pieces are linguistic structures, dependent for their effect on what the viewer brings to them.

Richard Long's art mixes contemporary and Romantic æsthetics. For Anne Seymour, Long 'has not only penetrated more deeply into the world of natural landscape than anyone since Turner, he has taken abstract art with him, creating a new art which allows all parties to retain their full identities' (OW, 54). Mary Rose Beaumont also places Long within a British Romantic tradition. This was a tendency of art criticism of the 1980s, as espoused by fine art gurus such as Peter Fuller and Robert Rosenblum. There was much talk in the 1980s of the New Romantics/ Neo-Romantics/ New Ruralists/ New Arcadians, and so on. Whether High Modernism or postmodernism, Classical or Romantic, Long's art is certainly a romance with the natural world, but always in an ecologically-friendly and Postminimal fashion. Long lives in Bristol, where the pagan/ New Age/ hippy influence is very prominent, and in all points South and West of Bristol (and Long employs many the sites sacred to pagans, New Agers, witches, hippies and tourists in his walks and works).

Richard Long often revisits places many times, Dartmoor being the most obvious case. Dartmoor's a large area of South-West England, but even after a few walks one would soon begin to repeat and revisit places and routes (Dartmoor's 365 miles square). As well as the journeys that Long repeats, he has also revisited particular artworks he'd made years before (which could be the route of an earlier walk, a crossing-place, or a stone cross). In *Dartmoor Time* (1995), a text piece, for instance, Long noted how he passed 'a pile of stones placed sixteen years ago'. If one was able to layer Long's walks in Dartmoor on top of each other, on a map, there would be lines and routes everywhere: Dartmoor is a patch of land that Long has traversed many, many times over the course of his art and walking career.

Richard Long has tended to concentrate on favourite sites

for making walkworks (most walkers have their special places). The Longian territories include America, Scotland, England, Ireland, Italy, Portugal, Tanzania, Turkey, Holland, Japan, Lappland, Nepal, India, the Sahara, Argentina, Malawi, Bolivia, Ecuador, Canada, Korea, Finland, Mongolia, Mexico, Patagonia, Iceland and Peru. That's a pretty big number of territories for anyone to visit, let alone an artist (artists often being poor). But Long hasn't made walkworks absolutely everywhere on the planet. On the European mainland, for instance, Long hasn't made as much art as one would expect in Switzerland, Norway, Finland, Denmark or Sweden, Belgium, Spain, the former Yugoslavia, Hungary, Austria, Germany, Romania, Bulgaria, Albania, Turkey, the Czech Republic and Greece. Many of those countries contain landscapes Long favours.[7]

Most land artists have their preferred spots (like the Americans with the New Mexico, Nevada, Arizona, and California deserts). Richard Long has tended to make art in far more countries than many land artists. For instance, Long has walked in Korea, Malawi, Zambia, Kenya, Tanzania, Ecuador and Bolivia, which are not the usual stops on the land art circuit. One of the reasons must be that Richard Long's art does not require huge resources, materials, trucks and helpers: it is made mainly by one person using only the items necessary for a walk. The larger pieces of land art require large sums of capital, easy access, transport, materials, and many assistants. Another reason is that Long's art is not backed by big corporations or patrons. The economics of it are quite different from the art of the Christos or big public commissions. Long undertakes many private commissions, like many artists (land or otherwise), but most of his art is not public or corporate.

Like Ana Mendieta and Hamish Fulton, Richard Long uses his hands and feet to make his art, not an array of machines and tools. No motorcycles, snowmobiles, jets, planes, steam machines, chainsaws, cranes, diggers, tractors, dynamite, tankers, scaffolding or trucks (but transport must be provided for the stones Long uses from nearby quarries for his indoor stone sculptures). The aim is to be unobtrusive, 'invisible', in tune with the Earth. So Long acts like many environmentally-conscious walkers and trekkers: he covers his tracks, does not leave behind trash, does not harm nature. So fierce is the 'right on', politically correct eco-friendly tendency of some walkers and campers, they worry about leaving even a footprint in grass as they pass by. Hamish Fulton declines to make any mark on the world as he moves through it, except footprints. 'The natural environment was not built by man and for this reason it is to me deeply mysterious and religious'.[8] Fulton doesn't want to buy it, own it, sell it, build on it, alter it, deface it, exploit it or ruin it (Long does not go as far as the more austere Fulton, who can make Tibetan Buddhist monks look like cigar-chomping industrial capitalists. Long does use parts of the Earth, and does buy and sell the Earth: his mud drawings, his stone rows and circles, his works on paper and wood).

Richard Long has tended to avoid featuring himself in the flesh in his art; although his art is full of all sorts of embodiments of the artist, Long does not include portraits of himself. In a book like *Walking the Line* (2002), although photographs of Long were included, they were over-the-shoulder angles, or pictures of his hands making artworks (such as the fingerprint sculptures), without showing the face in close-up. Long appears in his art like glimpses, a vague presence; it's not that he's just stepped out of the frame – he was never anywhere near it in the first place. It's very different from the long history of artists who included self-portraits as one of their major themes (Rembrandt van Rijn, Max Beckmann, Egon Schiele and Vincent van Gogh).

In the mega-visual postmodern world, even complete unknowns can become celebrities, but many fans of Richard Long's art probably have no idea what the artist looks like. Andy Warhol, David Hockney, Salvador Dali and Barbara Hepworth are familiar faces, but not Long's. For those who haven't seen Long, here's a description by Mark Irving of Long at age 59: 'impressive with his tall rangy frame, close-cropped hair, piercing eyes and straggling eyebrows, he looks half-purposeful evangelist and half-wild countryman' (2003a).

It's the same with television, radio, the internet, magazines, newspapers and Richard Long's own books. Few of them feature headshots of the artist. During the making of a BBC TV documentary in 2004 (*Art and the Sixties*), Long permitted the film crew to shoot only his feet (on a visit to the site on an early Long work of the 1960s). Later in the show Long relented, and agreed to be interviewed in the usual manner (i.e., a medium close-up on his face in a room responding to questions). Long has been interviewed many times over the course of his career, though; he's just averse to personal appearances in the visual or electronic media.

Richard Long is not a performance artist, but there is an element of performance art about his work. He always performs privately. If he makes a mud wall drawing in a gallery, or builds a stone oval or circle in a public space, it is always before the exhibition opens, never during it. The construction of a Richard Long stone circle is never a performance in public in itself. It's the same with the artwalks: they are always made by the artist on his own, without witnesses or spectators. Very occasionally Long embarks on walk(work)s with other people (most famously, his walks with fellow artist-as-walker Hamish Fulton: they walked in Peru, Nepal, Alaska, Mexico, Lappland, India and Spain). The time and place and performance of the walk exist in a quite different time and place and context from their consumption by spectators as artworks, Long maintained.

But Richard Long's art was developed at the same time that performance art was a big thing on the art scene (in the 1960s and 1970s), and some of the theories and ethics of performance art (and body art) also apply to Long's art. For instance, responding to an environment, letting an artwork be shaped by an environment. Allowing for spontaneity, chance, and the unpredictable. Creating work based on simple concepts. Repeating an action many times. Including sound in a work. Performing random/ arbitrary actions (such as throwing stones). All of these (there are plenty more to consider) are part of the philosophy and methodology of performance art, and they are also part of Richard Long's art. (In a performance piece in Amalfi in 1968, for the *Third International Exhibition of Figurative Art*, Long shook hands with twenty or so people in the town square. That was an early work, a specifically performance piece. Long hasn't undertaken many similar performances since).

The tone of Richard Long's art tends towards the laidback, the mellow, the chilled; although he doesn't have the long hair, beard, jeans and West Coast colours, Long's art comes across as hippyish. The ideals, politics and worldview chime with those of the Woodstock generation (and the retinue of hippy stereotypes: the stoner, the drifter, the music fan). Anger, anxiety, pain, self-doubt, lust, aggression, neurosis, or psychic torment are not really a part of Richard Long's art. His art is not the haunted torture of Vincent van Gogh or Edvard Munch, or the flamboyance, narcissism and self-publicizing of Salvador Dali or Andy Warhol, or fiercely feminist body art of Ana Mendieta or Karen Finley, or the stridently ideological combat of Barbara Kruger or Hans Haacke, or the ironic, fey discoursing on the postmodern condition of Jeff Koons or Robert Rauschenberg, or the crazy performances of Stuart Brisley or Annie Sprinkle, or the *avant garde* poses of media favourites Yoko Ono or Matthew Barney.

A LINE MADE BY WALKING, A 2 1/2 MILE WALK SCULPTURE AND OTHER EARLY WORKS

Richard Long's 1967 walkwork *A Line Made By Walking* is routinely cited in art criticism as Long's first major work, but let's use another early piece to illustrate Long's æsthetics. In *A 2 1/2 Mile Walk Sculpture* (1969), made when Long was 24, the artist documented how he walked along parallel 55 yard lines four times. The first time, he walked 32 times back and forth, travelling a mile; the second time, 24 times, going 3/4 mile, the third time, 16 times (= 1/2 mile), and the fourth time, 8 times (= 1/4 mile). As well as the text explaining the walk sculpture, there was a photograph of the grass and lines Long walked, and a diagram of the lines.

This work contains all of the key elements of Richard Long's art: there's a photograph, written text, and a diagram. Each of those three media are vital in Long's *œuvre*. The work was exhibited as a wall piece. It originated with a performance, made by the artist, alone, with no witnesses (although not in the wilderness spots he became famous for – India, Peru, Iceland, the Sahara. Even though it's not Ladakh, it's still on grass, without people, houses, roads, factories, telephone lines, trash, etc, cluttering up the picture). It was not made in (or for) an art gallery. It was not a commissioned piece (the idea for the walkwork came from the artist, not from anyone else), or funded (it was not paid for any anyone, and the artist owned the work). It was not part of an artists' collective. It did not have manifestos attached to it, or political aims. It was Conceptual: the work was planned beforehand, then executed. The artist knew he was going to document the walk in some way – it would require at least the text, to explain what the artist did; a photograph was probably considered too before the walk was made (Long had his camera with him, and film in it); the diagram may have been an idea that came after the walk. It was partly about the artist's relationship with nature. It involved measurement, time, distance, speed, and direction, all ingredients which Long would experiment with throughout his artistic career. It was Process or serial art: it involved repetition (and meant repeating a simple action). It was composed of small units which were added together to form a larger unit. The materials derived from Arte Povera (grass). It did not 'add' anything to nature (it was not an object; but it did leave the mark of flattened grass). It had a simple geometry and form:

straight lines. The written text described the action of the work, including precise accounts of distances and times (with numbers prominent). The photo was a fairly straightforward documentation of the location of the work, and the action of the work (the grass rubbed flat), but the artist was left out of the picture. The walkwork took place during daylight (as most of Long's walks do). The photo, text and diagram is all that is left of the work: the actual walk took place at some former time (which Long usually includes in the documentation of his walks). The walk had to come first, before the photos, textworks and diagrams; Long didn't create the documentation then walk the walk. The exact location of the walk is not included. And the work was primarily a *walk*: the walking was the single most important aspect of the work: walking is the experience upon which all of Long's art is founded.

A Line Made by Walking (1967) was one of Richard Long's early walkworks, which was a short line made on grass and daisies. How did Long make it? By walking repeatedly over the same area, back and forth. This work had all the hallmarks of the Long walkwork, as discussed in relation to *A 2 1/2 Mile Walk Sculpture*: a definite intention, clarity of image/ geometry/ form, a countryside setting (well, grass and trees at least – it was near London, not in the wilder zones Long later visited), a sense of process and formalism, the direct touch of humanity and nature, the sense of time and impermanence, the relation with nature, and the relation between conception and execution.

Ben Nevis Hitchhike (1967) was the first of Richard Long's recognizable walking works: in it, Long hitchhiked to Ben Nevis mountain (in Scotland, and back to London, over 6 days. It was a map, text and photo work. Early on in his walking career, Long established the idea of basing walkworks on different types of walking: straight walking, meandering walking, circular walking, and so on (in *A Ten Mile Walk*, for instance [1968], Long 10 miles in a straight line).

In 1994, Richard Long looked back at the *Line Made By Walking* and remarked: 'I definitely had a sense that what I was doing was really important and I had a terrific conviction and belief that it was interesting' (1994b). In 2003, Long acknowledged that *A Line Made By Walking* was 'an utter *Arte Povera* work – it's made with nothing and is yet something' (2003a).

For critic Irving Sandler, *A Line Made By Walking* was Richard Long's 'prototypical, perhaps consummate, piece':

> It had all the components of his later outdoor work: an underlying concept; a minimal form; a substance found in nature that reverted back to nature after the piece was completed; and photographic and/ or other documentation. (1996, 62-63)

Of *A Line Made By Walking*, Tony Godfrey remarked that it was a performance piece, which anyone could do (democratic), which was recorded in a photograph (the photo could be exhibited – and sold), it existed outside the commercial gallery system, it was Conceptual (based on a single idea), and was ecologically sound (didn't have a damaging impact on the landscape).

Artist Jeff Wall related *A Line Made By Walking* to Barnett Newman's

> notion of the establishment of a 'Here' in the void of a primæval terrain. It is simultaneously agriculture, religion, urbanism and theatre, an intervention in a lonely, picturesque spot which becomes a setting completed artistically by the gesture and the photograph for which the gesture was enacted. (1995)

Although the photograph of *A Line Made By Walking* was documentation or reportage, Wall maintained, it also moved 'in precisely the opposite direction, towards a completely designed pictorial method, an introverted masquerade that plays games with the inherited æsthetic proclivities of art-photography-as-reportage' (ib.).

In the late 1960s Long photographed some concentric plastic stripes in a variety of settings (such as a beach in

Ireland in 1967). The works recalled Dutch artist Jan Dibbets' plays with perspective in the landscape (such as *Perspective Corrections*, 1968). Long made sculptures by cutting into grass (*Turf Circle*, 1966 and 1969). In 1964 he created a Goldsworthyan sculpture on the hills near Bristol: the track a snowball made as he rolled it along (*Snowball Track*. Talking about artists being 'child-like' – it's a favourite thing for children and adults to do with snowballs). On a beach in Somerset Long constructed an open square from pebbles (1968). On a beach in Cornwall he fashioned a spiral from seaweed (1970). A square spiral was created with his boot heel in 1970 (Long later made a boot heel line in 1997 in Argentina). Cross-shaped sculptures included one submerged in the shallows of Little Pigeon River in Tennessee (1970); a cross on grass and daisies (1968); a cross made by walking on wet sand at half-tide (Ireland, 1971); and a very large, wide cross comprising pine needles in London (1971).

RICHARD LONG: HOW TO WALK

*Afoot and light-hearted I take to the open road,
Healthy, free, the world before me.*

Walt Whitman, 'Song of the Open Road'

It is worth remembering that Richard Long's art comes out of the tough fitness culture of professional and dedicated walkers. The ethos and practices of the professional hiker and trekker informs much of his art. The professional walker aims to go, for a start, where there are very few people.[1] This is not a Sunday afternoon stroll along the cliffs after a pub lunch with five pints of real ale. This is hiking in wilderness country for days on end, carrying everything one needs (however, Long's art is not about adventure and adrenalin activities or extreme sports: he's not going to make a blurred photowork taken on a bungee jump over a gorge in Oz, or a textwork based on some rad skateboarding in Detroit. Canoeing, cycling and walking and occasionally a bit of mountain climbing are more the order of the day).

The professional walker typically has a good pair of boots, which become like old friends, fully waterproof clothes, a backpack, a compass, a map, food, clothing, water bottle, hat, walking stick, rope, sleeping bag, stove, matches, flashlight and a tent, as well as other useful items. Many of these things feature in Richard Long's art – one sees the rucksack or tent in his photographs; the compass is used for walking in straight lines; water is tipped out of his water bottle to create sculptures that dry in the sun; and that all-important walker's tool, the map, is the subject of many works.

On his walking trips Richard Long said the tools he took with him for making art included leather gloves, a collapsible water bottle, and string (for drawing circles). For the walks in wildernesses, Long carries heavier gear, including heavier boots, fuel, a stove, camping gear, and all of his food. Sometimes he uses wood for fires, if there's any around. For the walks made on roads, or near towns or villages, Long travels lighter, buying provisions along the way, often staying in bed and breakfasts and hotels. A watch or clock is essential, too: Long is always logging exactly how long he walks for, and some walks, such as *North and South* (1991), are based around walking in one direction for a certain time, then changing direction. In other walkworks, Long walks for sixty minutes then stops (as in *Hoggar Hour,* or *A Sixty Minute Circle Walk on Dartmoor*, 1984).

Richard Long travels quite a bit, and has visited many countries to make his art or exhibit it. However, Long maintains that he is not a nomad, and is not constantly on the move. He always returns to Bristol, to his home, and to see his family, and do everyday, ordinary things, like shopping or gardening. Being at home is a way of recharging, too, so the artist has more energy and enthusiasm for future walks and works (1994b).

Richard Long's art suggests folklore and phrases to do with walking, some of which Long uses: 'walking the walk', 'walking it off', 'walking the dog', 'going for a walk', 'walking in circles', 'walking a line', 'walk alone', 'leaving no trace', 'leave nothing behind', 'travelling light', 'travelling is better than arriving', 'travelling without moving', 'like a rolling stone', 'free as the road', 'the open road', and so on.

Quite a few of Richard Long's walks (especially the later ones, such as *Heaven and Earth,* 2001) explore the notion of magnetic North (the compass is often mentioned, being one of the walker's chief tools). In *Natural Forces* (2002), Long writes of walking 'along magnetic force by compass'. In *A Walk of Thirteen Days in the Swiss Alps* (2000) he writes of 'turning around all points of the compass countless times'. Magnetic North is one of those invisible concepts to do with cartography that's bound to fascinate the boy scout in Long (the idea that submerged magnetic rocks hundreds or thousands of miles away can affect a tiny compass needle, and also guide a traveller even in an inhospitable and featureless wilderness).

In *Avon To Avon To Avon* (2001), Richard Long walked from one River Avon to another (a walk which could take place all over Britain, 'avon' being another word for river). Long limited himself to the River Avons flowing in Wiltshire, Warwickshire and Hampshire. In *A Highland Walk* (1988) the usual short phrases of the experience of the 244 mile walk, and things encountered on the 14 day walk, were printed in a pattern roughly corresponding to (or suggestive of) the actual route Long undertook. In *Hoggar Hour* Long listed his experience of walking for 60 minutes in the Sahara ('rock / yes / thinking / burnt / flies / boots / horizon').

Twelve Hours, Twelve Summits, made in Scotland in 1983, was a classic kind of professional walker work, a list of the summits Richard Long achieved over 5 days in the Highlands. Long has undertaken many classic routes favoured by hikers: coast to coast walks, walks around the tors of Devon, the Foss Way, the Ridgeway, and even Land's End to John O'Groats (that's *the* classic route across the British mainland, 900 some miles which remains very popular). Many ramblers will be undertaking those classic walks right now. (Little ol' Britain may not have New York to L.A., or across the Sahara, or the Silk Road through Central Asia, or the Great Wall of China, or coast to coast via the Amazon basin, but it sure as rock cakes has Land's End to John O'Groats. It may not be base camp to the summits of Everest or K2, but it's a good walk).

Water Way Walk (1989) was one of Richard Long's more complex textworks, recording a walk of 152 miles in England and Wales, and the many streams, drains, ditches and rivers encountered along the way. The text piece (printed in *Walking In Circles*) lays out the names of the rivers and streams in a pattern loosely approximating to Long's journey (and the work is complicated by Long printing the words in different sizes – i.e., 'River Severn' and 'River Wye', being big rivers for a tiny island like England, are printed large, while 'Ditch' and 'Stream', which don't have names, are printed very small).

From Tree To Tree (1986) was a textwork of a walk made in Avon, listing the trees Long encountered and how far along the walk he saw them:

OAK 9 MILES
SCOTS PINE 15 MILES
HAWTHORN 22 MILES
WILLOW 29 MILES (WC, 13)

Plenty of Richard Long's walks record pretty mundane, everyday events. *To Build a Fire,* made in Tierra del Fuego in 1997, registers nothing more amazing than building a fire at each campsite along a six day walk (Tierra del Fuego may be amazing, but building a fire isn't). *The Space of Time* (1999) simply records the number of days between two circular artworks, one made in Ecuador in 1998, the other in Greece in 1999 (Long likes to find ways of joining two separate walkworks together). In *Dry Walk* (1989), Long records he walked 113 miles between two rainfalls. In four walks on Dartmoor (*Distance and Time, Time and Distance*, 2000), Long simply lists how far he walked and how long he walked for on each day (that's the most basic Richard Long walkwork: how many miles, and how many hours).

In *Five Walks* (1993) the number 30 is the foundation: it comprised a walk of 30 miles, a walk over 30 crossroads, a walk lasting 30 hours, a walk passing 30 farmhouses, and a walk seeing 30 blackbirds. The number five is the star of another walk: five stones, five rivers, five tors, five bogs, five days. In *Up and Down* (1997) Richard Long produced a classic walkers' artwork: a record of the summits encountered on a 7 day walk in Eire:

FROM LECKAVREA MOUNTAIN 2174 FT.
TO LETTERBRECKAUN 2193 FT.
TO BENBAUN 2395 FT.
TO BENCOLLAGHDUFF 2290 FT.

The list of peaks and heights might appear in a walker's notebook after a hiking vacation in the hills.

Many of Richard Long's walkworks are illustrated with landscape photographs of the terrain traversed, and don't feature art objects such as stone circles or rows or waterlines. Instead, there are photos of clouds, mountains, forests, lakes, rivers, boulders, snow and trees: *An Eight Day Walk in Adamello* (2000), *An Eight Day Walk In the Rimrock Area of the Mojave Desert* (1994), *Wet Weather Walking* (1993), *Crossing the Duzon* (1992) and *A Southward Walk of of 220 Miles In 14 Days Across the Middle of Iceland* (1994).

While the photos of rows, lines, crosses, cairns, ellipses and circles attest to a recognizable art object made along the way of the walk, the works without these productions emphasize that the walk itself is the artwork (as in *The High Plains* [1974], a photowork of a walk in Canada). These photographs are not holiday snapshots, though, but they do serve a very similar function: they state *I was there*. The spectator is invited to interpret these photos as a record of the artist actually walking in those landscapes. Vacation photos have the same purpose. Buying postcards or mementos is not enough: tourists and holiday makers take their *own* photos or videos of places they visit, to personalise it. And tourists and visitors typically compose photos where they are standing in front of some monument, view or landmark, again to emphasize their presence at the site. That's not too far from Richard Long's photographs of his walkworks: note how many times Long includes mountains in the background, which say 'Andes' or 'Alps' or 'High Sierra'. Or parts of a desert which say 'Gobi desert' or 'Sahara desert'.

A Walk Across England was a walk from the West coast (in Devon) to the East coast (in East Anglia), with the results published in a book (1997). Richard Long was commissioned to produce the work by Children's Library Press of California. The work contained the usual images in Long's art: country lanes, wide views of hills and fields, streams, gates, bridges, cows, a white horse, boats, clouds, and a windmill. So far, so expected, so Longian.

But there were photographs in *A Walk Across England* not usually found in Richard Long's art, and many of these pictures featured smaller details of the landscape, such as: a dead fox, a snail, a red postbox, street signs, a dead tree, a church clock, a railway crossing, cow shit, bird shit, flowers, puddles, a horse chestnut leaf, crops, a railway station, a dead badger, railway lines, canals, a wooden stile, sunbathers by a river, trucks, canal locks, a pub sign, tree roots, a goat, a ladybird, a phone box, boundary signs, a brick wall, poppies, urine, a pothole, a rock, a canoeist, a feather, apples, pigs and horses. There were also traces of Long himself: his shadow on the road, his boots, his socks, his bare feet in a river, his rucksack, and his campsite. The semi-documentary approach Long took in *A Walk Across England* recalled the work of British photographers such as Martin Parr (Long's book *Dialog* has a similar look).

Different kinds of walking are sometimes valorized in Richard Long's work: meandering walking, fast walking, slow walking (but not strolling or sauntering), straight walking and walking in circles. Also, walking while kicking stones and walking while making lines in the dirt with a boot heel. Judging by the amount of terrain covered in the times stated in his walkworks, Long must usually walk fairly fast, in the region of 3 or 4 m.p.h.

Sometimes animals appear in Richard Long's walkworks and text-works, such as the dog sitting beside the stone circle in *Leaving the Stones* (1995, Norway), the raven on a cairn in *Walk of Seven Cairns* (1992), the moorhens in *Mountains and Waters* (1992), cows in *Dusty To Muddy To Windy* (1993), horses on the Mongolia trip (1996), and monkeys in *A Walk In a Green Forest* (1997).

During his career as the world's premier artist-as-walker, Richard Long would have encountered thousands of animals. In many parts of the world they're a constant presence (even in tame, stuffy, cold, damp Britain, sheep, goats, cows, horses, dogs, chickens, insects, birds and fish are everywhere).

For Richard Long, walking itself is the primary act of his art. Walking is mainly what he does, as an artist. His talent, he says, is to be able to walk. Walking clears the mind, it is a process and experience of simplification and purification. 'I will try to have in my work only what is necessary to it' Carl Andre said (1984). Walking purges the soul, Long says, it forces the self to concentrate on simple things such as air, sky, earth, rock.

> Like art itself, it [walking] is like a focus. It gets rid of a lot of things and you can actually concentrate. So getting myself into these solitary days of repetitive walking or in empty landscapes is just a certain way of emptying out or simplifying my life, just for those few days or weeks, into a fairly simple but concentrated activity which, as you say, is really quite different from the way that people normally live their lives, which is very complicated. So my art is a simplification. (RC, 23)

For Richard Long, as for many people, walking is a way of

simplifying life, of cutting through the clutter. When walking, one moves into a different space, a space set quite apart from the rest of life. The time of walking is not the everyday, day-in-day-out time of the working world. It is not the profane, boring time of working at a check-out in a supermarket, or slaving away in some factory in Korea, South Africa, Denmark or Bolivia. Walking takes one right away from that sort of everyday time, into a non-profane time and space. Walking in fact sacralizes space and time. As the walk takes places, sacred time is re-instated.

Walking therefore has a religious or philosophical dimension, which sounds odd only if terms such as religion or art sound odd to the ear. In walking, in travelling, in holidays or other escapes and adventures, people put themselves back together. Walking in wildernesses, people say, is invigorating and refreshing: walking returns people to themselves, and of course renews their contact with nature (inner nature as well as outer). These things can sound stupid, pompous, pretentious – 'renewing one's contact with nature'. But one can't avoid nature in the wilderness everywhere– it surrounds the self entirely. Plus, the walker is also nature themselves.

> I do the things that have a deep meaning for me [says Long]. I have the most sublime or profound feelings when I am walking, or touching materials in natural places. That is what I've decided to do and that is what I am showing you in my art. (RC, 224)

The sculptures that Richard Long made on his walks are a response to the walk (or part of the walk), or an embodiment of the walk, or an eruption of an aspect of the walk. Long said that the sculptures he made on walks were a kind of celebration of the experience of being in particular place at a particular time, a little like celebrating a moment with a poem or a song (1995a). The sculptures also arose spontaneously, they were not planned in advance (2004b). All sorts of things could inspire the artist to make a sculpture in a landscape – something he hasn't seen before, or a particular alignment of forms in the landscape, or a nice flat piece of rock for a water-pour work. Chris Drury said that the cairns he constructed then took down in particular places were about a positive, celebratory response to a moment in time and space.

The continuity that Richard Long sees between the idea and the walk, between gallery art and art made under the sky, echoes the precepts of Western magic, where the realms of inner and outer are unified, summed up in that key phrase in magic, 'as above, so below'. Magicians imagine that the outer and inner worlds are connected, even that they are the same. Thus, what occurs within the magician occurs in the outer world too. Psychoanalysis sees magicians as less mature than, say, religionists, because they have confused ego boundaries: the magician's self extends beyond her/ his body to the world outside, and the magician imagines the world revolves around herself in some ways.[2]

People who are not psychologists or anthropological behaviourists do not speak of anal or oral immaturity: instead, they might see magicians and artists as simply acting at times like children. Which is fine. The sense of play is especially important for Richard Long, as it is for many (most? all?) artists. Defining the qualities of his sculpture, Long says the child and the adult cannot be separated, so that

> all the sensibilities that energize you as a child sort of flow through. And being an artist that means you can use them. So when newspapers derogatorily talk about my work as being sort of playing, like making mud pies or skimming stones across rivers or damming streams – all these childhood pursuits that people leave behind – I say "great!" I don't deny that I'm doing all the same stuff. (WC, 14)

The sense of play is something apparent in every Richard Long art book, every Richard Long exhibition, and every Richard Long walk. Only an artist with a keen sense of child-like play could produce a work called *Two Stones* which is a four day 122 mile walk across the North of England based on nothing more complicated than being a stone's throw from the two seas, Irish and North Seas (featured in *Mountains and Waters*). Another work, made in the Sahara, consisted of the artist clapping two stones together a thousand times (*Two Sahara Stones*, 1988). For many folks, that wouldn't count as anything anywhere near art. It might count as something that could be fun to do, if you like that sort of thing. But for anyone who knows anything about performance art, action art or Conceptual art, it's quite familiar.

> Richard Long [wrote P. Rodaway] builds his art from walking across the landscape, from an intimate sensual experience with space and the materials of his environment and forms his 'sculptures' in pattern with the landscape, its structure and material substance...3

Richard Long himself is not quite 'in' his art, though, as are, say, Gilbert & George or performance artists such as Kate Bornstein, Hermann Nitsch or Annie Sprinkle. Despite this, adoring fans such as Anne Seymour go so far as to state '[t]here is also a sense in which the artist not only walks the path or the line, but is the path itself' (WC, 9). Eh? It's true to say that Long's walks are his art, but not that the artist himself 'is' the path. Here Anne Seymour makes the old mistake of humanist/ modernist criticism, by conflating artist and art, the sculptor with his sculpture.4 No, Long's art is, finally, 'art'. It's not him, the artist is always 'elsewhere' (and Long always asserts that, and his art does too).

Richard Long said on his website that his

> intention was to make a new art which was also a new way of walking: walking as art. Each walk followed my own unique, formal route, for an original reason, which was different from other categories of walking, like travelling. Each walk, though not by definition conceptual, realised a particular idea. Thus walking – as art – provided an ideal means for me to explore relationships between time, distance, geography and measurement.

Richard Long's æsthetics emphasize simplicity, purity,

practicality, physicality, actuality and subjectivity. He iterates the simple gesture or structure or idea: if it's too complex, the artwork won't work. The practical aspect of handling materials is always crucial in art. As with Constantin Brancusi, purity is always uppermost in Long's theory of art. The physical and actual nature of his sculptures is what's important. And subjectivity, as in late 18th century Romanticism, rules all – so that, as Donald Judd said, paraphrasing Marcel Duchamp, 'if someone thinks it's art, then it's art'.

In Richard Long's sculpture, the subjective dimension is prime. He exalts the personal, the intuitive, the emotional: '[m]y art is about my senses, my instinct, my own scale and my own physical commitment.'[5] These are some artistic statements of Long's which typify his æsthetics:

> I like the simplicity of walking, the simplicity of stones...
> I like sensibility without technique...
> I choose lines and circles because they do the job...
> My work is about my senses, my instinct, my own scale and my own physical commitment...
> My work is simple and practical. I may choose rolling moorland to make a straight ten mile walk because that is the best place to make such a work, and I know such places well. (in RL, 236)

In *Walden*, Henry David Thoreau exhorts '[s]implicitly, simplicity, simplicity!... Simplify, simplify'.[6] Walking for Richard Long was a way of dealing with the things that sculpture or art deals with but in a way which was not bound up in the rules and genres and formal aspects of traditional sculpture. It allowed Long to step outside of art history, perhaps. Or to bend the rules a bit. Or to rewrite some of the rules.

> Walking as a medium enabled me to bring a big increase in scale and space (distance) into a work of art. Time could become a fourth dimension. Walking can express many different ideas. For example, I have used riverbeds on Dartmoor as footpaths; I have carried stones in my pocket

for many miles to make sculptures about movement, transference and relocation. I can use it as a simple human measure of time, like walking across a country, or from one planetary event to another, or from one shower of rain to the next. (2004b)

Richard Long summed up his art with some words in a May 25, 1997 lecture in Japan:

REALITY | TIME | MEMORY | SLEEPING | COUNTING | LANGUAGE | BOOTS | SOLITUDE | MAPS | MUSIC | TENT | HUMOUR | DISTANCE | INTUITION | EXPERIENCE | CHANCE | LOVE (WL, 147)

Denying it or hinting at it, Richard Long's sculpture is definitely 'religious'/ 'mystical'/ 'spiritual'. Walking itself is sacred; making art is sacred; the allusions to stone rings are religious; circles themselves are religious; the awe with which viewers regard the sculpture has a religious aspect, and so on. Not all of Richard Long's works are circles – there are always the lines. Long continued to make lines in the shape of a cross from time to time, such as in *Two Places* (Bolivia, 1972), where a small cross was made on marshland in a pile of stalks. Another cross was built in Iceland from some stones (*Stopping Place Stones*, 1974), or in the Sahara (*Crossing Marks*, 1988).

The crosses are very much like geometric marks 'drawn' onto the landscape, as if to mark a place. Most of the single straight lines are short, like the crosses, such as *Walking Without Travelling* (Sahara, 1988). Occasionally, Richard Long makes a square zigzag line: short right angles are marked upon bare soil, as in *Campfire Ash* (Bolivia, 1972 – most of these works are from *Mountains and Waters*). Another zigzag line sculpture, in Antwerp in 1973, extends outwards to take over the gallery: each Long sculpture is made for a particular space, and expands to consume the gallery floor. The zigzag lines recall the Peruvian Nazca animals and symbols drawn on the lava plain (Long had walked along one of the desert lines in 1972: he also made sculptures which employed symbols such as the puma, condor, falcon, moon, sun and rain). For his 2004 show at Mario Sequeira, Long built *Five Paths* (2004), with a wavy line space between meandering rows of stones. Long has his visual motifs which he returns to time and again, like most artists (circles, lines, rows, and, lately, ellipses and arcs).

Richard Long spoke warmly of Carl Andre and Lawrence Weiner, important Sixties Minimal, Postminimal and Conceptual artists (IC 2, 24). He has exhibited a number of times with both Andre and Weiner. The links between Long and Carl Andre include an emphasis on place; seriality and repetition; simple geometric forms; an emphasis on the experience of making the artwork; nature; the use of unadorned, untreated materials; floor-standing sculptures without pedestals; and objects used as things-in-themselves with don't refer to things outside themselves.

It is significant, too, that Long felt he was working on his own in Britain when he started out (in terms of being an artist making the kind of work he did). But when he stepped out of Britain he realized there was 'a whole new world of ideas going on'. Long notes, perhaps wryly, that '[t]here was an immediate interest and understanding of my work as soon as I stepped outside England' (IC 1, 17). Although Long lives in England and makes many pieces in the British Isles, he has always been very much an international artist, and has exhibited internationally far more than in his home country (perhaps his art was understood best first outside the UK). Long himself declines being described as a Conceptual artist ('[m]y work is real, not illusory or conceptual. It's about real stones, real time, real actions' [RL, 236]). He speaks sympathetically of Arte Povera, the use of 'simple, modest means and procedures' (GL, 6).

Some commentators have negated the tendency to view Richard Long in Romantic terms. 'Richard Long's landscape is... as modern (in feeling) as the city of Bristol from which he sets out for a walk' claimed R.H. Fuchs, one of Long's supporters (1986, 43). Richard Long, Fuchs says, tries to play down 'as much as he can the romantic/ Romantic, poetic connotations' of his locations (ib.). Yet, surely wildernesses such as Dartmoor, Mexico, Nepal, Canada and Lappland, where Long makes his art, have been inscribed with connotations of Romanticism. They are places now described in terms of 'spirit' and 'soul', spaces that in contemporary romantic, nostalgic culture imbue the observer with a sense of infinity, solitude, pantheism, awe, eternity and all the rest of the Romantic æsthetic portfolio. 'A walk is also the means of discovering places in which to make sculpture in 'remote' areas, places of nature, places of great power and contemplation' says Long, speaking in Romantic terms of his walks (RL, 236). The starting points and the end points of the *Four Walks* (1977) sound like a list of destinations a landscape painter might make for a 1790s Grand Tour of Britain: the source of the River Severn, Snowdon, Chesil Beach, Sherwood Forest and Carantouhil peak.

In a walk such as *Straight Miles and Meandering Miles* (1985), Richard Long walked some 'straight miles' along the way, between Land's End and Bristol. As expected, these 'straight miles' were walked in wilderness or countryside or 'Romantic' locations, such as Bodmin Moor, Exmoor and the Mendip Hills (those were places where swooning Romantics swanned around 200 years ago, as they do now – except that Romantics these days are called Goths, neo-pagans, hippies, ramblers, poets and artists).

There are plenty of built-up areas along between Bristol and Land's End that Long could have walked through when he made *Straight Miles and Meandering Miles*, but chose not include in his work: parts of Street, Taunton, Exeter, Plymouth, St Austell, Truro, Redruth, Cambourne and Penzance aren't particular picturesque. Anyone who has visited those places and many others in the Western hemisphere will know that apart from being surrounded by luscious countryside and wild moors, there are service stations, freeways, out-of-town retail parks (with their multiplex cinemas, supermarkets, household, gardening and electronic stores, Burger King, Pizza Hut, KFC and McDonald's), shopping malls (Gap, Boots, Woolworth's, Virgin), warehouses, car pounds, junk yards, hospitals, clinics, cemeteries, factories, power stations, office blocks, electricity substations and poles, telephone exchanges and call centres, ring roads and by-passes, highways, railways, train stations, gasometers, police stations, trash heaps, landfills, water and sewage processing plants, housing estates, tower blocks, and heavy industry. Not far from Long's beloved Dartmoor, for instance, a huge area of Plymouth is taken up by industry, military barracks and naval dockyards.

Although he may downplay the Romantic associations with the art made in or about landscape, Richard Long describes landscape in romantic, emotional terms. He reacts to landscape directly, facing it straight on, as is apparent in all his interviews and writings. He speaks of the need for transcribing landscapes purely and clearly. So, for instance, Long's photographs are simply taken, without too much trickery, and they are printed in a straightforward manner (although the emphasis on 'simplicity' doesn't do away with the many philosophical and technical complications of photography itself).[6] At the same time, Long speaks of 'places of great power and contemplation', terms which William Wordsworth might have used a hundred and fifty years before Long, or Henry Vaughan, the Metaphysical poet born on the Welsh borders, before that. Robert Rosenblum wrote:

> An artist I would think of as still perpetuating an older unbroken tradition of Romanticism is Richard Long who really doesn't have the irony of the 1980s, but he's been doing this for a longtime. If I had to have a candidate for somebody who perpetuated the imagery, the feelings, the emotions of someone like Constable or Wordsworth, I'd vote for him... He is somebody who really continues those endless magical communions with nature by talking, touching, feeling and accumulating. I find this very direct in terms of his experience and really very moving as a kind of endangered species, but it still works with him. I think he is the last of his race.[7]

Stressing the Romantic heritage and tradition of Richard Long's art though, only makes up part of the picture. Like other artists of the 1960s (whether Pop, Conceptual, Minimal, Process, ABC, Arte Povera, body, action, performance or other art), Long suppresses notions of poetry and Romanticism, as if that interpretation is too limiting, too much to do with art history, and too traditional and conventional. 'My art is not urban, nor is it romantic' Long claimed (RL, 236). Looking at *A Line in Iceland* (1982), a line of boulders Long built in a wilderness space and shot against a brooding sky and a backdrop of snowbound mountains, one can see the affinities with the High Romanticism of William Wordsworth's poeticizing of the Lake District, J.M.W. Turner and his watercolours of Snowdonia or the Alps, or John Ruskin and his evocation of the sublime.[8]

True, *Red Slate Circle* (1980) in the Fogg Art Museum in Cambridge (MA), or *Sandstone Spiral* (1983) in the National Gallery of Canada, or the *Puget Sound Driftwood Circle* (1996) in Houston, or *Forte de Vinadio Circle* (Italy, 2001), or *13th Street Ellipse* (2004, NYC) are set on museum floors, in the clean, sparse gallery environment, and look Minimal and sophisticated and not obviously 'Romantic'. What concerns Richard Long is that '[e]ach work is appropriate to its place and context', and the wilderness works and the museum pieces are 'equal and complementary'. What counts, Long says, is the feelings that the work, whether inside or outside, arouses: 'my ambition is basically with the emotional power of the work, in both idea and image' (SF). Walking, nature and the landscape are at the heart of Long's work (GL, 8), but Long knows, as any professional artist must know, that the art world conducts its business indoors (and in cities – and the international art scene where Long works and trades is concentrated in a few major cities). The art may be 'natural' or about the natural landscape, but the art world in which artists operate is distinctly urban, sophisticated, wealthy, highly educated and high culture. The *content* of Long's art is walking in the natural world, but the *context* is as urban as

Keith Haring, Jean-Michel Basquiat, Frank Gehry or anonymous graffiti artists tagging the New York subway.

The slate, stick, wood and footprint circles of Richard Long look like late 20th century artworks, not 'Romantic', but Minimal, Conceptual and Arte Povera, like Carl Andre's copper and zinc plate squares or Donald Judd's Plexiglas and steel stacks and boxes. They have a coolness and clarity that one associates with Dan Flavin's fluorescent tubes, Anne Truitt's rectilinear slabs, Tony Smith's cubes and the white open boxes of Sol LeWitt. Long's stone circles make sense to the viewer partly because of a grounding in the discourses of contemporary art. Without assimilating the circularity of signs that flow around contemporary art, the spectator might not know how to make full sense of Long's circles. True, the circle as a shape has been around for eons, but only in the contemporary era have circles been made out of bits of the landscape, in galleries and in landscape settings in this particular way.

> I think circles have belonged in some way or other to all peoples at all times [remarked Long]. They are universal and timeless, like the image of a human hand. For me, that is part of their emotional power, although there is nothing symbolic or mystical in my work. They are also easy to make. (1995a)

TARAHUMARA CIRCLE, 1987

Take Richard Long's *Tarahumara Circle* (Mexico, 1987): it's what seems at first to be a simple shape. But it's not 'simple'. It's a 'negative circle', a circle made into a circle by the ring of rocks around it (like *Walking a Circle In Ladakh*, 1984). The line of rocks marks out the circle, but not evenly. Some of the rocks are piled deeper on one side of the circle. Hardly anyone will have seen this circle intact, in its situation, so it's known only from a photograph. The seemingly straightforward approach of Long's photography has made a few æsthetic decisions, which shape the viewer's perception of this artwork. For instance, the viewer sees the stone circle in the centre of the frame, in the lower third, in the sort of classical composition that was taught in the fine art academies of yore. Behind the circle the trees and hills of Mexico are glimpsed. Long's photograph thus 'captures' the stone ring amidst the Mexican landscape, placing it firmly within a wilderness landscape. The setting is impressive and it is meant to be. With its wooded slopes and hills receding into the blue haze, the photograph is worthy of the ærial effects described by Leonardo da Vinci in his treatise of Renaissance painting. The composition of *Tarahumara Circle*, the more one studies it, becomes increasingly 'classical' and carefully controlled: there are even two small trees either side of the stone circle, in the foreground, framing the circle, a compositional device favoured by Turner, Girtin, Cotman and other late 18th century landscapists.

So *Tarahumara Circle* is actually a complex cultural artefact. The elements in *Tarahumara Circle* that could be called 'natural' or 'organic' (the landscape setting, the material used for the circle) are actually the last aspects of the work to be considered:. Sure, for the artist, they may be the most important, but they're just one component in a highly sophisticated manifestation of 'high culture'.

Although the photographs and textworks in Richard Long's output were part of a recording or documentary process, Long said he would not want his art to be entirely about documentation. That would appear too 'second hand'. He also had to make something; hence the indoor sculptures (2004b). That way, Long could present both aspects of his art – the faraway places in the photographs, and real artwork on the floor or walls of the gallery.

Richard Long says he has conceived particular walks precisely so he can document them in a textwork (1995a). In other words, the walk may come first, the walk may be primary, but while walking Long is also making art, and walks have been planned so they will fit into the format Long has developed for his textworks. It's an important point, because it indicates that sometimes something does come before The Walk, and that is The Idea. The Walk may be absolutely primary, and absolutely the foundation of Richard Long's art, but occasionally The Idea is as significant.

A RICHARD LONG EXHIBITION: ANTHONY D'OFFAY, 1993

Richard Long's Summer 1993 show at Anthony d'Offay in London was typical of his kind of art exhibition: in the three galleries of his UK dealer, Long showed a mix of sculptures and text/ map/ photographic works. In no. 23 Dering Street, London, Long exhibited a number of framed works, mostly of text, though there were also maps and titles of these works explains much of Long's typical preoccupations: *Mount Whitney Stone Circle*, *Orkney Stones*, *Old Year New Year Walk*, *Watershed* and *Walking a Circle on Hoy*. These works, from 1992 and 1993, contain the usual Longian obsessions (for instance, walking between two rivers, the Avon and the Thames, in *Watershed*, 1992). Other titles indicate the spiritual nature of Long's work: *Dorset Song Lines* (1991), for example, explicitly relates to the Australian aborigine 'songlines', and with ley lines in Britain of folklorists and occultists. The notion of Aboriginal 'songlines' is taken up by Richard Long in a number of works. Only in a few works, though, does Long directly refer to this notion of the leyline/ song line/ *feng shui* (dragon lines). In *Dorset Song Lines*, a textwork referring to a 7 day walk, Long draws in thick black ink the squiggly lines of his journey through the landscape, an artwork that is halfway between map-making and graphic art. Underneath each line Long prints the names of Dorset's sites, which are familiar as some of the places beloved of Thomas Hardy and his Wessex: Weymouth, Swanage, Cerne Abbas, Milton, Puddletown and Lyme Regis.

Upstairs at d'Offay's no. 23 Dering Street, Richard Long produced one of those circles for which he has become famous: *Midsummer Circles* was a slate circle (1993) over five metres in diameter: the definitive Long form. At no. 9 Dering Street, Long displayed a series of works on paper which were distinctly Oriental in content and appearance. They were calligraphic swirls and splodges of mud and ink on handmade paper, Japanese paper and Korean paper. All these works on paper were titled *Untitled*, which is *the* archetypal title for any 20th/ 21st century work of art. Some works, such as *Untitled* (1993) were described as 'Korean mud on Korean paper'. Other works, such as *Untitled* (1992), were billed as 'River Avon mud on Japanese paper'. The combination of the two elements: mud from near Long's home in Bristol and Japanese paper, is typical of Long's fusion of Eastern and Western culture.

At Anthony d'Offay's no. 21 Dering Street gallery in 1993 were the familiar large-scale Richard Long works: a huge spiral made from terracotta bricks, and a wall painted black and smeared with terracotta. *Footprint Spiral* affirmed the primacy of the body, of feet, of feet walking on the Earth. Each brick was a small unit with the imprint of Long's foot embedded in it. As with the stones in the lines or circles, each brick formed a chain in *Footprint Spiral*, creating a spiral. Walking is simply one step followed by another, and *Footprint Spiral* affirmed the significance of walking, the simplicity and beauty of it.

Untitled (1993) was a large area of liquid terracotta smeared or thrown at a wall. This work could only have occurred after the drip paintings of Jackson Pollock and the furls and curtains of Morris Louis's huge poured canvases. The splashes and smears of the ochre-hued terracotta on the black wall created a sculpture which absorbed the æsthetics of both painting and sculpture. Long's terracotta-smeared wall had affinities with 1960s painting, with installation art and performance art of the 1970s (Michael Craig-Martin and Andy Goldsworthy have produced flat, mobile wall-drawings).

It was not quite an 'installation', though the wall and its terracotta covering were specially prepared. It was not a 'performance', because Long had smeared on the terracotta at some earlier time, although the visitor to the gallery could see the splashes on the other walls, and on the floor. It was not, either, a 'painting' in the usual sense of paint on canvas. Nor was it truly sculpture, for it was essentially two-dimensional, a relief perhaps (or, more accurately, just a 'thing'). It was a thin layer of liquid over black paint, not really exhibiting enough volumetrics to be a 'sculpture' in the traditional sense. What mattered about the terracotta splashes, then? It was, perhaps, the actual look and feel and atmosphere of the liquid. For, as in Morris Louis's unfurled and curtain paintings, where the acrylic paint was poured directly onto unprimed cotton duck, Long applied the terracotta directly. The result is an immediate, tactile work. It is simply terracotta on a wall, like Carl Andre's bricks and metal slabs are just those things in themselves. This is, of course, the foundation of Long's art, this fusion of simplicity and complexity, thereness and otherness, inside and outside, nature and art.

THE HUMAN TOUCH

Richard Long uses his own life in his works. His walks are what he does much of the time, and these walks become his works.[1] To produce all those sculptures, have all those exhibitions around the world, and embark on those walks (plus preparation, admin, transport, accommodation, flights, etc) takes a lot of time and effort (and he must really enjoy it). There is an æsthetic and philosophical continuity between Long's life and his art. 'My art is the essence of my experience, not a representation of it' Long says (RL, 236). All art, though, is representation, isn't it (among other things)? Long tries to underline notions of essence, where art is always, if nothing else, a form of representation.

> I can use words and they can give me different possibilities than I would get from using a camera [says Long]. So, taking photographs does a certain type of job, records one moment, makes an image. And words do a different job. They can usually record the whole idea of a walk, maybe much better... (IC 1, 7)

Discussing the textwork *A Three Day Bicycle Ride* (1982) –

BIRTHPLACE   BRIDGE   THE FAST YEARS
1977 CROSSING PLACE   FOSS WAY   CHALK VALLEY
FELLOW TRAVELLERS ON THE SAME ROAD   FLINT
SOURCE

– which used many autobiographical elements[1] (Silbury Hill, the Foss Way, Bristol, his birthplace, etc), Long said: '[t]ime, distance, memory, history, and what the land is made of, places you meet, strangers you meet, the friends you stay with, it is actually a very dense work' (IC 1, 21).

True, the experience of making this work might have been very dense for Richard Long,[2] but for the viewer? True, Long may have put together many elements to make a rich work of art, but what does the viewer actually see? The viewer sees a few words printed in capitals in a book or on a piece of framed paper. For the viewer, the text piece may be nothing more than semantics, a semiotic game, arcane wordplay. The viewer has to *imagine* the whole artwork, build it up. The viewer has to put the walk back together, from those few words Richard Long has supplied. For the artist, these words are an abbreviated notebook form with key words to remind her/ him of certain experiences. For the viewer, the experiences are vastly different. The single word 'family' in *A Three Day Bicycle Ride* Long glosses as '[a]nd 'family', well, I cycled back home' (IC 1, 21). But for the viewer, the word 'family' might mean anything and everything. Like 'love' or 'art' or 'world', 'family' is one of the broadest, most general words in the language.

In the textwork made on the Mendip Hills, near Long's

home, one finds a vertical list of words: 'turf/ gorse/ trees/ field/ trees/ field'.[3] These are simple words which aim to communicate some aspect of the walk. There is so much to experience in a walk, though (in any walk) that Richard Long's notebook form of art must inevitably be extremely reductive. These words read like a stream of consciousness text, or the utterances of someone lifting up their eyes from their feet every few seconds to speak in a dull monotone into a tape recorder, Samuel Beckett-style: 'hillside/ swift/ scrub/ bush/ scrub/ bush'.

So all those things that Richard Long himself experiences – '[t]ime, distance, memory, history' etc – are open to any interpretation. Anyone who's been on a walk knows that there are many, many elements to it. One might list temperature of the body, heartbeat, pulse, sweat, cramp, aching, rubbing, blisters, movement, feel of wind, cloud, rain, water and sun on the body, and a host of other experiences to do with the body; then there is the way the body reacts to the environment; the things seen, heard, smelt, touched; then the mind thinks about the immediate and long-term past and future; people seen; and so on. To list all these in a short textwork is impossible. Poets know the 'inarticulate' nature of words. Simply, one cannot 'capture' a walk in words. And only the very, very greatest writers – such as John Cowper Powys, or Arthur Rimbaud, or Friedrich Hölderlin (great walker-poets) – have come anywhere near describing in words the sensual experiences of walking. Richard Long, who is not a poet of the stature or talent of Powys or Rimbaud or Hölderlin (now that would be an incredible combination), is not as adept at communicating the experience of a walk.

Why, then, is Richard Long's work so popular? It must be that before he made the text pieces he made very sensual works to which people could relate instantly. Long's (relative) fame or popularity must stem (partly) from his stone and slate circles and rows, which people can see and touch and discuss. If Long had never made a stone circle or line or mud wall, would he be as popular as he is today? That is, has a painter or sculptor become successful simply by sending words to a typesetter to be printed and framed and put on gallery walls? It's an interesting question. Imagine a sculptor who produces no objects, no images, no visual material and no photographs of works made outside the gallery. The ultimate post-Conceptual, Postminimal, post-performance, postmodern, post-everything artist. Who doesn't exist, of course. Even the most exquisitely post-Conceptual artist must produce something, even if they produce nothing. As Yves Klein found out, even exhibiting a galery with 'nothing' inside it is something. (It's still too early to see if these Conceptual and post-Conceptual artists will stand the test of time like, say, the ancient Athenian sculptor Praxiletes, who was sculpting statuary between 375 and 330 BC).

Of course, Long was making the textworks *as well as* the slate rings and mud walls. Even Conceptual artists such as Gilbert & George had actual objects people could see. They might have been 'living sculptures', but they also made colourful, easy-to-digest (if mundane) works. There are few artists, it seems, who have become famous merely by manipulating and exhibiting words in frames. And the other important factor explaining Long's success is his use of the Great Outdoors, the wilderness landscape which is so dear to Anglo-American-European art audiences (Long's photos depict gorgeous wild zones in Bolivia, Iceland, Scotland, the Sahara, Nepal). In stinking, sweltering, freezing, abysmally grey and drab cities, Long's works suggest wide open spaces, vast cloudscapes, cycles of growth and decay long obliterated from the Western city. Long commented in 1994 that 'for preference I'm attracted to the empty wilderness places... Through choice I'm not an urban artist – my work is about being in the natural world. Most of the world's surface is still open landscapes' (1994b). It's not that he doesn't travel through built-up areas, of course. 'The map works and also many of the road walks take me through towns and villages because that is where I can buy food, or find a bed and breakfast, find shops' (1994b).

In using walking, Richard Long employs one of the most basic of all human activities, and dance, theatre, and some sports, derive in part from walking.4 'Walking is the most primitive, the most immediate, the most corporeal medium for human transportation'.5 And Michel de Certeau saw walking as comparable with speaking: for him, walking, like the speech act, realizes space and place, and sets up relations between form of movement and enunciation.6 In de Certeau's system, Long is 'speaking' as he walks: clearly, for Long, walking and making art are part of the same thing.

In Richard Long's art, there is often no 'exterior' object, such as a painting or a sculpture, there is The Walk itself. At the same time, the area bounded by The Walk or Cycle Ride can be regarded as the sculptural object. When Long started to make walks as art, he could encompass huge areas and incorporate them into art. Discussing the changes in art, Long said:

> I could make a piece of art which was ten miles long. I could also make a sculpture which surrounded an area of 2401 square miles. All I have to do to make that was just to cycle around the countryside and leave it as a sculpture. (IC 1, 16)

The spectator knows about the Richard Long walks from the maps, text and photos. So, as he walks, Long is making art. It is not quite the same as with Joseph Beuys, Hermann Nitsch or Gilbert & George, who were performing, who were 'living sculptures'. Long's absence from his photos and texts is part of his ecologically-friendly, non-destructive stance. 'I consider my landscape sculptures inhabit the rich territory between two ideological positions, namely that of making 'monuments' or, conversely, of 'leaving only footprints'' Long remarked (WL, 68). The walks, though, are not a 'performance'.7 The walk is not 'performing' something, a performance *of* something, a representation, a reference to something outside of itself. It's not an illusion of space or place, a 3-D illusion, in the post-Renaissance manner of most traditional art in the West. It is about movement in space, a lived experience.[8] The walk is the walk. To call it art is also to call it life, in Long's view. The two things are continuous. 'My work has become a simple metaphor of life' he says.[9] The central thing to grasp with Richard Long's art, as also with other land artists, such as Heizer, de Maria, Nash, Fulton, Aycock and Holt, is the essence of their work, the mythic centre, which may be an idea, an essence, a structure or an experience. For Long, doing the walk itself is pleasurable:

> spending a day walking across the moors following the compass point... which is a very enjoyable way to spend the day. But it was also enjoyable because of the fact that I knew I was making a very original, a unique and dynamic work of art which had a new scale to it, which was a sculpture which was invisible and in many other ways was interesting as art. So, for me, it is a domination of things, as I said in my statement, *common means given the simple twist of art*. My work is about ideas and actions, it is a balance of the mental and physical. A good work like the Exmoor walk should be a fantastic idea and also fantastic to actually do. Everything comes together at the right moment. (IC 1, 16)

The walk is also a physical, energetic thing to do. For Richard Long, walking as art is more 'heroic' than painting (though plenty of painters might disagree with him):

> [the walk] takes a lot of work, it demands a lot of energy and time. If I have the idea to walk a thousand miles it's great to have the idea but I also have got to do it, I want to do it. That is what I mean by commitment. Doing a walk is far more physical than making some 'heroic' easel painting. (IC 2, 5)

The walk *Hours, Miles,* for instance, when Long walked 82 miles in 24 hours and 24 miles in 82 hours, was about the two walks, one balancing the other, not just the effort and heroism of walking 82 miles in 24 hours. The idea was to explore a 'kind of symmetrical inversion or balance, between difficulty and ease, because the other half of that work was to walk 24 miles in 82 hours' (2004b). As the *Tao Te Ching* put it, 'the difficult and the easy complement each other'.

Like Hamish Fulton, Bruce Chatwin and Chris Drury, Long has travelled to some wild places in pursuit of interesting spaces: Lappland, Africa, Australia, Peru, Alaska and the Himalayas. It's easy to see Long's art as simply pure Romanticism, a 'back to the land' art that utterly ignores political, societal, ideological, racial, economic and gender issues. True. Long's art is not concerned with the urban world of issues and daily news at all. It doesn't address political movements, revolutions, entertainment, celebrity gossip, wars, famines, floods, pollution, scientific breakthroughs, baseball, charity events, advertizing, pop music, royalty, terrorists, prison riots, crime syndicates, industries, air crashes or assassinations. You won't find Long's art discussing the price of oil, the Superbowl, or stocks and shares, or unions and strikes, or corporate mergers, meltdowns and takeovers. And it looks odd to see Long's work in galleries in cities, to see the stones in a setting quite different from the wildernesses. Rather, Long's sculpture comes across as deeply poetic, personal, subjective and romantic. It is *all* about a response to nature, about getting into connection with nature,[10] as with Chris Drury and David Nash. On his website Richard Long says he has been exploring 'some of the variables of transience, permanence, visibility or recognition'.

> In a way art demands an act of faith from the viewer as well [writes Long], like we accept Carl Andre's bricks as art as well as bricks, or my stones being art as well as stones. Especially when working in a wilderness, art for me is a personal and not a social experience and must be understood like that. (IC 2, 6)

RICHARD LONG'S EASTERN TURN

*A journey of a thousand miles
Starts from beneath one's feet.*

Tao Te Ching (LXIV)

Richard Long has sometimes made direct use of Far Eastern visual culture in his art: he has produced calligraphic art on Japanese and Korean paper, quoted from the *I Ching* (a favourite text), and based art around Chinese and Japanese ideograms and symbols (in a way, Long may be making his own, Westernized version of the *I Ching*, his own *Book of Changes*). A typical example would be Long's mud wall drawing *Heaven and Earth* (Glarus, 2002). Long has used the trigrams from the *I Ching* as the basis for work, such as the trigrams for mountain, heaven and earth (or the floor-piece *Following Thunder Tranquillity*, 2001, which reproduced the hexagrams from black bricks). Long said he liked the idea that the Chinese ideograms were partly language and partly graphic or abstract images, but they also had a meaning. Long was also attracted to the meaning of the *I Ching* trigrams: 'the symbols have really strong, epic, classic meanings like Wind, Tranquillity, Transience, Change, which give them a power and a strength' (SS, 309).

The eight *pa kua* (trigrams) of the *I Ching* are built from short lines (*yin*) and long lines (*yang*). The trigrams represent water, mountains, earth, thunder, fire, vapour, heaven and wind. Consider *Heaven* and *Earth* (2002): Richard Long has fashioned two wall drawings in mud on a black backing: for *Heaven*, Long built up six long lines of mud, while for *Earth*, there were twelve short lines.

The Chinese Taoist mystic, Chuang-tzu (the 'Groucho Marx of Taoism' as Lawrence Durrell called him), wrote: '[l]eap into the boundless and make it your home.'[1] This statement perfectly describes an artist's act of faith and risk, which is so essential for good artistic creations. As Søren Kirkegaard said, without risk, life is not worth living. Again, these Existentialist and Taoist notions of risk and leaping into the boundless are perfectly in tune with 1960s land art, 'expanded field' sculpture and Long's art.

Richard Long spoke about Japan:

> I do feel very close to the spirit of many of their points of view. Zen is quite pure and philosophical, it's close to art, and the Japanese religion, Shinto, is based on nature, and nature is universal. Nature belongs to every culture. (1994b)

Comparisons can be made between the shrines and temples in Shinto religion and some of Richard Long's art; the notion of *kami*, fundamental to Shinto, also chimes with Long's art (*kami* is a vague term which can indicate anything awe-inspiring, including living and inanimate things). Shinto shrines with their abodes of *kami* are typically situated in forests and mountains, surrounded by trees and rocks (mountains, tree and boulders may themselves be objects of worship). Long's stone circles are also obviously reminiscent of *mandalas*, the magic circles of Eastern religion (which are forms of *yantras*. The idea of the *mandala* was famously later taken up by C.G. Jung).

The great books of Far Eastern mysticism – *Tibetan Book of the Dead*, *Chuang-tzu*, the *I Ching* (*Book of Changes*) and the *Tao Te Ching* – have many correspondences with Richard Long's art. In some cases, he has drawn on them directly to create artworks.

Among Western mystics and philosophers, one could cite, in connection with Richard Long, Heraclitus (everything's in flux), Empedocles, Paracelsus, Meister Eckhart, Jan van Ruysbroeck, Plato, various Neoplatonists (such as Philo and Plotinus – Platonism and Neoplatonism is everywhere in Western philosophy), and William Blake. Maybe some theosophy, some Quietism, some alchemy definitely, and all sorts of bits of occultism and hermetic philosophy. Pantheism (or nature mysticism) is there in abundance, of course.

American Indian spirituality is a big influence too, as well as Australian aborigine religion, with their profound reverence for the land.

Clearly, Long's encounter with Oriental mysticism in the Sixties was profound and has proved long-lasting. There are far fewer references in his art, for instance, to Catholicism (the Mass, say, or sin and repentance), or Anglicanism, or Protestantism, or Calvinism, or Judaism, or the *Qabbalah*, or Zorasterianism. The repressive notions of Western religion – guilt, sin, the Fall, body-hatred – seem to be absent from Long's art (however, the fundamental utopian theme of Christianity is still there. Christianity is haunted by the idea of paradise, some earlier Eden or 'pure land', before the Fall of Man). Note that, although he must have walked beside Western churches, cathedrals and cemeteries thousands of times, Long's art doesn't employ much Christian iconography at all (those early crosses, for instance, were Minimal X's, not references to the Crucifixion).

And when it comes to Eastern religion, Richard Long's art tends towards the Far East, rather than Islam, Sufism, Christianity and Judaism in the Near East, or the religions of India: Hinduism, Jainism and Sikhism. It's far more likely to find references to the *I Ching* in Long's art than the great books of Indian mysticism (the *Upanishads*, the *Bhagavad Gita*). At times it can seem as if Long were creating his own form of the religions of the East: walking as yoga, walking as *zazen* (Zen Buddhist meditation), walking as *tantra*, walking as 'the Way' ('Tao').

CRITICS OF RICHARD LONG'S ART

Richard Long's art polarizes critics and art consumers. People tend to love him or loathe him. For fans, Long's a New Age, eco-friendly mystic, making cool, Conceptual art that doesn't harm the environment. It's art that has a refreshing simplicity and clarity. And it reminds them how beautiful the world is, how complex and multi-layered its landscapes and processes are.

Herman de Vries said he liked the work of Richard Long 'very much', in particular his 'feeling for poetry'.[1] Long's supporters include Rudi Fuchs, Anne Seymour, Robert Rosenblum, John Haldane, John Beardsley, Anne Dyson, Mel Gooding, Colin Renfrew and Hamish Fulton (and many curators and gallery owners, such as Konrad Fischer, Anthony d'Offay, Jean Bernier and Gian Enzo Sperone). Detractors include Peter Fuller, Jonathan Jones, David Sylvester, Rasheed Araeen and David Lee.

For sceptical critics, Richard Long's output is pretentious, shallow, repetitive, unoriginal, arrogant, conservative, apolitical and spiritually bankrupt. Modernist critics moan that there's no object to grasp in Long's art – for them it's a series of empty Conceptual gestures. Postmodernist fans can admire how Long plays the art market, trouncing conventional views of the art object. For Long, a sculpture can be two hundred and thirty miles long if he wishes. If a sculptor wants to make a 'real', physical object 230 miles long, s/he has to have a lot of money (like Christo with his *Running Fence*). Long, however, retorts that his 230 mile long sculpture really is a physical thing: he walked those 230 miles, physically. He might record sensual aspects of the walk: wind direction, incidents along the way, weather, etc. So, 'conceptual' though it seems, Long's sculptures are 'real', physical objects. A walk, after all, is one of the most physical, and fundamental, activities for humans.

Critics of Richard Long's art concentrate on the same things they find lacking in land art in general: its avoidance of political or 'important' or problematic issues, such as AIDS, poverty, 'Third World' debt, globalization, sexuality, gender inequality, colonialism, war, terrorism, and so on. They dislike its romanticizing and spiritualizing of the natural world; its conservatism; its nostalgia; its escapism; its self-indulgence; its élitism; its repetition and lack of imagination (many critics have called Long's art repetitive); its lack of formal experimentation (Long just does the same thing over and over, critics carp); and its over-simplification of its subjects. Tony Godfrey, describing *A Line Made By Walking*, said that Long's art could be seen as political:

> In so far as Long was positing the possibility of being in nature, not just seeing it, but *being* in it, he is also making a political statement. We can escape from alienation and false consciousness: by a wilful act we can be wholly in the world – reconnected. (1998, 130)

Of course, all art, and all artistic activity, is always (at least) political or ideological. But for nay-sayers, Richard Long's art doesn't engage directly (or obviously) in political issues, and appears to be avoiding them.

Richard Long acknowledged that his art could be seen as repetitious, because walking is endless repetition, and because the forms he employed were repetitious. But: although his forms were repetitions, Long said his sculptures were also about the infinite variety of the cosmos, so that every footprint, every mud or water splash, every individual work of art was individual and unlike any other in its precise forms and details. 'I could make a million stone circles and they'd all be different' (2004b).

For the negative critics, Long's art and land art in general is a romantic retreat into escapist, nostalgic fantasies about nature, with nothing to say about the anxieties, problems and challenges of living in the contemporary, 21st century world. It's hippy-dippy art that panders to the Western middle class's nostalgia for nature, seen from the perspective of neurotic city dwellers who hanker for the peace and quiet of the countryside. It's also an art that flatters and assuages the bourgeoisie's liberal guilt over wrecking the natural world with its ceaseless, unstoppable and vast consumption and pollution. It's an art that doesn't seem to say much about the particular world critics valorize – a late capitalist, technological, post-industrial, consumer society.

For critics like Jonathan Jones, British land art is hopelessly detached from 'real life'. Jones claimed that Andy Goldsworthy's art 'says nothing about the violence, hypocrisy and waste of our relationship to nature and is about as radical as the Body Shop'. While the United States of America had big, romantic works of land art, such as Robert Smithson's *Spiral Jetty* or Walter de Maria's *Lightning Field*, which were authentic attempts to grapple with the sublime in the natural world, Britain had tree huggers and Goldsworthy's 'twee arrangements of twigs and stones' (2001).

Oddly, critic David Sylvester claimed that Richard Long has had too much adulation:

> He has too many admirers. A quarter of a century has passed since he began to gain an international reputation at about the time he left art school, and this reputation has steadily grown upwards and outwards. Mounting stacks of books, catalogues and articles have ensured that his very particular, ascetic, ritualistic methods and their mystique have become common knowledge.

Can an artist become *too* popular? The downside of popularity is perhaps queuing for four hours to see a Claude Monet show at the Met or trying to peer over people layered five deep in front of Leonardo da Vinci's drawings at the National Museum of Art, Osaka. Long hasn't reached this point of superstardom yet. *Very* few living artists have. To be an artist superstar, you have to be dead (preferably a genius dying young, like Mozart, Arthur Rimbaud or Vincent van Gogh).

Peter Fuller, who advocated a distinctly *British* form of modern painting, saw spiritual bankruptcy in land art. Of Richard Long, one of Fuller's targets, Fuller intoned:

> It is, I believe, a tragedy that consideration was given to inviting an artist such as Richard Long to create a piece within Lincoln Cathedral. His work, for me, is symptomatic of the loss of both the æsthetic and the spiritual dimensions of art. He shows little trace of imagination, of skill, of the

transformation of materials. Seen in contrast to the greatest achievements of the British tradition in art, Long's relationship to the world of nature is simply regressive. His work is sentimental and fetishistic... claims that his work is worthy of 'spiritual' attention are preposterous...[2]

One sees clearly Fuller's outrage that Richard Long might sully the building beloved of John Ruskin, Nikolaus Pevsner and D.H. Lawrence, one of the finest English cathedrals. But surely Fuller is missing the point with Long, who is clearly as mystical, as in awe, as deep in his feeling for nature as Fuller's cherished Brit artists, Cecil Collins, Henry Moore, J.M.W. Turner or Patrick Heron.

One wonders what happens when Richard Long bumps into members of the public while making his walks and works. Sometimes artists can encounter suspicion or hostility when working outside their studios. Imagine that Long is walking in some wilderness somewhere in South-West England, and meets an inquisitive soul. The following conversation might be heard by the surrounding rocks and bushes.

(Do not read this if you are a big fan of Richard Long's work):

SCENE: EXTERIOR. SOMEWHERE IN ENGLAND. DAY.

Inquirer (sporting a heavy West Country accent): 'Allo there.
Richard Long: Hello.
Inquirer: Noice day, innit?
Long: Yes.
Inquirer: What, out for a walk, then?
Long: Yep.
Inquirer: Do a lot of walking, do yer?
Long: You could say that.
Inquirer: Be noice to just walk for a livin', wouldn't it?
Long: Well, actually...
Inquirer: What you doin' wi' that stone?
Long: [*lifting up the stone in his hand*] Well, I'm carrying it.
Inquirer: Oh.
Long: Yes, I'm carrying it from the Dorset coast to

	Weston-Super-Mare.
Inquirer:	*Really?* Why?
Long:	It's a coast to coast walk, English Channel to Bristol Channel. It's what I do.
Inquirer:	You carry stones around? Just that?
Long:	Yes.
Inquirer:	Blimey! Anything else?
Long:	Yes. I make lines in the snow, or circles out of rocks. Or I splatter mud on walls. But mostly I walk.
Inquirer:	Walk?
Long:	Yes.
Inquirer:	What, you *walk* for a living?
Long:	Yes.
Inquirer:	And make money out of it?
Long:	Yes.
Inquirer:	Lots?
Long:	Sometimes.
Inquirer:	Money just from walking? How's that? Are you sponsored, loike, by a charity? Is it some benefit for cancer research thing?
Long:	No, I finance it all myself (but there is the gallery's percentage, materials, transport, agents, flights, hotels, frames, film, printing,...) Oh, and sometimes commissions. And sometimes there's public funding. Oh, and the limited edition prints, and artists' books, and posters, and so on.
Inquirer:	Wow. But... [*ponders slowly*] how do you get paid, then? How do they – your bosses – *know* you've done your walk, eh?
Long:	Sometimes I write about it. Sometimes I take photos.
Inquirer:	Ah, yes, I see the camera. Nikkormat; nice camera. Then what?
Long:	Then I show the pictures in a gallery.
Inquirer:	Oh God, you're an *artist!* You should've said. That explains *everything*. Must be goin'. 'Bye.

[*Inquirer exits rapidly*]

7

Circles, Lines, Rows, Splashes and Other Forms in Richard Long's Art

There are a lot of things theoretical and intellectual to say about lines and circles, but I think the very fact that they are images that don't belong to me and, in fact, are shared by everyone because they have existed throughout history, actually makes them more powerful than if I was inventing my own idiosyncratic, particular Richard Long-type images. I think it cuts out a lot of personal unwanted æsthetic paraphernalia.

Richard Long (RC, 22)

STONE CIRCLES

The reasons for making a work are many says Richard Long, ranging from time, measurement and mileage to an idea, or a line:

> A walk, and place, can be chosen for any reason. For no reason (or on a "hunch"), or to follow an idea, or in a place I know, or in a place I don't know, to complete a time, or to complete a mileage, to go from place to place, or to walk in one place, to cross a country (to "measure" it by footsteps), from sea to sea, or border to border, to follow a river, to follow a straight line. (SF)

The closer one looks at Richard's Long's circles, the more

one finds differences between them. The unifying principle behind them is a circle set flat on the gallery floor or outdoors. Beyond that, there are many variations. The slate circle, which seems to be a Long standard, is not simply a circle full of slate, evenly packed or spread through the area of the circle. The size and shape of each slab of slate varies. Although he favours long oblong chunks of slate, the pieces vary in size and shape: some are triangular in cross section, and short; others are long and rectangular in cross section (the stones in the gallery sculptures usually come from quarries). Some of the slate circles consist of pieces of slate grouped tightly together (such as *Slate Circle* [1979], or *Cornwall Slate Circle* [Bordeaux, 1981], or *Berlin Circle* [1996], or *Bilbao Circle* [2000]); others, such as *Slate Circle* (Amsterdam, 1980) are open circles, with a lot of space between each piece. *Stick Circle* (also Amsterdam, 1980) is another open circle, comprising short (one foot long or so) sticks (other open stick circles include *Black River Circle* [2000] and *Dead Wood Circle* [2001]).

Red Slate Ring (1986) was installed for the 1986 show at the Guggenheim Museum: pieces of slate of a roughly similar size were overlaid to produce a wide open circle, each piece of slate covering the ones below so that no part of the floor showed through. *Stone Lake* (1988) was a large solid circle of stone slabs made in a field of long grass in Schloss Crottorf. *Chisos Circle* (1990) was a medium-sized open circle drawn in the stones in Texas. For the Haunch of Venison show (2003), Richard Long produced irregular, curved rows of stones (*Cornwall State Lines*, 2003), and a *Norfolk Ellipse* (2003).

A 1994 circle, *Merrivale Circle*, shown at Anthony d'Offay, London, is an open ring about thirteen feet in diameter made from Dartmoor granite. The stones are not touching, and the circle is full of light. The openness and relaxed stance of the circle is emphasized by the pale hue the granite. Although each block of stone is weighty, *Merrivale Circle* is not as heavy or opaque as some of Long's other circles (such as the slate circles which're dark toned, filling up the gallery floor with grey and black shapes). In *Circle of Memory Sticks* (1996, made at Long's German art gallery), a collection of short, neatly cut sticks were arranged in an open circle, each stick pointing towards the centre of the circle.

Other stone circle forms by Richard Long include concentric circles. A series of three circles is often favoured by Long (a group of three circles was employed in prehistoric earthworks, such as the Hurlers, on Bodmin Moor, a landscape that boasts at least thirteen stone circles). Three concentric stone circles include *Napoli Circles* (1984), *Midsummer Circles* (1993), and *Little Tejunga Canyon Stone Circles* (Los Angeles, 1984). *Turf Circles* (1988, Cambridge) comprised concentric circles made using cuts in the grass.

Unlike the stone circles of Nancy Holt or Robert Smithson, Richard Long's concentric circles (like all his stone circles), are constructed from small stones, stones that can fairly easily be carried. These are stones that could be found in the landscape, by hand, not carved out of the earth (the outdoor works are constructed from existing stones; but although the art gallery rings use stones from quarries, Long still opts for small-sized stones). In contrast to the bigger, more bombastic earthworks, such as those by American land artists, Long's circles are distinctly 'human-scale', in the sense that each stone in the circles relates to the human touch, the human hand. One feels one can pick the stones in Long's circles: they are friendly artworks, not domineering. They do not overpower the viewer, but entice the viewer with notions of presence, the natural world, the texture and feel of materials.[1] Among the more ambitious concentric stone circles are *Six Slate Circles* (London, 1982), which consists of about 103 stones, and *Six Stone Circles* (England, 1981). Long has also produced flattened concentric circles, such as *White Foot Circles* (1986, Finland).

Some of Richard Long's circles are open at the centre (such as *Helsinki Circle* [1983], or the large open stone circle in the Gobi desert [*Nomad Circle,* 1996]), a shape also favoured in

Long's wall circle drawings created with River Avon mud. The open centre circles allow for a larger circle to be constructed using the same quantity of materials. Most of Long's circles are between 4 and 6 metres in diameter: Long likes to make his circles fill up a space (if it's an indoor circle). There is room to walk round the edges of the circle, but also the room is not allowed to dominate the circle. The circle must not be overwhelmed by the gallery space; rather, the circle must assert its own presence in the gallery.

Some of Richard Long's circles are very large – such as the *Red Slate Circle* (Boston, 1980), which is over nine metres in diameter, *Lightning Fire Wood Circle* (1981), which is 8.8 metres wide and *Bushwood Circle* (Melbourne, 1977), which is also nine metres wide. 1982's *Ring of Stones* in Ottawa was an open circle 10.68 metres in diameter.

Pine Tree Bark Circle (1985) is a solid circle, not one of Richard Long's largest, but it dominates the gallery. The slabs of bark, mostly two or three feet long, offer many points of interest for the eye. Each chunk of bark is individual, with its own shape and size, just as in the Orkney 1994 Bob Dylan stone sculpture, where the stones are untreated, made to stand as they are. The circle shape gives the bark a formal unity, while the textures of the pine bark make the sculpture very varied. The wood circles are quite different from the stone or mud circles. The way Long uses wood is to break it up into similar sizes, but to leave the shapes of the pieces of wood alone. So there are irregular edges and points, bits which stick out, as in *Circle in Africa* (1978). This latter is a large open circle made with sticks of wood from the small trees which surround the sculpture in its archetypal Longian wilderness setting.

Some circles in the landscape are created by Richard Long taking away snow (or drawing in the snow) in open circles, so the the ground underneath shows through, as in *Early Summer Circle* (1997), *Shirakami Circle* (1997), *Sunrise Circle* (1998) and *Walking a Circle By the Beagle Channel* (1997), or the snow is cleared away around a closed circle, as in *Tierra del Fuego Circle* (1997) and *Throwing Snow Into a Circle* (1991), or stamped out by the act of walking in a circle (as in *Footprint Circle* [1989, Italy]).

Brough of Birsay Circle (Orkney, 1994) is a large open circle which relies on plants and their blooming in Summer to make it work. Like his late 1960s lines and crosses made by walking, for this work Long has walked in a large circle on a field of flowers. The plants have been pressed flat, leaving a circular mark. In essence, *Brough of Birsay Circle* is no different from the walk sculptures the artist was creating 25 years previously. There is no sense of progression in *Brough of Birsay Circle* compared to the earlier works, no addition, and nothing new. It's the same countryside setting, the same wide shot encompassing the work (taken, as usual, during the daytime), the same notion of grass (and flowers, here) being pressed flat as a trace of the artist's boots, act of walking and route, and it's the same sort of fundamental geometric shape. But that's part of the charm of Long's art: there is, really, no attempt at development or progression. Long really does follow the maxims of Donald Judd and Jasper Johns of doing one thing, then another... and another. Long adds new shapes sometimes, or coloured stones, or alters the paper backing of wall drawings from black to white, but it's all really the same sort of art he's been making for decades.

The largest of circles in Richard Long's art are of course the circular walks he undertakes, which could be many miles in diameter. Some of these find their way onto maps (they begin as circles on maps before they're walked), and some are suggested through words in textworks. These are 'imaginary' circles but no less significant than the tactile stone circles.

Only occasionally has Richard Long ventured into using the spiral, the form of the most famous piece of land, Robert Smithson's *Spiral Jetty*. Long's spiral works include *Along a Four Day Walk In Norway* (1973), *Sandstone Spiral* (Toronto, 1983), and *Rhône Valley Stones Spiral* (Switzerland, 2000). *Whirlwind Spiral* (1988) was made in the Sahara, producing a close-knit white spiral form. The spiral is a shape many land artists progress towards after exploring the circle.

In a 1996 Tokyo circle (*Hemisphere Circle*), one of Richard Long's permanent installations, comprised of large boulders set in a circle, each rock is level underneath, so it is laid flush with the ground. Long sometimes creates rows or groups of circles, such as *Tierra Del Fuego Circle, Santa Cruz Circle* and *Bhubut Circle* (all 1997), *Hogwallow Flat Circle, Stony Man Circle* and *Hazeltop Circle* (all 1993), or *A Line of Circles* (Milwaukee Art Museum, 2001). *Continents Circles* was a group of five large slate circles installed in Barcelona in 1992. The groups and rows of circles are a way of fitting the circle shape into long, narrow galleries. Plenty of art galleries are not 'white cubes', but lengthy rectangular interiors (sometimes they're a bunch of rooms knocked together, and often they're buildings converted from other uses, such as industry). The long rectilinear spaces (sometimes 50 or more yards long) are not the ideal space for Long's sculptures. Hence he often produces lines of stones for those spaces (or more lately ellipses), or mud drawings. But situating one normal-sized circle next to another, in a series, is another method of dealing with galleries which're more like narrow corridors.

A broken circle occasionally appears in Richard Long's œuvre, as in *Earth Circle* (Porto, 2001), a stone floor circle split apart down the centre, or *Heaven and Earth Circle* (Glarus, 2002). The broken circle didn't have any hidden meaning, Long asserted. It was 'just another way of doing a circle'. It was just a bunch of stones. 'Stones are what they are… With symbolism there's a fixed meaning. All good art is open-ended' (SS, 310). Long said he had the idea for the broken circle by coming across one on a walk, seeing a path or track made through a patch of land on a hillside (SS, 309).

One or two of Richard Long's stone circles are small: *Circle of Standing Stones* (1983) is 26 stones arranged in a circle of a half metre in diameter, *Cornwall Slate Circle* (1982) is 34 stones in a 2 metre circle, and *Standing Stone Circle* (1982) is 36 stones in a similar size circle. The small stone circles are often made of standing stones, and many of the outdoor circles are of this type (*Evening Camp Stones*, 1995, for instance). Long's use of standing stones, rather than ones laid flat, echoes prehistoric stone circles – for instance, the Scottish stone circle *Stones and Stac Pollaidh* (1981), or *Sincho-lagua Summit Shadow Stones* (1998).

Richard Long's small stone circles are intimate works compared to the broad, large pieces. In Britain there are a number of small stone circles which produce similar atmospheres of human-scale and intimacy (such as the small circles on the ridges of hills in Dorset). 'I like simple, emotional, quiet, vigorous art' remarked Long.[2] While the large circles in the galleries of Western cities spoke of polished, upmarket art, the small, 1.5 metre stone circles evoked small wayside shrines. The large gallery circles are planned and organized sometimes months in advance, but still look spontaneous. Long's small outdoor stone circles, though, are direct and immediate responses to a landscape, a moment, an atmosphere, a feeling.

Richard Long has also used animal bones for circle sculptures (as in *Mojave Bone Circle*, 1995). In Ecuador (in 1998) Long placed bones in the direction of his walk. Bricks with footprints on them formed the basis of *Footprint Spiral* (1993). Driftwood was another favourite material for floor-based sculptures (in *Sea Mills Driftwood Circle* [1996], *River Avon Driftwood Circle* [1978 and 1996], *River Avon Driftwood Line* [1977], *Puget Sound Driftwood Circle* [1996], and *A Circle in Alaska* [1977]). Bark was also employed in many solid circles: *Pine Tree Bark Circle* (1985), *Bark Circle* (1993, Paris), and *Bark Circle* (1994, Australia).

In the late Nineties, Richard Long started to fashion floor-based stone circles using different coloured stones: black, white, purple, green, and blue rocks. Each circle comprised coloured stones which were grouped together in single colour. Thus, in *Black White Green Pink Purple Circle* (1998, Galerie Tschudi, Glarus), about half the circle is green stone, a sixth segment is white, a smaller chevron-shaped part is black, a slightly larger zigzag section is pink stone, with purple placed along a third of the circumference. This was also the form of *Black White Blue Purple Circle* (1998, Glarus), and the circles installed at Museum Kurhaus, Kleve (2001). *Mohawk* (2002, Florida) was an ellipse made from white and grey stones, the grey placed in a wide zigzag through the middle. At *OPENASIA 2004: The East Meets the West*, Long showed a *Blue Sky Circle* (2002) comprising different coloured stones.

As one can see from the above examples of Richard Long's stone circles, Long has probably made more circles in land art than any other artist. It's hard to think of any artist who has created more circles out of stone, wood, snow, mud and slate than Richard Long.

New shapes appeared in Richard Long's floor-standing sculptures in the 1990s: solid ellipses (as in *Spring Ellipse* [Salisbury, 1999], *Basalt Ellipse* [2001, Kleve], *Cornwall Slate Ellipse* [New York, 2000], *Trento Ellipse* [Trento, 2000], and *White Quartz Ellipse* [New York, 2000]); open ellipses (as in *Periphery Stones* [1999], *Antibes Ellipse* [Antibes, 1999], *Porfido Ellipse* and *Red Mud Ellipse*, Italy, 1998), and a wheel (as in *Circle of Life*, 1997. This latter sculpture is reminiscent in shape of a Swedish prehistoric stone circle, at Sola, Nerike).

And in the wall and mud drawings, Long developed new forms: the arc (*Glarus Arc* [Glarus, 1996], *Gulf of Mexico Arc* [Houston, 1996], *River Avon Mud Arc* [Bilbao, 2000], and *Fast Hand Mud Arc* [Athens, 1999]); the open ellipse (*River Avon Mud Ellipse* [London, 2000]), and the demi-circle (*From One To Another* [Houston, 1996], or *Seminole* [2004], a half-circle shown at Seminole, Florida). One of the largest of the upside-down arcs was made at the new Guggenheim museum in Bilbao (2000).

Richard Long also created mud drawings on the gallery floor (as in *Sicilian Mud Hand Circle*, 1997). 'Mud Walls' were also a favourite form, a rectangular block of white or brown or red spread high up on the wall, and allowed to drip down the rest of the wall below: *Muddy Water Wall* (Glarus, 1993), *Muddy Water Line* (Rome, 1994), *Setagaya Mud Line* (Tokyo, 1996), *Waterfall Line* (London, 2000), and *White Water Lines*

(Hanover, 1999). Some were muddy splash marks (as in *Muddy Water Falls*, 1984). Sometimes Long opted for the visual device of alternating a block of one colour of mud with another, as in *River Avon Mud and China Clay Wall* (2001) and *Red and Grey Mud Wall* (Italy, 1994). These were rarer, because Long prefers a single colour or material for most of his indoor sculptures.

In his 2004 show at the Kukje Gallery, Richard Long made mud works on handmade paper, which were mounted to the wall, as well as stone circles and spirals (*Spring Spiral, Monkey Spiral* and *Magpie Circles* [all 2004]). Another new development was finger-printing on objects such as flat, round stones or small pieces of oak or driftwood. For the fingerprint sculptures, Long elected to use the geometric forms he'd developed over his career: circles, concentric circles, spirals, lines and ovals: *2000 Fingerprints* (Los Angeles, 2000), *Fingerprint Stone* (New York, 2000), *River Avon Mud On African Mud*, *River Avon* and *Mud* (Switzerland, 2000). To print on the stone or wood, Long used china clay or his beloved River Avon mud, and placed the fingerprints beside each other, in rows.

STONES

> *A sculpture may be moved, dispersed, carried. Stones can be used as markers of time or distance, or exist as parts of a huge, yet anonymous, sculpture. On a mountain walk a sculpture could be made above the clouds, perhaps in a remote region, bringing an imaginative freedom about how, or where, art can be made in the world.*
>
> Richard Long[1]

Stones are *very* important in Richard Long's art (and that's an understatement). No other contemporary sculptor has made stones, boulders and pebbles so central to their art.

They are kicked, thrown, picked up, put down, carried, written on and stacked. 'A walk is an event in space-time, and I may carry, scatter, concentrate or place stones, or exchange their places along a walk, as required. My stones are like sub-atomic particles in the space of the World' Long said in 2001 (WL, 69). Some stones are kicked into a row (as in *A Line In Bolivia*, 1981), or thrown into a line or a circle (as in Morocco in 1979). Sometimes Long throws stones. In *Two Stones* (1991), a walkwork across the North of England, the walk was a stone's throw from the Irish Sea and North Sea. *Skimming Stones Across the Rio Grande* (1990), which was made in Texas, comprised a photograph of the river, a cow, distant hills, and part of Long's tent. In *A Line of 164 Stones* (1974), Long placed a stone on the roadside after every mile, creating a 164 mile long sculpture. In *Stones Added To a Field Circle* (1999), Long added his stones to an existing open circle. In *All Ireland Stones* (1995), a 12 day walk from the South to North coast (ending up at the Giant's Causeway), 32 stones are formed into a line 'randomly spaced along a walking line of 382 miles'. In *Wind Stones* (1985) Long turned 207 stones to point into the wind in Lappland. 'There are millions of stones in the world, and when I make a sculpture, all I do is just take a few of those stones and bring them together and put them in a circle and show you' Long explained (WC, 45).

Sometimes Richard Long writes on the stones and follows the instructions for walking on the pebbles as he draws them from a bag (in two very Conceptual works, made in Dartmoor in 1998: *From Uncertainty To Certainty* and *Walks of Chance*). In *Walks of Chance*, Long wrote a word on each stone and followed the instructions as he drew out the stones one by one (the words included 'North', 'South', 'Straight', 'Fast' and 'Meandering'). For instance, in *From Uncertainty To Certainty*, Long pulled the ten pebbles out of a bag one by one, at random, at indeterminate intervals, puts the pebble on the ground, and follows the instructions on the pebble. The procedure is repeated until all of the pebbles have been used up. The instructions include:

FIRST PEBBLE WALKING EAST
SECOND PEBBLE WALKING STRAIGHT
THIRD PEBBLE SLOW WALKING (WC, 151)

From Uncertainty To Certainty, Richard Long explained, 'uses language, stones, chance, walking and Dartmoor'. One can see too that this work required a certain amount of preparation: it was not a spontaneous walk which was written up later as a textwork. It required the artist to collect the pebbles, decide what to write on them, then write and put them in a bag.

In *Time Flowing and Time Repeating* (1999), a walk in the maritime Alps (Villanova to St-Étienne-de-Tinée), Richard Long built columns of stones on the mountain passes. Sometimes he carries a stone a certain distance or a certain time, puts it down and picks up another one, as in *Stone Walk* (1984), *Walking Stones* (1995), and *Heavier, Slower, Shorter, Lighter, Faster, Longer* (1982, England). *Walking Stones*, Long explained, was a walkwork in which '[e]ach day I carried a different stone in my pocket. From stone to stone, from day to day. So the work was called *Walking Stones* and it was eleven days and eleven stones' (WC, 147). Sometimes Long carries a stone from one coast to another (as in *Crossing Stones*, 1987, a walk between the North Sea at Aldeburgh and the Irish Sea at Aberystwyth). 'My work is another agent of change and placement. And walking is simple; stones are common and practical' (WC, 69). Sometimes Long rolls them down a hill, as in *Ten Stones* (Iceland, 1994). (This was also a crossing place walk, between walks made – and stones rolled – in 1974 and 1994). In *Stones Steps Days* (1985), Long combines stones with footsteps, days and the cardinal points:

FIRST DAY A STONE MOVED ONE STEP WEST
SECOND DAY THE STONE MOVED TWO STEPS NORTH
THIRD DAY THE STONE MOVED THREE STEPS EAST
FOURTH DAY THE STONE MOVED FOUR STEPS
SOUTH

FIFTH DAY THE STONE MOVED FIVE STEPS WEST[2]

Sometimes he makes a line of stones in water, as in *Europe Asia Stones* (1989), made at the Bosphorus in Turkey. Sometimes he counts the stones and boulders, as in *Granite Stepping-Stone Circle*, a circular walkwork in Dartmoor in 1980 ('passing over 409 rock slabs and boulders'). Sometimes Richard Long exchanges stones in certain places, after a certain duration, as in *An Exchange of Stones At a Place For a Time On Dartmoor* (1997). The description of the walkwork reminds the viewer of the enigmatic behaviour of the artist:

BRINGING A STONE FROM TIERRA DEL FUEGO
PLACING IT ON SADDLE TOR FOR THE
DURATION OF A THREE DAY WALK AROUND
DARTMOOR
AND REMOVING IT AT THE END OF THE WALK
TO BE DROPPED INTO THE RIVER AVON IN
BRISTOL (WC, 56)

Richard Long related this walk to particle physics, his stones as analogies of sub-atomic particles (WC, 69). What Long has actually done for this walkwork is: carry a stone from his home in Bristol, put it on a tor in Dartmoor, walked for three days, then came back and collected the stone, travelled back to Bristol and dropped it into the Avon. To an observer, it would seem as if Long were engaged in actions that appear like obscure rituals.

Sometimes he throws stones into every river or stream he comes across, as in *Splashing Around a Circle* (1997). This was a four day walk around an imaginary circle 41 miles across in Wiltshire, on Salisbury Plain and the Marlborough Downs. It was a textwork, which described the actions performed, and a circular textwork, with the words 'SPLASH' written around the circle at irregular intervals, to indicate where Long had thrown stones into rivers and brooks on his walk.

Or he carries a stone from one river to the next, as in *Dartmoor Riverbed Stones* (1991). In this walk around the edge of Richard Long's sacred ground (Dartmoor), Long carried stones between Dartmoor's many rivers and streams: from the River Dart to Holy Brook, from Holy Brook to River Mardle, from River Mardle to Dean Burn, and so on. Or he places 1449 stones on a cairn at 1449 feet above sea level (again on Dartmoor, in 1979), or 82 stones at 82 feet above seal level (in *Footstones*, 1979).

Sometimes Richard Long places stones by the road on each day of a walk, as in *Portuguese Stones* (2001). The textwork of this walk is a simple numerical progression ('one stone in Monção, two stones in Braga, three stones near Lixa, four stones near Cinfães', and so on [WC, 66]). Sometimes Long moves a certain number of stones (ninety stones were moved 'each one step' along the route, North, South, East and West, in *Dartmoor Stones*, 1992). 'My work is a balance between the reality of seeing real stones, and then a photograph of perhaps a stone circle made many thousands of miles away' (WL, 147). This is part of a stony text piece, 1996's 'Dolomite Stones:

STONES THROWN OVER A PRECIPICE
STONES PLACED ON MOUNTAINTOP CAIRNS
STONES DISLODGED FROM THE PATH
STONES USED TO SECURE THE TENT
STONES THROWN INTO A CLOUD[3]

A 1998 walk across the British Isles, from the Southern-most point, the Lizard in Cornwall, to Dunnet Head in Scotland, the Northernmost point, was entitled *A Line of 33 Stones, A Walk of 33 Days*, because Richard Long put a stone down in the road on each of the 33 days of the walk. The stones were there to mark and measure Britain, Long explained, to measure the speed and distance and the route of Long's walk (WL, 69). Each of the stones represented a day's walking along the 1,030 miles that Long traversed. 'Each stone has its geological history, yet perhaps momentarily, conceptually, symbolically or privately becomes 'something else' as well' Long remarked (WL, 69).

Cairns are markers along the way which walkers encounter. Richard Long sometimes photographs them, writes about them, or creates his own cairns: as in *Walk of Seven Cairns* (1992), a four day walk in the Brecon mountains and Fforest Fawr in South Wales, where Long built cairns in 'a windy place' or 'after a roll of thunder'; and *Road of Three Cairns* (1992), where he built three cairns on a 586 mile walk from Bordeaux to Turin. Sometimes Long adds to the cairns, piling up stones, as in *Stones On a Cairn,* in Dartmoor (1992, fashioned into a roughly circular form.

Stones are small, portable, and come from the Earth. All very obvious attributes, but vital ones. Unlike plants, grass or trees, stones don't fade away. They are intimately connected to the ground where they're found. They don't decay and die on you like flowers or plants when you pick them, so using stones in art can tie in nicely to an eco-friendly ideology. They're small and easy to carry (vitally important for a walking artist). And they're free. And there's a plentiful supply. And they can be found in almost any territory. And stones also have links with Oriental mysticism (such as Zen Buddhist gardens), and they are one of the fundamental elements that Eastern religion is always talking about (such as the clouds, the wind, the sky, the Earth, water, the sea, pools, rivers, mountains, trees and stones).

Stones always photograph nicely (especially in black-and-white, which Richard Long favours many times over colour photography; it enhances the surface texture of stones). For these, and other reasons, one can see why stones would feature so prominently in the art of Richard Long. 'In my sculptures, a stone is a stone, and I also use other raw materials like dust, water and mud, only to show their own innate natures' Long said in 2001 (WL, 69).

Richard Long could be said to have a 'sacred' relationship

with particular objects – stones, mud, water – which is often exactly like the shamanic, animistic relationship of ancient peoples. It's the artist's *relationship* with particular things and places that's as important as the stones or places in themselves. 'Sacred stones or trees are not adored in their natural capacity', Mircea Eliade wrote in *Myths, Dreams and Mysteries*, 'but only because they are *hierophanies*, because they "show forth" something which is no longer mineral or vegetable but *sacred* – "wholly other"' (125). (*Hierophany* for Eliade means 'the act of manifestation of the sacred'). Long's reverence for stones is only surpassed in modern sculpture by perhaps Constantin Brancusi.

Like John Cowper Powys, like the Romantic poets, like the archaic shaman, Australian aborigines and 'primitive' peoples, land artists sometimes develop an intimate relation with the landscape. Very likely Richard Long has favourite spots, such as familiar prehistoric standing stones, or oak trees he's watched grow over the years, or a favourite crossing place over a stream, or a particular viewpoint on a hillside overlooking the West Country. Even small stones or bushes can become familiar to a walker over oft-trod routes. And one place in particular has come to act as Long's spiritual home: Dartmoor.

LINES AND ROWS

Everywhere the human 'touch' is present in Richard Long's sculpture, as in all sculpture. The shapes might be 'organic' – circles, spirals, zigzags – but the appearance of Long's sculpture in their wilderness settings is always of some sophisticated (not archaic) human gesture at work. Long's work has not changed that much since the late 1960s, when he found and developed his way of working. Critic Penelope Curtis commented: '[h]is way of working over the last two decades has been unusually consistent' (136). Still one finds circles, lines and spirals in his work, thirty years and more after his first works. Presumably circles and rows will remain in Long's repertoire right up until the end, until the last artwork. (There has to be a final work, a Last Walk, some time or other. It would entirely fitting if it was a circle or a line).

The early Richard Long pieces, from 1965 to the early 1970s, contained many more spirals than he makes now. One finds spiral works in Arizona (1970), in *A Sculpture Left By the Tide* (Cornwall, 1970), at Oxford (1971) and in *A Line the Length of a Straight Walk From the Bottom to the Top of Glastonbury Tor* (1974). Zigzags appear too, but much less frequently than the lines and circles (in *Inca Rock Camp-Fire Ash*, 1972, for instance). Rows also feature in the early pieces, as in *Stone Rows* (London, 1977).

The rows are really lines – Long calls them lines. *A Line in Ireland* (1974) is a short pile of flat rocks in a line, while *A Line in Australia* (1977) is a wider line, more like a row of red rocks (RL, 54-55). *A Line in Scotland* (1981) is a row of small flattish rocks that were stood on end at Cul Mór, like a row of prehistoric standing stones. In *Ash Line* and *Bushfire Line* (both 1994, Australia), Long dropped wood ash in a short line in a forest. In Yorkshire in 1977, as in Bolivia in 1981, Long cleared a space each side of the line as he picked up rocks (RL, 124, 126). The opposite of this line is the 'negative' line, made by leaving a path through a tangle of rocks, as in *A Line in California* (1982).

Richard Long's lines or rows are, typically, photographed end-on. This viewpoint emphasizes the direction of the line, the relation of the direction of the line to the horizon, and the sense of motion, of 'walking the line'. And also the stupendous backdrop which's often situated at the end of the line. The *Line in the Himalayas* (1975), for example, is seen from one end: the other end points up the slope, towards the mountains and the sky beyond (other angles on this work don't have quite the same effect). In *A Line In Scotland* (1981) mountains recede behind the line of rocks. In *Snow Stones* (2002) the misty, snowy Alps form the backdrop. *Cloud Mountain Stones*

(2001) frames the mountains of Oregon behind the widely-spaced row of stones.

Photographing the line end-on encourages the eye to run along the line, to follow the line to its destination – somewhere on the horizon – or, in the case of *A Line in the Himalayas* – right up into the Tibetan sky or void (the *Tibetan Book of the Dead* speaks of the 'Clear Light of the Void'). The skyward direction of this particular line is wholly appropriate – the Himalayas are called the 'roof of the world'. Mountain climbers have said it's exhilarating standing on Everest, knowing there is nothing else on Earth higher than that point. Long's *A Line in the Himalayas* emphasizes the sense of ascension, flight and transcendence, the archetypal motifs of religion and shamanism. One recalls the asceticism and talk of emptiness of Tibetan Buddhist mystics such as Mila Repa, of the 'clear light of the void' in the *Tibetan Book of the Dead*, of the harsh light and fabulous, transparent air of the Himalayas.

Talking about Tibetan Buddhism, the void, and the 'roof of the world' no doubt romanticizes Richard Long's *A Line in the Himalayas*. But the compositions encourage this reading. Another line or row of stones that echoes *A Line in the Himalayas* was made on Mount Fuji (*A Line in Japan*, 1979). Again, the line of stones is photographed from one end, the lower end, so the line stretches up the mountain, into the mist. Like the Himalayan line, the Mount Fuji line emphasizes the sense of the infinite, the religious/ Romantic reaching up into the heavens. The photographs of the other rows of stones mentioned above (*A Line In Scotland, Cloud Mountain Stones,* and *Snow Stones*) do the same thing.

In galleries, Richard Long's lines are often wide rows of sticks which directly recall Tony Cragg's spreads of found (sometimes painted) objects. *Somerset Willow Line* (1979), like *192 Pieces of Wood* (Switzerland, 1975) and *Forêt du Porge Line* (Bordeaux, 1981), is a large row of widely-spaced sticks, plenty of room between each stick on a gallery floor. These rows re-order the irregularity of nature, shaping the odd lengths and volumes of the branches into a humanmade, geometric structure. These row/ line sculptures inevitably codify and control the natural world. The actual materials used – wood, slate, pine needles – seem less important than the geometric (human) shapes the sculptor makes with them. The lines are partly about time and process, of moving from one place to another, the significance of moving along a line, which is following a predetermined structure. The line takes the viewer from one place to another, yet it looks roughly the same at each point along it. The line, like the walk itself, is different yet the same. Each stage along the line offers a new viewpoint, a new way of looking at the landscape. Yet each stage of the stone or wood line or row looks roughly like the last stage. The beginning and the end of the line thus becomes crucial: and, significantly, Long emphasizes the beginning of the line by choosing to take the photograph beside it. The end of the line is also emphasized: it stretches away into the distance, sometimes lost in mist, sometimes pointing towards a mountainous background, and sometimes pointing up to the heavens.

COLOUR IN RICHARD LONG'S ART

Note how Richard Long sticks very often to black-and-white photography, even when colour photography is easily attainable, technically, and cheap too (and, since the 1980s, large colour prints have become *de rigueur* for any artist or photographer). The preference for black-and-white photography gives Long's photographs the aura of classic photography, in line with the great photographers from the history of photography. Long's photographs can be read as part of the long tradition of landscape photography, then, the canon which includes Ansel Adams, Edward Weston, Paul Strand, Walker Evans and Bill Brandt. There's no suggestion, though, that Long's photographs come anywhere near the sublime heights of those photographers. He is no Ansel Adams or

Alfred Stieglitz (and I don't think he would put himself in their class). But photography is absolutely vital to Long's art. Rather, he is one of those artists who is also a photographer: like David Hockney, Andy Warhol, Robert Rauschenberg or Man Ray.

Note how Richard Long tends to avoid colour in his art (and especially rich colours). His text pieces are nearly always typeset in large Gill Sans lettering on white paper. Occasionally, Long allows himself red type (usually for the titles of the works). Very rarely brown, or green, or blue (again mainly for the titles). (Hamish Fulton, for instance, employs all sorts of colours and fonts). But the black-and-white with occasional red colours in Long's art gives the textworks (and the photos) a very Minimal look (which also evokes Chinese calligraphy). Compare with contemporary artists of Long's, such as Donald Judd or John McCracken, who happily took up car spray paint, lacquer, and Plexiglas in pinks, reds, yellows, blues and greens.

Most of Richard Long's photos are in black-and-white, but there are plenty that do use full colour. Even so, the colour photographs, partly because they are of landscapes, partly because of the way Long frames and selects them, tend to use blues, greens, browns, whites and greys. Deeper or more saturated colours are usually avoided in Long's art (look at any magazine newstand or billboard: saturated colours are easy to achieve). Long's stone sculptures inevitably tend towards black, grey and brown (although, more recently, Long has employed different colours, such as pink, purple, blue and green).

Richard Long has based walkworks around colours. In *Red Walk* (1986), Long recorded the items he encountered which were red: an apple, a sunset, a rose, a shoe. In *White Light Walk* (1987, Avon), Long recorded the colours of things he met along the way, the colours making up the rainbow of light (red leaves, orange sun, yellow parsnips, etc).

The Zen or Taoist harmonizing approach is very much that of land art. Land artists can be seen as an ecological artists,

artists committed to ecological issues. Chinese gardens were designed by balancing the principles of *yin* (feminine) and *yang* (masculine), water and mountain. Land artists reorganize the landscape, building mountains, digging holes, creating pools, as in *feng shui*. Land art, including some of Richard Long's art, can be seen as a kind of modern *feng shui*, a Westerner's way of harmonizing the *yin* and *yang* elements (being in harmony with the world is often evoked in Long's interviews).

Perhaps the most famous of the Japanese Zen gardens is at Ryoanji, Kyoto. It is a must-see for anyone interested in land art (along with James Turrell's *Roden Crater*, Michael Heizer's *Double Negative*, Robert Smithson's *Spiral Jetty* and Donald Judd's Marfa site).[1]

TOUCH, PERFORMANCE, REPETITION

Richard Long makes circles again and again, and it in these repetitions, as with Minimal, Process and serial art, that the insights of his art are to be found. Although Long's work is 'repetitive', it is in this very repetition that his art flourishes. On the one hand, each walk is just another walk, whether in Dartmoor or Nepal, Bolivia or Lappland. On the other hand, look closer, and the viewer sees that every walk is different. The light's different, the weather changes, the ground changes, the route changes, the duration changes, so many things change. And the walker changes too, *during* they walk, as well as between each walk. So a walk, whether Richard Long does it or anyone does it, is always different. Using the terminology of Eastern philosophy, each walk is always different, but always the same. Each walk repeats the first ever walk. Each walk is part of one walk (the One Walk, one might say).

Richard Long sprinkles snow in a circle, or smears mud, often from the River Avon near his home in England, in huge circles or arcs or lines on walls, or he makes marks on grass using his feet, or he dips his feet in white paint and makes footprint circles and lines. The use of hands, feet, the body, mud, soil, stones, snow and sand chime with many land artists' practical methods. Land artists, as David Nash insisted, like to get right in there when making their art.

> I like the idea [Long said] that I can make a show anywhere by just going down to the river taking a few handfuls of mud... and literally get on a plane and go anywhere and make a big show with the mud from my bag. (IC 1, 12)

Richard Long's art ethic – *have mud, will travel* – fits in with the notion of a pared-down, simplified, 'essential' æsthetic that was current in the 1960s and 1970s (one wonders how often Long's had to unpack his bags at airport customs: 'what's in the bag, sir?' 'Mud.' 'Uh-huh. Dave, call security'). The great thing is not so much that Long can splatter mud on a wall and call it art (he does the former, not the latter), but that people around the world accept mud splattered on a wall as art.

> In the early days, if I was doing a mud circle in New York, I would take a plastic bag of mud from the Avon. One part of my work is the practical aspect – it is possible to take a big handful of mud from the Avon on the plane to New York, mix it with a bucket of water when I get there and make a huge work in New York with my River Avon mud. (1994b)

(Richard Long – one of the success stories of the British art school system (along with David Hockney, Patrick Caulfield, Peter Blake, Barry Flanagan and Shirazeh Houshiary) – knows only too well from his days at St Martin's School of Art that he is lucky to be able to travel the world with a bit of Avon mud in his bag, and have gallery audiences lap it up, because for every major (successful) artist there are thousands of students pouring out of the art colleges each year. And these art students are often producing work just as rich and challenging as that of Long, Blake, Houshiary, Hockney and

Flanagan.)

The sense of touch, of gesture and of sensuality is crucial in Richard Long's art of 'circles', 'lines', 'cairns' and routes. 'It's the touching and the meaning of the touching that matters' says Long (OW, 59). Long likes the idea of touching something where people have been or where they will be, of 'touching' history and the future (if it's possible to 'touch' history or the future). Thus, he will brush leaves and stones off a path with a stick (in Nepal in 1983). Not when the people are there, watching him. No, Long is not interested in 'performing' in front of people. He is interested, though, in 'touching' people – directly yet indirectly (all artists want to have some kind of effect on their audience. Otherwise, why bother to reach an audience?).

The idea of this sculpture 'was that the sculpture was absolutely on the line of people's everyday walking' (IC, 2, 14). Long wants to connect with people, but not directly, not by performing to or with them. Long likes the invisibility of the artist, so that his photographs look as if the artist has just stepped around the edge of the frame, is just out of shot. Long's paths have *just* been walked on, *just* been brushed with a stick, *just* been splashed with water. The photographs record a unpremeditated creative act, but do not show the artist doing it. (There are very few published records of Long making his art, in photography, film, TV or written accounts).

Often the 'touch' in the art of Richard Long is the foot. The touch of the feet on grass, rock, soil, sand, water, mud, paper, wood, stone. The walk itself is an artistic 'statement' in Richard Long's work. The walk is a mark, a gesture, an interaction of artist and 'material', the material being the world. 'My talent as an artist is to walk across a moor, or place a stone on the ground' Long says modestly (in RL, 236). If that's Richard Long's only talent, then, perhaps anyone could become a much celebrated land artist? If all it takes is to walk over Dartmoor, the Glarnish Massif (Switzerland), the Sahara, Bolivia, or North India a few times (perhaps picking up a stone, perhaps not) then everyone could have major retrospectives at the Guggenheim or Hayward. If walking makes one a celebrated artist, then anyone can be a celebrated artist. Except this is not the case. Long is in fact a clever manipulator of expectation and perception, shaping his artistic discourse to fit in with the changing times, like most successful artists, whether they are Andy Warhol, David Bowie or Federico Fellini. Long's art has stayed pretty much the same over the course of his artistic career since the mid Sixties, but notice too how he has subtly shifted the way it's presented, carefully altering the framing, the content and marketing so it fits in with the continually changing cultural climate.

Sometimes Richard Long will make a line of stones, or a line of water, or a circle of stones. But always he sticks to simple geometric shapes, the line or the circle (and sometimes the cross and ellipse). The circle speaks so directly and concisely of nature and organic growth. No other shape, it seems, can so swiftly connote nature. Perhaps only the gentle curve – seen in the ridges of hills, or the branches of trees, is more 'organic' and 'natural'. When Long puts his circles into urban galleries, which are nearly always, like most buildings, rectangular, he creates, instantly, a natural, organic presence in the gallery space. At the same time, though, these large circles are also 'unnatural', in the sense that one rarely finds such near-perfect circles in the landscape. So a stone or wood circle built by Long will always stand out, very distinctly, from the surrounding landscape. The stone or wood circle always speaks of 'humanity', even while it is 'natural', and a shape found everywhere in nature. (Note that Long draws out his circles using string, so they are nearly always very accurate circles. But then he often deliberately roughens up the circumference slightly, by allowing stones to be placed on the gallery floor or ground over the line, or letting his mud handprints smear across the line.)

The line or row in Richard Long's *œuvre* more directly relates to humanity – in the sense that although straight lines do exist naturally, they are much rarer than the circle. The line in Long's art relates more obviously to movement, to walking, to distance, to direction, and to time. While the circle connotes cyclical time, time coming back to its starting point (endlessness, and everything is ultimately the same), the straight line speaks of a segment of time (and space), of time with a definite beginning and end, of time being started and stopped, time being measured. A work like *A Walk of Flux* (1999) celebrates movement and change (sticks floating, thunder clouds, tides, water pouring), as does *Half-Tide* (1971), an early work, an 'X' inscribed on the beach in Bertraghboy Bay in Ireland with stones and seaweed.

The indoor lines and rows of stone fit much easier into a gallery space, and Richard Long always relates the size and shape of his stone lines to the space where they are shown. The *Line of Lake Stones* in Turin (1984) is large because the space is large (nearly 22 metres long). *Bordeaux Slate Line* (1985) is over 42 metres long. The line or a cross of lines is as far as Long goes in the direction of 'human' geometric shapes. He does not employ the triangle, for instance, the pentagon or other complex geometric shapes (as so many postwar and contemporary artists have done). Although these may be found in nature (in crystals most spectacularly), Long keeps to the simplicity of lines and circles (with later variations, such as the oval, the broken circle and the demi-circle).

In *Walking a Line Through Leaves* (1993), made in Korea, dead leaves were kicked aside, to form a clear line (but it's not a perfect straight line, it bends slightly, reacting to the terrain and the leaves). In Scotland (1991) Richard Long walked over burnt heather to create a short line. Sometimes snow is heaped into circles and lines, or rubbed out, as in *Along the Way* (1992), made in Japan, and *Throwing Snow Into a Circle* (1991). In this sculpture (created during a 7 day walk in Switzerland), Long picked up snow and threw it onto some grass (where snow had melted away). The result resembled Long's stone rings, where small units are gathered to form a geometric shape. *Dustlines* (1995), in El Camino Real, New Mexico, used kicked up dust to create a line.

White River Line (1994), installed at the São Paolo Bienal, was a large floor sculpture made with splashes of white in a tightly-knit serpentine form. The long, narrow sculpture stretched across the gallery floor in close curved thick lines. It was a continuous snaking line within a rectilinear form (the unbroken line suggested the flow of a river, but also a walk. The line could have been followed on the floor on foot, like a turf maze).

In another riverwork, *The Rivers of France* (1993, Paris), Richard Long drew the courses of rivers on the floor in thick white lines. It certainly wasn't an accurate map of the rivers, and had no sense of distance, scale, terrain, or tributaries. Rather, *The Rivers of France* at the Arc-Musée d'Art Moderne de la Ville de Paris offered only a vague suggestion of the courses the rivers took. In *Atlantic Lava Line* (1995, Iceland) Long placed stones on the gallery floor in snaking loops.

Some of Richard Long's walkworks concern clouds (a section of *Walking the Line* is given over to them). Cloud works included: *A Cloudy Walk*, a walk across Scotland in 1978, coast to coast; *In the Cloud* (1991) was a walk across Scotland with three-quarters of an hour spent inside the clouds while traversing Ben Macdui (the highest point on the walk); *Cloud Circle* was a stone circle built on a hillside in the Tyrol in 1996 (the photowork reveals a cloud drifting behind the sculpture); and there have also been Dartmoor walks following clouds. Clouds crop up in many textworks, such as *Planes of Vision* (1983), part of a list of things encountered on a walk: 'rocks', 'trees', 'cloud', 'sky' and so on.

In *A Cloudless Walk* (1996), Richard Long walked in France under blue skies and decided to halt the walk when he saw the first cloud. Of *A Cloudless Walk*, Long remarked in 1997 that '[t]he walk started at a very solid geographic place, and ended, by chance, with an ephemeral phenomenon like a cloud. One of the things I like about walking is that just the simple and very normal act of days of walking can carry quite interesting ideas' (WL, 147). To anyone not versed in Long's kind of art, stopping a walk when you see a cloud might seem nuts. Stopping when it rains, or blows up a storm, or snows, maybe, but a cloud?!

TIME AND HISTORY

> Give me the clear blue sky above my head, and the green turf beneath my feet, a winding road before me, and a three hours' march to dinner – and then to thinking!
>
> William Hazlitt

There is a historical and human dimension to Richard Long's walks, because he is always aware (and persuades the viewer to be aware) of the personal and social history of a place, even when it is a wilderness. 'A walk is just one more layer,' Long says, 'a mark laid upon the thousands of other layers of human and geographic history on the surface of the land.'[1] Long talks in terms of walking as a kind of palimpsest, where one layer is written upon the next (a notion central to Lawrence Durrell's *The Alexandria Quartet*, where no view is privileged over any other, but everything is relational). Long is conscious of re-activating history as he walks through landscapes. Some of his walks are founded on archæological and historical principles.

Take, for instance, the *Windmill Hill to Coalbrookdale* walk of 1979, where Richard Long travelled from two centres of human 'industry': Windmill Hill is where the inhabitants were the first 'to make permanent changes in the landscape', Long tells the viewer. Ironbridge and Coalbrookdale, as the place name implies, was 'the birthplace of the Industrial Revolution'. These walks of Long's require much imagination and background knowledge on the part of the viewer: s/he has to recreate the significance of the Windmill Hill people, or the Industrial Revolution. When one visits Windmill Hill, or other sites on the Wiltshire Plain, there is not much to see (compared, say, to Aztec temples or the Colosseum in Rome). One has to recreate the past in the mind (as so often in Britain). Similarly, when one goes to a city like Alexandria in Egypt, which has a history far more exotic and extraordinary than most places in Britain (only London could compete with Alexandria), there is hardly anything to see. Pompey's Pillar, a few catacombs, a Roman theatre, and not much else. No sign of the marvellous Library of Alexandria, or the Temple of Serapis, or Cleopatra's Palace, or Alexander the Great's Tomb.

Richard Long's historical walks and works, then, trade on people's capacity to imagine and dream. Even at Ironbridge, a relatively recent historical site, where things haven't had much time to disappear under mounds of soil, there is not much to see. There's the famous bridge, of course (not as big as it looks in pictures), some old houses, railway tracks in the road from factories, but not much else. Instead, Coalbrookdale is now a 'heritage' site; it has been made-over by fervent 1980s Thatcherite heritage mentality. It is full of museums of one sort or another (museums of industrial archæology, of rivers, of engineering, etc). Although it is but two hundred years old, Coalbrookdale requires museums and the 'heritage industry' to explain the place to the visitor. Even something as in-your-face and hard to ignore in the landscape as heavy industry seems to disappear rapidly, so that industrial sites soon slip into the post-industrial decay that Robert Smithson so loved to explore.

Richard Long's works, too, require the viewer to know (and yet not know) exactly where the stones or sticks he deploys in his sculptures were gathered from: the place, time, season, weather, etc. All these things Long reckons are important, and so he includes them in the captions and texts that go with his works. Indeed, sometimes, these captions and texts *are* the works themselves.

Richard Long is aware of walking into his *own history*. As he walks in Dartmoor, for instance (moving into the very familiar 'Dartmoor Time'), he goes over ground he walked on years ago. Year after year of walks. Dartmoor is 'full of memories' for Long. 'More and more I keep intersecting my own past walks, all across England. There is no way I can go down to Dartmoor now and not be aware of what I've done there before. It's full of memories' (WC, 104). There's a desire here to visit Dartmoor again as if for the first time. As if there could be, once again (like a First Dartmoor Visit), a First Walk. But there never can, of course, be a First Walk again.

England has become crisscrossed with Richard Long works and walks, so that Long can 'perceive the same place (England) at different times, from different directions and from artistically different points of view' (RL, 105). A map of Britain with all of Long's walks drawn on it from the mid-1960s onwards in different coloured inks would be a mass of squiggly, interconnecting and overlapping lines. (But then, if many people sketched out all of the journeys they'd made in adulthood on a map it could well look similar).

Mircea Eliade, the 'historian of religions' whose thoughts chime with Richard Long's at many points, spoke eloquently of this nostalgia of revisiting old places. For Eliade, though, it is a joyful nostalgia, in which one meets one's former selves. Eliade spoke of the continuity of one's life which re-emerges when one revisits places of one's earlier life: '[i]t is a comforting experience: you feel you haven't lost all that time, wasted your life. Everything is still there...'[2] (A lost, fondly remembered childhood lurks behind Long's art, which's linked, in the classic nostalgic fashion of the religionist or poet, to an earlier period of history).

Richard Long's art often evokes the past, and for the poet, this layering of one's own life is not a burden but a richness. Long in interviews expresses the doubt that the artist can 'start afresh' each time s/he makes a work (the desire for a First Ever Walk). The artist is conscious of having already made many poems/ songs/ dances/ paintings/ sculptures. This is the challenge for the artist, though: to make each work as if for the first time over the years. This is what everyone has to face: to wake up to another day, to the whole round of life starting again, every day. The anxieties, pains, joys, impossibilities, idiocies, boredoms and chores of each day.

What art can do, and what Long's art can do, is to exalt certain moments of life, to make certain aspects special again. The best art refreshes life (among other things). It renews the sense of life. And for some artists it becomes a life on its own: the art *is* the life. Not a 'substitute' life, André Gide might say, but rather the life the artist has chosen (or it has chosen for them).

An essential ingredient of the impact of Richard Long's walks is that they have a history, that Long has been undertaking his walks for many years. Without that history, the viewer might find it harder to accept that the walks were even made in the first place, as Stephen Bann noted.[3] Certainly it's a significant element in Long's art, the sense of layers of history and memory, both personal and social ('travelling is almost like talking with men of other centuries' wrote René Descartes).[4] In some territories, Richard Long is walking upon many layers of previous art and earlier walks. The South-West of England (and Dartmoor in particular), and the Scottish highlands, for instance, are thick with layers of Richard Long walks. Sometimes Long acknowledges earlier artwork-walks in his exhibitions and books. So when Long sets out to walk in Dartmoor or Scotland again, he's going over terrain that he has walked over many, many times. 'I have done so many walks in England – it is really my landscape, my home turf. I think accumulated experience is really great, and that too becomes part of the art' (1994b).

So there's nothing *new* in Richard Long's art: a walk made in the 2000s or 2010s would very likely be not a lot different from one made in 1999 or 1994 or 1986 or 1978 or 1973. In this sense, Richard Long is very like the Conceptual, serial and Process artists of the 1960s and 1970s, such as Donald Judd and Carl Andre, who do 'one thing then another', whose art-works are not grounded in liberal, humanist notions of 'development' and 'progression', of something getting refined or improved, but of simply repeating very similar forms and methods and processes.

> My work is just another layer on the surface of the world that has been shared by all these different generations, so it's really about continuity [Long opined]. But it's also about new ideas about time and space and walking. (2004b)

Richard Long acknowledged that, after decades of making art, repetition was more common, that it was impossible to walk in certain landscapes without being aware of his artistic history. 'Repetition can reinforce significance', however, Long reckoned (2004b). There could be a new kind of value or significance from the accumulation of one walk on top of another.

So if Richard Long makes a walkwork right now, or next year, or in five years' time, or twenty years' time (if he can still walk), it will very likely be a walk of a certain number of miles, a certain number of hours or days, and probably over wilderness terrain, and probably walked alone. And it will probably be recorded (embodied, manifested, expressed) with a photograph, or maybe some short phrases framed on a large piece of paper on a wall, or in a book. Maybe some stones will be picked up, carried, put down, thrown or piled up. Or maybe not. Maybe a stone circle will be constructed. Maybe water will be splashed over rocks. Or not.

8

Idea/ Text/ Desire: Textworks

THE IDEA AND THE TEXT

Art possesses nature and yet does not possess nature: something always remains elusive. What's there, in nature, is no longer there in the artwork. As David Reason noted of Hamish Fulton's work, and this applies to Richard Long's text pieces: '[i]n the work, everything derives from what cannot be shown and shared – walking and camping in close relationship to a specific patch of the natural world.'[1] The viewer does not experience the real subject of the work, which is the walk, the camping, the experiences the artist had. Instead, the viewer has to place herself or himself into the role played by the artist, as she or he walks in the landscape (it's impossible to reach the experience of the walker-artist, so the spectator has to drawn on her/ his own experiences. It's the same when a novelist writes: 'a man sat on a wooden chair'; the reader has to put that image and reality together for themselves, drawing on their own lives). The text pieces can be seen then as sophisticated forms of holiday snaps, those little coloured slips of plastic, pixels and photochemicals which record two weeks' escape from labour. Mementoes; memorials; mnemonics.

Richard Long's art is always an art of memory (as well as everything else). Long's textworks do not 'describe' the landscape, in the usual manner. Short phrases, and sometimes single words (as in Hamish Fulton's work), stand in for (a description of) the landscape. Reminders or hints of the experience of walking (living, breathing, camping) in the landscape. Long's textworks do not claim 'this is the world', but record tiny parts of the world seen from a particular subjective perspective on a particular day in a particular season and frame of mind. The particularity of each work is emphasized by Long's placing of the time and place in the final sentence of each text piece (everything is meticulously recorded). Sometimes, as with the art of Fulton and Chris Drury, a distinct date is mentioned; at other times, just the year. The duration of each walk is also critical: thus the viewer can get an idea of when and where the walk took place, and how much mileage was covered in a certain amount of time.

Instead of trying to depict or describe nature, then, Richard Long's art (like Fulton's) may be about the impossibility of representing landscape in art. At the same time (here's the paradox again), both Long and Fulton (and other land artists) are consciously making art in or about the landscape. Even though the impossibility of the project is stressed, they are still making art. That is, still indulging in a particular kind of Western, bourgeois, intellectual, creative activity.

Richard Long's textworks are set in Gill Sans, a popular typeface (the artist roughs out the textworks in pen and pencil on ruled lines to be set by the printer). Eric Gill's sans serif font is admired for its stylish simplicity: it is, like Helvetica, an unfussy typeface which typographers and designers admire for its clarity, its economy and its all-round usefulness. It is not a typeface that pulls any tricks, that is fiddly or precious or self-conscious (unlike many display, fancy or joke fonts). Gill Sans is also, like the London Underground fount from which it's partially derived, distinctly 'modern' looking ('modern' in the sense of modernist – early 20th century).

Richard Long's intention with the text pieces is to be as simple and unadorned as possible: the typesetting and design is not intended to draw attention to itself as design (but of course it can't help doing that). Similarly, with his photographs, Long uses the same 35mm Nikkormat camera and lens: '[t]here is always the emphasis on the art and not really on the technique. It should look good but it should not look designed or special' (IC, 1, 18). The idea is to be artless, undesigned, unprecious.

Hamish Fulton, Richard Long's contemporary (he was born a year later than Long), who's has been a companion of Long's on many journeys and walks (and works), commented that his 'work is about the experience of walking.' This could be Long talking here. Fulton continued: '[t]he framed artwork is about a state of mind – it cannot convey the experience of the walk.' This is true also of Long's works (and is the inescapable melancholy of art; that art is always 'after the fact'; that it always comes afterwards, or last; that it can never replace what occurred, or desire, or what was lost).

What counts in Hamish Fulton's work may be the communication of a particular state of mind (in Zen Buddhist fashion). The reduction to one or two words, like Chinese or Japanese *haiku* or a modernist poem by Gertrude Stein or Ezra Pound, plus the clean design of Fulton's text works, plus the lack of extra æsthetic paraphernalia, attest to his desire for clarity of communication. Fulton's *Seven Days (Whistling Elk): a seven day walk in the Rocky Mountains of Alberta Canada* (1978) is similar to Long's text and photoworks: a large black-and-white photograph (of pieces of wood on soil, it seems to be) is set above a caption which is also the title of the work. Another Fulton artwork is a text piece, just like one of Long's text pieces: four words are printed in capitals in red and black: 'ROCK/ FALL/ ECHO/ DUST'. When it comes to typography, however, Fulton is far wilder than Long, and much more experimental.

Have a look at this:

A LINE OF GROUND 226 MILES LONG

ROAD COAL TIP ROAD ROMAN MOUNTAIN ROAD ROAD

WOODLAND RIVERBED ROAD STONY TRACK ROAD

This is part of a 1980 Welsh work by Richard Long, with no picture, no map, no funny little arrows dotted around to indicate wind direction, no 'SPLASHES', no squiggly lines for routes or rivers, and no reference to anything other than itself. It's not a painting *of* something, a sculpture *of* something (a place, perhaps, or a walk), or an object brought back from the making of the work. This textwork is simply these words (reproduced in *Richard Long* [1986, 164]).

At the same time, Richard Long's textworks have all sorts of possible readings. He chooses particular words, often seemingly plain words (*road, lane, rock, mud*), or words used in simple phrases and clauses (*a line of ground, the lark in the morning, ashes blowing in the wind, 120 miles in 4 days*). The vocabulary Long employs – *night, place, clouds, ground, sea, river, grass* – is simple and direct, with few embellishments (one might call it 'plain English', an unadorned vernacular that prefers words with roots in Anglo-Saxon rather than Latin or Romance languages).

Nevertheless, Richard Long's textworks echo concrete, modernist and visual poetry or typewriter or graphic art at many points. In *Mountains and Waters* (1992) there are works with distinctly 'poetic' titles: *November Sunshine, A Spring Walk, In the Cloud, Dorset Song Lines, Walking Up Cedar Creek, Dartmoor Stones and Mind Rock*. Long also uses descriptive words which are usually the province of poetry: for instance, a textwork from Nepal (1983) reads like cut-up poetry, a poem with verbs and pronouns excised:

GREAT HIMALAYAN TIME A LINE OF MOMENTS
MY FATHER STARLIT SNOW
HUMAN TIME FROZEN BOOTS[2]

The observer needs to insert their own phrases into this *haiku*-like shorthand: '[I'm remembering] my father... [walking in] starlit snow... [this could be called] human time... [I have] frozen boots', and so on. There are some lovely phrases of Long's in textworks like this: 'great Himalyan time' for instance, or 'a line of moments'. But the really explosive phrase is: 'my father'. It suddenly turns the textwork documenting a walk into something personal and emotional.

While we're referencing *haiku* poetry, this is a good moment to illustrate the form with a classic example (from Basho):

A branch shorn of leaves
A raven perching on it –
This Autumn evening.

Another textwork, one of Richard Long's most poetic, the title piece of *Mountains and Waters,* employs techniques such as different coloured text; variable sized text; indented text; and white space.

One of the most obvious comparisons with Long's textworks (chosen from the long history of visual poetry) is the poetry of Gertrude Stein, the feisty and startling American poet who lived in Paris, was a guru to many an aspiring artist, and who wrote *avant garde* poetry way before James Joyce and T.S. Eliot. Two of Stein's celebrated pieces, 'Patriarchal Poetry' and 'Lifting Belly', employ repetition, like Long's poems, but in a highly controlled, stylized manner. Though some people have found Gertrude Stein's poetry difficult to read, a chore to wade through, it forms the foundation for 20th century concrete/ visual poetry, of which Long's text pieces are a part. It always repays a little effort. This is from Stein's 'Lifting Belly' (a gorgeous, highly erotic lesbian pæan):

Kiss my lips. She did.
Kiss my lips again she did.
Kiss my lips over and over and over again she did.
I have feathers.
Gentle fishes.
Do you think about apricots. We find them very beautiful. It is not alone their color it is their seeds that charm us. We find it a change.

> Lifting belly is so strange...
> Lifting belly is so kind.
> Lifting belly fattily.
> Doesn't that astonish you.[3]

There are plenty of other poets in the modernist/ cut-up/ concrete/ visual mode (Stéphane Mallarmé, Kusano Shimpei, Paul van Ostaijen, Tristan Tzara), but Stein provides a suitable illustration (as well as being one of the best).

Richard Long also utilizes quotations from pop music, from artists such as Bob Dylan, John Barleycorn, Johnny Cash (in *Reflections In Little Pigeon River, Great Smokey Mountains, Tennessee*, 1970), and country singer Nanci Griffith. His 1994 work in Orkney had a verse from a Bob Dylan song printed with it which ended: '[b]ut we still ain't going nowhere'.[4] The Johnny Cash song which accompanies the photo work *Reflections in the Little Pigeon River, Great Smokey Mountains, Tennessee* ends: '[b]ecause you're mine / I walk the line' (in *Old World, New World*, 56).

Music, Long feels, is another way of dealing with the emotions of a work. It expresses something in a work which words and photographs cannot (IC, 2, 15). Music is something important for Long – he refers to it a number of times in his works (it is one of the phrases he used to sum up his work in his 1997 Japan lecture). The kind of music Long uses in his art is generally American, country and western or folk or soft rock. Long's favourite time and place in music would probably be the late 1960s in America.

In 1994, Richard Long commented: 'I couldn't imagine life without music. I think it is really a fantastically emotional feel-good kind of art form' (1994b). When he visited art schools to give lectures and slide shows, Long said he used to play a piece of music to accompany just one slide, so the students had to look at one image for the duration of the song. (Andy Goldsworthy recalled a visit from Long to his art college in Northern Britain in the 1970s: how Long played Country and Western music during his 'lecture', but refused to answer questions from the students.)

> But the one piece of music that always got the most rapt attention, where you could almost hear a pin drop, was Roisin Dubhn, the slow air played on a tin whistle, with people looking at the circle in Ireland. That was always the most moving piece in the slide show. (1994b)

Roisin Dubh ('a slow air') was cited in the photowork *A Thousand Stones* (1974).

Sometimes, in a text piece, Richard Long will record the wind direction with a series of arrows – as in *Wind Line Walk* (1992) or *Wind Line* (1986) (The wind's a sound that accompanies so many walks). Long's first wind walk work, he recalled, was *Wind Line,* made on Dartmoor:

> that was very much to do with the fact that not only does the wind blow from a prevailing part of the sky, but it also reflects the shape of the land... I very much liked the idea that in a subtle way the wind line was also reflecting the shape of the land. (WC, 66)

In *Circle of Autumn Winds* (1994), made (where else?) on Dartmoor, Long recorded the direction of the wind during a 46 mile walk inside one of his imaginary circles. Wind is a huge physical presence on many walks in any territory (and certainly is almost constant blowing in places like Dartmoor). For a walker, in the open landscape, it's impossible to get away from the wind. But the little black arrows dotted about the place in Long's textworks seems fairly arbitrary and pointless, having little to do with the reality, force, sound, sensuality, speed or direction of wind blowing.

Stephen Bann has commented that some of Richard Long's works can be a little confusing. Of *Hundred Mile Walk*, made in Ireland, Bann wondered if the 100 miles also included miles up and down hills, or detours for fording rivers, or if it meant out and back (1994b). The mileage in Long's walkworks, presumably, means the no. of miles walked once the walk started, and doesn't count the mileage to the start of the walk, from the hotel, the town, the airport, or Long's home in Bristol.

Richard Long's text pieces are not poems, but they do, like poems, aim to transmit some of the experience of walking, or some idea of walking. The maps, photographs and texts are 'second hand' works, Long remarked (GL, 8). Though they're not poems, Long's text pieces employ many of the formal aspects of poetry (repetition, rhymes, alliteration, visuals, sounds, and so on). First comes the walk, Long says, then the art made from the walk. Other people may make walks, but, Long says, 'what makes me an artist is the art I make from the walks' (IC 2, 19).

In an article on sculpture in the Forest of Dean, David Lee spoofs Richard Long's textworks, calling them 'certain fashionable but pretentious word sequences which nowadays masquerade as art'.[5] David Lee wanders around the Forest of Dean in the following manner:

MOSSY TREE STUMP
CORNED BEEF SANDWICH
RIBENA

It's easy to parody Long's textworks. But Long's text pieces, though, are not 'pretentious', as David Lee attests: Long is not 'pretending' to produce art, he *is* producing art. Long has, too, written notes just like Lee's spoof: his diary entries (such as in *Walking the Line*, 144) record cups of tea and coffee, orange juice, cereals, bread and cheese, soup, scrambled eggs, and bars of chocolate. For instance, this is day 13 from a diary entry in *Walking the Line*, describing a walk (*A Line of 33 Stones, A Walk of 33 Days*, 1998) in Long's beloved West Country:

> Watery dawn. Good sleep. Bounty. Into Melton Mowbray: 1. Bank 2. Paper 3. Breakfast, full monty by market. Out on small road north. Post back map No. 2 from first village. Mixed skies. Dry tent at 12, stop on village green, ring Mum. Next village, Kit-Kat, Lilt, ring B from place with closed pub. On straight (down off high land now) to Granby.

> Look around for pub, very obscure, closed, but Irish lady opens up, makes a cheese sandwich. (WL, 64)

Nearly two weeks later, on day 26 of a 1,030 mile walk, now up in Scotland, Richard Long records similar everyday aspects of his walk:

> Lady a bit late for 7.30. Bran flakes. Gear up immediately in pouring rain with Dutch (?) cyclist in doorway. Straight, to Crieff. Buy map in info place. On 2 hours in pouring rain, first stop, an Inn. Coffee pot, with hot milk – 80p! On down, then up Sma 'Glen, over river, then up. Coffee rebounds... bit of diarrhoea behind rock. Next stop a tea room at junction with small road to glen. Great thick veg. soup and tea-cake. Chat to Eng. proprietor about walkers. (WL, 64)

In *All Ireland Walk* (1995), Long registers 'mince beef and onion pie... sharing a pot of tea at a garage... a coffee in a flooded bar'. Some of the text pieces involve simple descriptions of acts that are vivid and easy to grasp. For instance, Long often moves a stone, or carries a stone then drops it. In the text pieces *A Moved Line in Japan* (1983 [In RL, 210]) and *A Moved Line* (1983), the whole line moves, or is constructed from short movements, each of which constitutes a 'moving line' when imagined together: *A Moved Line*:

**PICKING UP CARRYING PLACING
ONE THING TO ANOTHER
ALONG A STRAIGHT 22 MILE WALK**

**MOSS TO WOOL
WOOL TO ROOT
ROOT TO PEAT
PEAT TO SHEEP'S HORN
SHEEP'S HORN TO STONE
STONE TO LICHEN
LICHEN TO TOADSTOOL
TOADSTOOL TO BONE
BONE TO FEATHER**

FEATHER TO STICK
STICK TO JAWBONE
JAWBONE TO STONE
STONE TO FROG
FROG TO WOOL

To make a 'line' out of these acts needs the force of human imagination. Such artworks require culturally sophisticated people to make sense of them (and spectators steeped in contemporary Western art). 'The photos and texts etc feed the imagination, the sculptures (in a gallery) feed the senses' is one of Richard Long's mantras.6 To some observers in the landscape, watching Long pick up beech nuts or feathers or frogs or toadstools and carry them to another object found on the ground, it might seem that he was mad. An alien, observing Long from a flying saucer, might not be able to make any sense of the land artist working away in Dartmoor (though a child might). For culturally sophisticated people, which is everyone on Earth (all cultures make art, use language, etc), Long's acts would make more sense. To those who know something of contemporary Western art, Richard Long's travels through the landscape make some sense (even if they hate them). Long, though, works on his own. People are used to seeing television crews around the world, and other media folk who use tape recorders, cameras, laptops or notepads. The land artist, though, doesn't go around with a film crew (well, sometimes they do): s/he often works in the landscape without machines or tools.

Richard Long's activities would make sense, perhaps, if the casual onlooker saw the camera. In photographing the artworks made outdoors, the artworks are valorized, memorialized, mythicized. Just as some commentators joke that nothing is 'real' until it has been videotaped, land art may require the mythicizing process of photography to become 'real'. In a heavily mediatized cyber-tech-info world, maybe building a cairn with stones wouldn't make sense to an outsider, but taking a photo or video tape of it afterwards might.

The textwork *A Seven Day Circle of Ground* (1984) is a large circle in which words are placed spatially to suggest where the artist was at various times (*A Circle of Middays* is a related walkwork conducted in 1997). In capitals the word 'MIDDAY' is placed inside the circle. There are seven 'midday' points, showing where Long was at noon on each of the seven days during the random walking. This in itself is a bizarre idea, a little like a map an army general might use, to plot the positions of a roving battalion (although without a grid, references, cardinal points, contours, buildings and measurements, it's meaningless).

Richard Long has written in italic some of the geographical aspects of the circle of land: 'Quickbeam Hill', 'Avon Head', 'Ditsworthy Warren', and so on. *A Seven Day Circle of Ground* is thus halfway between a text work and a map work, and requires the imagination to make sense of it. The clue to the work's interpretation is in its title: the word 'imaginary': 'seven days walking within an imaginary circle 5 1/2 miles wide'. *A Seven Day Circle of Ground* does nothing more, it seems, that plot in an abstract space the artist's physical position at certain times of the day. Apart from the words denoting topographical features, such as 'Erme Plains' or 'Stall Moor', there is no other attempt at the usual elements of cartography (contours, for instance, which are so important for the walker, or streams, or bogs, or paths, or boundaries, or rights of way). Long abstracts just the key features of this landscape, features that he might know well (Avon Head, for instance), and sets them afloat in white space.

How does one walk in a circle over miles? The very notion is intriguing (or baffling, or just silly), just as walking in a straight line is perplexing (though perhaps a little more understandable. There are many ancient straight roads, for instance. A straight road suggests purpose, function, movement, progression). It's one thing keeping to a straight line, by following a compass or map reading. It's another thing to follow a circle with a radius of a few miles, a route which requires constant checking and realignments (a circular route doesn't suggest an obvious function). There's an indifferent arbitrariness about Long walking in an imaginary circle which could either appear to the spectator as haunting or dumb. Either this is cool Conceptual art which has a compelling physical equivalent or embodiment in the real world (i.e., Long actually does walk in imaginary circles), or it's just idiotic.

Whether presented as a map (*Low Water Circle Walk*, 1980) or text (*A 2 1/2 Day Walk In the Scottish Highlands* [1979] or *A Circle of Middays* [1997]), the circular walks are designed as fascinating artworks. While some people might organize a circular route in a town (bank to post office, then to the fruit stall then home), Richard Long makes the circular walk a matter of Conceptualism and geometry. The casual circular walk of everyday life (once along the boardwalk and back through the town/ once round the junk yard/ skirting the town centre to avoid the militia's machine guns and drug dealers), becomes in Long's art a living sculpture founded on 'universal and common' principles. 'My work has become a simple metaphor of life... I am content with the vocabulary of universal and common means,' writes Long: 'walking, placing, stones, sticks, water, circles, lines, days, nights, roads.'[7] In *Concentric Days* (1996), Long walked (meandered) within five concentric circles a few miles wide in the Cairngorms.

Early Morning Senses Island Walk (1982) is a poetic record of the sensory input of a walk on the Isles of Scilly, a group of islands 28 miles off Cornwall. Just as Richard Long likes to record how far he travels in a certain amount of time, the recording of sensory details is quite in tune with the project of communicating the experience of the walk. Listing the things that he felt or tasted or touched might be enough for Long, as a sculptor, but for a poet it is probably not enough. A Georges Seferis or Osip Mandelstam would have to do much more with the sensory data. In Long's pared-down, Postminimal or Arte Povera art, though, the simple printing of information ('distant surf roar', 'pebble maze', 'warmth', 'blackberry', 'earth lane') has a richness about it (or it does if the reader or viewer can supply the rest).

In *Rain Drumming On the Tent* (1997), another sensory work, Richard Long recorded the sounds he heard during a seven day walkwork in Ireland. *Sound Line* (1990) documented the sounds Long heard on a walk (with Hamish Fulton) in Spain over 21 days (622 miles): geese, skylarks, dogs, buzzards, surf, fires. Rain and water are the subject of some walks: *Rain Miles* (1989) recorded the number of miles walked in the rain in (inevitably) Ireland ('174 to 175 miles / 170 to 171 miles'). *The Wet Road* (1990) documented the number of hours spent walking on a road wet with rain during a North-South walk across France.

Ten Mile Places (1986) was a walkwork in the West Country, a list of short phrases describing things the artist encountered during (the making of) the walk:

A SINGING SKYLARK TWO SHEEPDOGS
A FLAT DRY EMPTY STRAIGHT ROAD (WC, 48)

Of Richard Long's many walks – *A Ten Mile Walk, A 24 Hour Walk, A Day's Walk on Honshu, On Midsummer's Day, A 100 Mile Walk, Early Morning Senses Island Walk, Four Walks, A Line of Ground 226 Miles Long, A Four Day Walk* – one of the longest has been *A Thousand Miles, A Thousand Hours*, made in the Summer of 1974. This is a textwork and a drawing: of a large square spiral. Long explained that the walk took in the whole of central England, so that the whole of central England became part of the walkwork. *A Thousand Miles, A Thousand Hours* had an appealing simplicity about it, spiralling over central England: it was about the 'geometry of time and distance' (RL, 103).

Some Richard Long walks have rules of space (a 22 mile walk, for instance), while others use time as the framework (like *Hours, Miles*, 1996). Some walks last one hour, such as *A Sixty Minute Circle Walk on Dartmoor* (1984). This is a textwork of a circular walk. In a circle 60 single words are printed. How did Long make it? Did he write the words every minute, i.e., walk for a minute than write 'slant' on a pad; walk for another minute and write 'squint', a minute later another word: 'sheep'.[8]

It's possible to write poetry while walking – actually walking, not stopping to sit down for a few minutes. It works best in a certain frame of mind – relaxed, open. This relaxed openness does seem to be Long's basic frame of mind while walking (and other walkers have recorded similar feelings). In the 1983 Nepal visit, he writes of being 'happy alert balanced'.[9]

One of the important tasks on any walk is to find a good campsite. It has to be out of the wind, somewhere sheltered, and preferrably near fresh water and firewood. Note that Richard Long camps in wild spots, usually – or at least, places away from cities, towns, villages. Or that's the impression the viewer gains from his photographs and text pieces (Long may quietly excise pylons, telephone wires, restaurant signs and highways from his photos). Long is not, for instance, part of the culture of holiday makers, campers, tourers and tourists who travel around with RVs, trailers, camper vans and caravans. Somehow, one can't imagine Richard Long setting up his tent in a municipal campsite, with its little shop or office, its kids' playgrounds, washrooms, toilets and maybe a swimming pool. No, Long's campsites are strictly no star, open-air affairs, in a forest somewhere, or a hollow in the hills, and not in the *Rough Guide*, *Lonely Planet* or *Fodor's* guidebook, or the handbooks of travel and camping clubs.

Richard Long has put sleeping places and campsites in his walkworks. He's even recorded the spots where he pissed during a walk (on a 96 mile walk from Dawlish to Bristol: *Urinating Places Line*, 1993). It's bizarre and grotesque, when you think about it. Next thing he'll be doing a *Defecation Walk*: places he's shat in. *Look, mama, here's where I shat today!* Well, Piero Manzoni canned his own excrement, didn't he? And those wall drawings Long does with smearings of brown mud, the sceptical onlooker could call them shit. (Actually, Long has used fæces: *Herd Droppings*, made in Mongolia in

1996, is an open circle which uses what appears to be excrement).

Richard Long often photographs his campsites without the tent, recording the marks on the ground his tent has made: in *Light Snow in the Night* (1993) and *Breaking Camp, Moving On*. In Korea (*Stony Ground*, 1993), Long records that the stones he used to secure his tent were left behind in the shape of the tent. The photos register the grass pressed flat, or the remnants of snow, or the shadow of dry ground; the pictures have a similar function to the images of grass or heather trodden flat by the act of walking. A trace of human presence (but not a lasting trace). *Sleeping Mark* and *Sleeping Place Mark* (1990) were further instances of the marks made by Long's tents and sleeping places. 'Leave no trace' is a maxim followed by Long (and Fulton). 'One who excels in travelling leaves no wheel tracks', said Lao-tzu (XXVII).

Richard Long has often based walks around celestial events, such as sunrise and sunset, or full moons, or lunar eclipses. The lunar eclipse was the focus of a 1996 walk (*Walking To a Lunar Eclipse*). *Midwinter Night's Walk* (1999) was made by the light of the full moon at the Winter solstice. Another lunar event – the tide – was the subject of *Tide Walk* (1992), a continuous walk of 'two and a half tides relative to the walker' (Long said that the walk was about measuring time and distance using the moon, which controls the tides: 'that walk was very much about relativity... It was like measuring the walk with two different clocks' [SS, 308]). In *Highland Time* (2002) Long noted that during the walk the Earth had travelled 5,740,000 miles in its orbit around the sun.

In *Phenomena*, a walk made in Richard Long's home county of Avon in 2002, Long referred to high tides, the Spring equinox, sunrise and moonrise. *High Tide To High Tide* (1992) was a walk between the tides on two rivers, the Medway and the Severn. The solar eclipse of Summer, 1999, was another celestial event that was the basis of a walk (*Walking To a Solar Eclipse*), as Long walked from Stonehenge (of course) to

Cornwall.

In *Speed of the Sound of Loneliness* (1998), made on Dartmoor, Richard Long related the time and distance and circularity of his artwalk with the rotation of the Earth, the Earth's orbit around the sun, and the Solar System's orbit around the galaxy. There's something child-like about this listing of big astronomical figures. It's like children who write their addresses with every possible line added to it:

Joanna Wilson
Apt. #8,
1575, South Ellis Avenue,
Chicago,
Illinois,
60637,
U.S.A.,
World,
Solar System,
Milky Way,
Universe

Yep, and in the time it's taken me to write that address the Earth has spun 10,743109 miles further around the sun. And the Solar System's span a few more million miles along in the spiral arm of the galaxy. And the Milky Way has drifted a fraction of a light year closer to the Virgo cluster of galaxies.

The measurement of most of Richard Long's walks is by days — that is, by solar time. The tidal walks are controlled by the moon, by lunar time (1994b). As Mircea Eliade noted, the moon is the symbol *par excellence* of 'the flow, passage, waxing and waning, birth, death and rebirth, in short the cosmic rhythms, the eternal becoming of things, Time'.[10]

Some of Long's walks are about how far he walked in a single day, either from sunrise to sunset, or continuously, for 24 hours, such as in *Hours, Miles* (1996), or a 24 hour continuous walk on Dartmoor (in *Dartmoor Time*, 1995). In 1994 he walked for 59 miles between sunrise and sunset on Midsummer Day. In *Old Year New Year Walk* (1993) he walked for twelve hours at the close of 1992 and for twelve hours at the beginning of 1993. The concept of this walk was repeated (inevitably) at the millennium: *Walking From One Millennium To Another* (1999-2000), a walk which ended up (inevitably) at Glastonbury Tor.

Rivers are often the basis or starting-point for Richard Long walkworks. In the river walk, *Mud Walk* (1987), Long walked from the mouth of the River Avon to the source of the River Mersey, throwing some mud from the Avon into the Thames, the Severn, the Trent and the Mersey rivers along the way. In *A Cloudless Walk* (1995), Long walked along the course of the River Loire from its mouth (stopping when he saw the first cloud). In *Muddy Water Walk* (1996), Long walked from his favourite river (the River Avon) to Devon, keeping the Bristol Channel in view along the way. Long walked between two bridges (in Bristol and London) in *Watershed* (1992). *Mississippi Waterline Walking Line* (1988) was a photowork of the shoreline and the imprints of Long's boots in the sand. In *Rio Grande Canyon Stones* (1993) Long threw stones into the rivers in Colorado and New Mexico (a photograph peppered with the superimposed word 'splash' apparently marked where the stones fell into the water). *Stone Water Sound* (1990) recorded the sound of splashes in water in the rivers encountered along the journey of a walk in Wales. In *Water Walk* (1999) Long carried water from one river to another. *River Po Line* (2001) was a serpentine line on the ground which looked back to Long's first land artworks.

In *Four Days and Four Circles* (1994), Richard Long walked within four imaginary circles, drawn on a map of Dartmoor. Long walked for eight hours within the area circumscribed by the map circle, each circle being bigger over the four days of the art-walk. In *A Circle of Middays* (1997), Long walked around Southern England within an imaginary circle 63 miles across. The Monadhliath mountains of Scotland was the site of *No Where* (1993), a 131 mile walk crisscrossing the terrain within an imaginary circle (the 'circle' was a few miles in diameter).

Richard Long walks in time as much as space (so does

anyone who walks – or lives). His works emphasize the temporal, historical dimension: for instance, Long will pick up a stone, carry it for a mile then drop it, or spend a certain length of time building a sculpture before moving on. 'A walk marks time with an accumulation of footsteps. It defines the form of the land. Walking the roads and paths is to trace a portrait of the country'.[11] Sometimes Long set out on a walk carrying a stone he picked up from a previous walk (as in *The Same Thing At a Different Time At a Different Place*, 1997).

North and South, made in Blighty and Cymru in 1991, is a truly strange walk: according to the textwork, Richard Long walked for 8 hours along the same road. On the 1st day he walked for 8 hours, North (from Chepstow to Saddlebow Hill). But on the 2nd day he walked for 7 hours North and 1 hour South (from Saddlebow Hill to near Leominster). On the 3rd day he walked for 6 hours North, and 2 hours South. And so on. There's a mathematical system there, which recalls Sol LeWitt, and a wilful arbitrariness which reminds one of Jan Dibbets or Hans Haacke.

WALL DRAWINGS AND HANDPRINTS

Richard Long works with his hands – touches of the hand not to be seen, perhaps, in the walks or the lines of stones amidst rocky valleys – but seen in those circles, lines and ovals of mud smeared on gallery walls, the handprints on the floor and walls, and the fingerprints on bits of wood. (It's not so easy to smear mud on walls with one's feet – although Long has made 'feet' sculptures by making an impression of his foot in terracotta – *Footprint Spiral*, 1993). Some of Long's mud circles allow the handprint to be seen on its own, without being smeared, as in *Kilkenny Circles, Mud Hand Circles* (New York, 1984), *River Avon Mud Hand Circles* (Dublin, 1984), the Rome *Muddy Water Circles* (1994), and *Rhône Valley Mud Hand Circles* (2000). *White Mud Hand Circle* (1996, Tokyo) was a handprint circle made on the floor (against a black backing). *White Hand Spiral* (1990) comprised white handprints on black paint on a wall.

The mud hand and fingerprint circles underline Richard Long's insistence of making art without machines or tools. The physical manufacture of this area of Long's art consists of his hands only. The mud is usually allowed to drip (especially in the lines and rows of mud), and to splash onto other walls. Other mud circles smooth all the mud together, as in *River Avon Mud Circles* (Paris, 1982 and Malmo, 1985) and *Cuckoo Circles* (1987), so that only the short strokes made by the fingers are apparent. These short strokes of the fingers make the mud circles look like the floor circles made with sticks. The short groups of strokes echo Jasper Johns' late paintings, which consist of small crosshatched brushstrokes.

In Richard Long's mud circles, the small, human-size unit (the handprint, the finger stroke) is gathered together to make up a large artwork. As in Long's walks, which are one step followed by another, Long's mud circles are one touch of the hand followed by another. Long's works are always clusters of small units. Each stone, handprint, stick or step goes towards constituting the whole. The totality is manifestly clear: the circle is *the* symbol of psychic, cosmic totality and unity. But each of Long's totalities consists of small fragments (the interrelationship of the macro- and the micro-cosmic, the one in the many, the many in the One). For Oriental mystics, each breath one takes is linked together, to form the basis of one's life. Similarly, in Richard Long's art, a single stone can be added to another to form an artwork.

The eroticism of such mud-smeared works is obvious, as is the sensuality of rites such as mud dancing, where people smother themselves with mud for its healing properties (and today, echoing mud rituals, women – nude, of course – mud wrestle in pornography). The forms themselves, though – circles, lines, ovals, spirals, cairns – are not, Richard Long maintains, the key point of his work. The forms are 'universal', they are forms which don't 'belong' to anyone, which sets

Long free to explore other aspects of the work.1 'The creation of my art is not in the common forms – circles, lines – I use, but the places I choose to put them in.'2 Long uses stones because they are simultaneously common and unique; they exist everywhere ('stones are stones' he says), but each one has its own characteristics. Context is absolutely crucial in land art. It is the *place,* not the circle or line, that 'makes' the work. The location is the poetry of the work, not the circle, oval or the line. The circle, oval or line of stones must be sensitive to the place, otherwise it won't work.

Yet Richard Long's lines are not 'organic', like his circles. The stone circles look right on the earth, maybe because so many objects in the natural realm are circles or transcribe circles in their orbits (planets, stars, atoms, electrons, cells, eyes, mouths, etc). The straight line, though, looks instantly odd. The line of a path bends slightly, and the ancient tracks which Long walks on (such as the Foss Way in 1977) are not absolutely straight, but veer and swerve with the lay of the land. The lines that Long walks along, though, are quite different. They are (usually) utterly straight, whether walked in reality or drawn on a map.

Of course, when Richard Long draws on a map, he uses a ruler or straight edge, so he can easily create a near-perfect straight line, just as the Minimal artists produced pin-sharp straight lines (Sol LeWitt in his wall drawings, Robert Morris with his rectangular solids, Isamu Noguchi with his *Red Cube*). Long, though, could not walk in a purely straight line across uneven ground, could he? Isn't it a physical impossibility? He follows his compass, reads the map carefully and walks in a straight line. But it is, as in so much of Conceptual Art, the *idea* of the straight line walk that is important. One knows that the actual walk in a straight line outdoors may be fraught with problems, but in the mind, all things can reach perfection. In theory, at least. The idea of 'perfection' disturbs some people, because, they say, 'nothing can be perfect'. But an *idea* can be 'perfect'. Similarly with other absolutes, such as infinity. Though astrophysicists state that infinity is an 'impossible' concept, one can still use the *idea* of infinity. Ditto eternity, timelessness, nothingness, imagelessness, all those notions of Buddhism, Hinduism, Taoism and Oriental mysticism which entered the art world in the 1950s and 1960s.

'Purity' is perhaps a better term than perfection, and artists of all ages have been concerned with purity, not just the Minimal artists or Conceptualists (though a term like 'purity' is as philosophically and ideologically problematic as 'perfection'). One can see in Richard Long's *œuvre*, though, a craving for artistic purity (a purity which an artist can conceive of and works towards, which is not the same as the purity of the philosopher or the ideologue). Towards 'pure forms', such as lines and circles, and for the 'pure' work of art. Long says: 'for me art is the possibility to do something pure and focused and simple in a chaotic world' (IC 2, 19).

It is the *purity* of the straight line that fascinates Richard Long. The actual line he makes in his walks may be wobbly, as satellite tracking or mapping might prove. But the purity of the straight line walk is the thing. The *conceptual* dimensions of the shape of the line are crucial for Long. Thus, he made a spiral line in a gallery in Amsterdam which was 'the length of a straight walk from the bottom to the top of the Glastonbury Tor', and another spiral line sculpture was entitled *A Line the Length of a Straight Walk From the Bottom to the Top of Silbury Hill*. The idea of the line being the same length as the walk to these sacred sites is the important thing. It suggests a connection that is both physical (a walked line, a path walked on) and spiritual or conceptual. This is Long's ideal artistic response: something that is both physical and conceptual, both matter and spirit.

In the gallery, confronted by the spirals, the viewer has to make the conceptual connection between what s/he sees in front of them, and the place to which Richard Long refers to in the title. The spirals make more sense when one knows that they refer to Glastonbury or Silbury (and even more, perhaps, if the viewer knows Glastonbury and Silbury well, or has visited them, or has even walked the same walks, walks which visitors undertake most every day of the year). The titles of Long's works are crucial, because without them the piles of stones, the slate lines, the spirals, could come from anywhere. And Long doesn't want that response. It's very important that his works arise from *particular* places. Those stones on the gallery floor are not from simply *anywhere*, but from somewhere in particular (and they're exhibited somewhere in particular too). As Long says, the 'creation' in his art stems from context and places, not from using circles or lines.[3]

The titles of Richard Long's works nearly always have the name of a place in them, so the works are sited firmly within (the context of) a certain place. *Little Tejunga Stone Circles, Napoli Circles, Kilkenny Circles, Crossing Place of 2 Somerset Walks, Bordeaux Slate Line, Walking a Circle in Peru, Trento Ellipse, Tennessee Stone Ring* – these titles make it clear that Long is dealing with particular places: the look, atmosphere, texture, lighting, colour, tone, shape, pattern, sound, taste, smell, touch, history and psychology of specific places.

Although Richard Long celebrates particular places, he likes to keep the locations a secret,[3] as if knowing about his locations, the public would somehow lessen their impact, or disturb them (Long's interventions in the landscape are his own; the public is not invited to share in their construction). Besides, Long's works do not last: only works such as the cairns that walkers use to mark a path, to which Long added some stones, will last. The other pieces fade into anonymity, or melt away to nothing. At the same time, (nearly all) Long's works exist somewhere, as all material artworks exist somewhere, in one form or another.[4]

There is a random aspect to Richard Long's art, an ad lib, arbitrary quality, a sense of the spontaneous. Minimal and Conceptual artists often spoke of not wanting to be too clever, to manipulate things. Robert Barry wrote: 'I try not to manipulate reality. What will happen, will happen. Let things be themselves.'[5] In his instructions for *Slate Circle*, which consists of 214 chunks of Welsh slate in a circle 6.60m in diameter, Long writes:

> First, the perimeter of the circle is marked out lightly on the floor (e.g. in pencil). The circle is then filled in stone by stone in a haphazard pattern. Each stone is placed on its longest, flattest, most stable side, not touching another stone. The stones are chosen at random. There is an even density of stones throughout the sculpture, and a fairly even distribution of sizes and lengths amongst the stones. All the stones should be used.[6]

Richard Long's sculptures, then, have a random, intuitive aspect in keeping with Long's Conceptual stance. Despite his fastidiousness (in his recording of time, measurements and geography), Long lets his sculptures be constructed any which way, but within a loose structure (the pencil-marked circle on the gallery floor). One could equally argue, though, that Long's instructions to museum curators are extremely exact. A curator and assistants installing the work should get something close to the one Long originally built. Long maybe doesn't want a stone circle being constructed which doesn't look like a Richard Long artwork.

There is nothing *special* about Richard Long's choice of location: it could be anywhere on the planet, because he regards the whole planet as a single space. 'My art is about working in the wide world, wherever, on the surface of the earth' he says (FS, 236). His lines and circles, he implies, could occur anywhere. This is not true, though, for Long is very careful about his selection of potential art sites. He makes sure the places have the right atmosphere, background, foreground objects, etc. Although his walks take him in all manner of directions, which conform to a mathematical or geometric formulation, although he includes much spontaneity in his walks, he also makes sure the locations are right. He reacts to places, like any place-sensitive artist. 'I must have a strong feeling' says Long (1986, 2, 21). Sometimes the feeling is so strong, or the 'place is so good' that Long doesn't make any art there.

RICHARD LONG'S BOOKS

Richard Long produces lavish, full-colour books to go with his exhibitions (or rather, his art dealers and publishers do). The coffee table art books and limited edition artists' books reach a market that couldn't get to the exhibition. They act as a substitute for, and a parallel of, the art exhibition. They are expensive books, often with a tiny amount of text in them, consisting mainly of colour photographs of land art. (Although Long may wish to be ideologically anti-capitalist and pro-ecology, colour art books cost plenty to manufacture, and they are probably not all made from sustainable materials. And Long has produced lots of them. So Long has contributed plenty towards deforestation just like everyone else).

Richard Long's 1988 *Old World New World* is typical of the art books that the artist publishes: a landscape-format colour hardback book, with twenty artworks illustrated, as well as photos of Dartmoor, Sniougoutse La and Bolivia (the Anthony d'Offay books are probably the best series in the Richard Long canon). Some of the artworks in *Old World New World* are Conceptual text pieces, such as *Pitching the Tent* (1987, France), which prints two words ('first night', 'second night') in different directions, because this shows, Long says, 'the direction of my tent and my sleeping place each night along a ten day winter walk in the Dauphine Alps' (and don't say you don't care one bit which way his tent was facing during his walk). Here is the typical Long artwork: Conceptual text made out of biography. What one gets in the Richard Long art book is a strange mixture of photography and concrete poetry, a use of graphical text more usually associated with 'concrete' or 'visual' poets.

The text piece *Ten Days Walking and Sleeping on Natural Ground* (1986) is one of Richard Long's most complex textworks: it consists of phrases and lines of words printed in a scattered, 'random' fashion within a circle. It is the lingual equivalent of Long's circles made of slate or sticks. The phrases themselves are the familiar ones taken from a Richard Long walk, those phrases which are usually printed in a vertical column with no punctuation. Here, in *Ten Days Walking and Sleeping on Natural Ground*, the phrases – as usual set typographically in Gill Sans capitals – create a visual poetry record of the Long walk: 'deer tracks… the line of a day's walk the arc of the sun… following a desire… dawn chorus… stepping-stones milestones… bone… frogs… raven… drumming rain… mist all day… scent of heather' (OW, 23).

Ten Days Walking and Sleeping on Natural Ground offers, though, a contradiction in terminology. What does 'natural ground' mean? Does the artist mean ground that hasn't had a human mark placed upon it? Does he mean ground that is not built over, that is not a city, a road, a gas station, a trash heap or some other human edifice? When he walks on 'natural ground', what is the opposite? '*Un*natural ground'? Anyhow, the 'natural ground' walked on in *Ten Days Walking and Sleeping on Natural Ground* is not 'natural': it (Scotland) is crossed with the memories of human feet, it bears the marks of campfires and campsites, of animals husbanded, of people altering the landscape in small ways (walls, fences, tracks, paths, posts, gates, etc). Also, the area is thoroughly mapped, measured, quantified, and the artist makes use of maps in this very work: even as he walks 'on natural ground' he 'follows a map' (OW, 23). Also, a great many of the 'natural' features of the landscape are named by humans (in traditional magic there's a link between naming something and controlling it). The artist logs these names in a single column of text, which is itself another artwork:

RIVER FEHSIE
ALLT A'CHAORAINN
SCARSOCH BHEAG

CNAPAN GARBH
BYNACK BURN
BRAIGH COIRE CAOCHAN NAN LAOGH
CARN GREANNACH (OW, 22)

Though he employs photographs of 'natural ground' or wildernesses in his work, Richard Long revels in the names given to the natural land in his artworks. A large part of the 'poetry' of Long's works derives from the poetry of place-names: Carn Ealar, Sierra Tarahumara, Hangingstone Hill, Aldeburgh, Lamayuru, Twyn Tal-y-Cefn. There is nothing 'natural' about a place-name: it has essentially nothing to do with the place except the fact that humans have associated the name with the place. There is plenty that's not very 'natural' about Long's wildernesses or 'natural grounds', to be pedantically semantic, unless humans making art is 'natural'.

See the 1984 Welsh Marches walk, in which the evocative names of the Welsh borderlands are cited: 'Hay Bluff to Tympa, Tympa to Y Das, Y Das to Gist Wen'.[1]

> You can tell from many of my works, especially the text works, that place names play a really important part. I think the way places are named affects the way we know places. It's like language, how we talk about things is part of our understanding of the world. (1994b)

This part of Britain is particularly beautiful, a true wilderness. Central Wales is one of the least populated areas of the UK (unlike on Dartmoor, you really can be miles from the nearest human). The mountains are magnificent. The Welsh place names are poetic, but they resonate more poignantly if one knows something of the rocky, wind-swept landscape of Wales. (One can assume that Richard Long will never make a walkwork in somewhere like Disneyland, or the Beverly Center shopping mall, highly artificial, intensely commodified spaces).

Perusing 1992's book and show *Mountains and Waters*, one finds another textwork, entitled *November Sunshine*. In

Blighty, the two words 'November' and 'sunshine' are a contradiction in terms. The work is a textual record of the amount of time Richard Long spent in sunshine, 'walking with my shadow'. The result is that, on the second day of the walk, there was six and a quarter hours of sunshine. But this was lucky, for the fourth day revealed 'no sun', while the fifth day had only a quarter of an hour of sunshine and shadows. *November Sunshine* wasn't a failure as a work of art, however. Long was not attempting to walk in sunshine as much as possible, as the Sunday afternoon stroller might have done. Long's walks and works can never be 'rained off'. He doesn't care if it rains, snows, shines or blows. His aim is simply to record his walk, sun or no sun.

In holding a Richard Long art book, then, one holds a Richard Long work of art. The text in the exhibition catalogues and books is exactly that of the large prints and paper works, seen on the gallery walls. In the case of *Ten Days Walking*, the text is coloured brown, to evoke landscape perhaps. Long's works, like Hamish Fulton's, are a little different when seen on a gallery wall instead of a book, but not much different. The context is the biggest difference: the upmarket art gallery is quite a different space from a private home, a bus, a plane. It's true that the scale of the gallery text pieces is different from that of the art books, that one cannot handle the works (unless you're buying), that the works are seen in frames, on a vertical wall, during the gallery's opening hours, in a particular location in a city, and so on. But these differences are not that important, finally. What counts is the idea of the experience that is trying to be communicated.

Richard Long said he didn't have people in his photographs because he has chosen to make art 'about lines and stones and walking'. The social aspect of his work was separate. People were important for hospitality, help finding the way, or for food, Long acknowledged, but 'it's just that people are not the subject of my work' (WL, 146).

One sees Richard Long's rucksack propped up against walls, or his canoe drawn up on the bank of the River Severn,[2] or his tent in some romantic wilderness (as in the photographs of *Campsite Stones*, 1985, or *Sleeping Circle*, 1987). Long himself seldom appears in the photos of his walks. In *Old World New World*, though, he mentions 'friends' once or twice, indicating people he meets on his walks (or people he's walking with). And there are some photographs of two rucksacks leaning against a shrine in India, Mexico, and in other wildernesses (Long walked in India with Hamish Fulton in 1984, and in Mexico with Fulton in 1987). It's understandable that, of any item, the rucksack should appear in Long's photos, for the rucksack is one of the walker's totems, vital source of his/ her food and shelter, where the maps, spare shoes, sleeping mat, tent, poles, clothes, water-bottle, etc, are stored (in *Four Walks of Known and Unknown Factors* [2000] Long writes that he carried a hundredweight).

Anne Seymour says that Richard Long 'sets out upon his journey... *only* with a length of string for making, pencil, notebook and camera for recording things perceived, map and compass for finding the way, gloves for lifting rocks, a water bottle for making water drawings, and a pair of well-worn boots' (WC, 15, my italics). Seymour implies that Long travels lightly: yes, but walkers also carry a lot of items too. They travel lightly but prepared. And the water bottle is not primarily for 'making water-drawings', as Seymour asserts, it is for drinking. It is perhaps the most important item a walker has. [3]

9

From Photography to Installations

The personal details of each sculpture in land art are important, and artists catalogue themselves and their works meticulously. It is curious to visit a Richard Long exhibition and be confronted by lots of large pieces of paper with Long's documentation of his 'walks' or 'sculptures' printed on them (walks as sculptures, sculpture as walks). (Curious, but no different from a Dennis Oppenheim, Robert Smithson or Lawrence Weiner exhibition.) 'My photographs and captions are facts which bring the appropriate accessibility to the spirit of these remote or otherwise unrecognisable works' said Long (RL, 236).

Typical is Richard Long's *Three Moors Three Circles* of 1982, an archetypal Long artwork – a walk in his beloved Southwest terrain, in three of the main moors in the region (Dartmoor, Bodmin Moor and Exmoor). The whole artwork is a large piece of paper (one can buy it framed or unframed if one likes). There are three concentric rings of words, printed in red, which read: *Three miles on Exmoor, two miles on Dartmoor, one mile on Bodmin Moor.* The words are printed in circles clearly to indicate a number of things – the walk itself, on the earth, in circles, and stone circles, and circles in general, as symbols and as Long's primary motif. The next line, also in red, is the title: *Three Moors, Three Circles*. The next line of type, in black, reads: *A 108 mile walk from Bodmin*

Moor, to Dartmoor, to Exmoor, walking around three circles along the way. The next three lines read: *Liskeard to Porlock, Richard Long, England 1982*. That's it. That's the whole artwork, a cursory, matter-of-fact description of the walk. The words being a certain size, or colour, or in a particular frame, 'is all about how they look like' revealed Long (IC 2, 19). The words on the paper, though, have little if anything to do with the actual experience of walking on England's wild moors, with their sudden rainfalls out of nowhere, their amazingly impenetrable mists, their seemingly vast marshes, and their occasional utter solitude.

HEAVIERSLOWER	SHORTER
LIGHTERFASTER	LONGER

A FOUR DAY WALK IN ENGLAND
PICKING A STONE UP EACH DAY AND CARRYING IT.
A FOUR DAY WALK IN WALES
SETTING DOWN ONE OF THE STONES EACH DAY[1]

Everyone's experience of walking in wildernesses is different. Most people would be aware of things such as a vast sense of space; of no human habitation or marks for miles (or less marks than a city or a theme park); the presence of the weather; the ever-changing nature of the weather; the attributes of the landscape; the myriad sounds of the natural world, as well as silence; the rhythm of walking; awareness of one's body (feet, thirst, hunger, breathing), and so on and on.

What one misses in Richard Long's representations of his walks is the silence, the ever-present stillness and silence behind, in and over the landscape. True, on windy days (of which there are many in the Southwest of Great Britain) one cannot say the world is 'silent'. But there is often an immense sense of silence, or near-silence (like a giant ear listening), which adds to the sense of solitude. This is what people hanker after when they speak of 'getting away from it all', 'walking it off' by 'going for a walk'. Contemporary life in the

Western, 'First' World can be very noisy. In favourite Richard Long places, such as Nepal, Ladakh, Lappland, Iceland, Mexico and Dartmoor, one can escape that technological, mediatized, late capitalist environment, and drink in the (near) silence.

In Albion, one can walk for miles in the counties of the South-West (Wiltshire, Devon, Somerset, Cornwall and Dorset) and not see anyone at all. In these places, one is aware of the faint susurrus of the wind: this is one primal reality that's missing in Richard Long's works. Yet the faint sound of the wind about the ears is such a prominent element of a walk.[2]

To be dumb and obvious for a moment here: perhaps Long should move into multi-media and interactive presentations of his walks? Perhaps he ought to have the sound of recorded atmospherics and wind in the gallery. Nautical museums, like the wonderful one that used to be in Penzance, have the sound of the sea playing through loud speakers. The incessant sound of the waves helps to create the all-pervading environment of the sea in the museum. Perhaps Long ought to try bringing more of the multi-sensory experience of a walk into the gallery space, something more than textworks, photoworks, wall drawings and circular sculptures. Perhaps he ought to encourage someone to spend a proportion of the next exhibition budget on employing some museum designers and curators to create a multi-media *Walk Show* installation. Sounds tacky and silly, and the kind of so-obvious solution a naïve young art student might come up with? Of course it is. But isn't having a framed Ordnance Survey map on a wall and presenting it as an artwork and record of a walk tacky and a little silly? (One knows it doesn't cost much to produce a map work: eight bucks for the map, 150 for the frame, a few cents for the pen to mark on the map). The stone circles 'cost' nothing, it seems, like the River Avon mud (forget transportation from the quarry, admin, overheads, and accommodation for the moment). Long's main materials for his sculpture seem to be 'free' – the walk itself seems to be 'free'. Seen in one way, Long's works can strike the viewer as 'cheap', tacky and pretentious. Mr Average might wander into a Richard Long show and exclaim, *it's just a few stones on the floor, innit? Jeez, anyone could do that!*

So Richard Long's works can appear tawdry, 'low budget' and affected. Unlike Carl Andre, though, Long doesn't 'risk' everything on the socio-cultural context of a gallery. As his sculptures relate to walks, they always have a solid, straightforward, no-nonsense element. No one can argue with the importance of walking. Walking is not namby-pambying around with a paintbrush and canvas like a Sunday afternoon amateur painter. It's not twee arrangements of twigs and flowers. No, walking is good, solid, dependable work. It's only when walking is portrayed as 'art' that the problems occur. (If Long had started out thirty years later, and launched his artistic career in reality TV mode in the late 1990s, rendering his walks in the form of video documentaries, rather than as textworks or stone sculptures, his notion of turning walks into art might well have been accepted wholesale).

Richard Long's bits of paper are word games which only hint at the reality of walking in wildernesses. They are Conceptual, semiotic games which point towards the powerful nature of Long's 'landscape of the soul'. The 'reality' of Long's work is clearly 'out there', in the world, in the landscape. Yet much of his art is conceptual, fictive, images, representations of representations.

> So the walk [Long said]... the idea of the walk just exists in the words or a photograph, or as I said before, the idea exists to be remade whenever I want to remake it. The works themselves disappear but the idea goes on forever. (1986, 1, 9)

There is much ambivalence in Richard Long's importing of 'natural' forms and materials into the urban space of the art gallery. The walks themselves are the reality of his art. Everything else is secondary, something for the punters and art critics, something, perhaps, to do on cold Winter evenings in Bristol in between walks and travels to wildernesses.

One can see how the text pieces, of all Long's works, would be a favourite with the artist. The textworks Long sees as simply another artform, no better or worse than photographs, walking, or mud circles (like many Conceptual, Process and Postminimal artists, Long doesn't privilege any particular form his art takes: it's always all part of the same thing. And it's unified by the artist himself and his experience). The text pieces, however, can actually describe (or try to describe) acts in walking which photgraphs cannot evoke. For instance, some of Long's sculptures consist of stones being picked up and put down. One might see a photograph of a stony landscape, but without a caption saying that the artist walked, say, twenty miles picking up a stone and carrying it for a mile before putting it down and picking up another, one wouldn't know exactly what had happened in the work. The text pieces enable descriptions of events or concepts which don't necessarily occur in the photographs.

Richard Long's atmospheric 35mm photographs of Dartmoor are powerful on their own, but without a caption saying 'Dartmoor, 1987', one wouldn't know that the photograph was Dartmoor. After all, Long is careful to ensure that very few signs of humanity are seen in his photographs. So one wilderness photograph can be interchangeable with another. The artist can recognize this or that place, Dartmoor or rural Japan, say, but the viewer needs the text captions to make the connections (certain landscapes, like Mount Fuji, or the Tibetan mountains, are more recognizable). In one sense, the locations Long walks in (makes art in) are anonymous, or vague, and could be in any of fifty different countries. On the other hand, it is crucial to know that one of Long's most haunting images, *Mountain Lake Powder Snow* (1985) was made in Lappland.

Some of Richard Long's works are photographs of places where a stone was picked up then put down. There is a photo, for instance, of a rocky hillside in County Kerry, Ireland, in mist. Just that: no artwork on display, no stone circle, no line of turf pressed down by Long's boots. Just a hillside of stones and grass. The title of this piece is *Throwing a Stone Around MacGillycuddy's Reeks*. The text then explains the artwork: 'Starting from where I found it, I threw a stone, walked to the landing place and from there threw it forward again' (RL, 53). So Long follows the trajectory of a stone. These moving stone works exist in a strange relation with the viewer, who sees merely a photo, all very nicely shot and framed, of an Irish hillside, a Lappland moor, a path in Nepal.

There's no image, for instance, of the artist picking up or dropping the stone, as many performance or body artists would include (and plenty body artists would find an excuse to take their clothes off too). No image, even, of the stone itself, but a wide shot of the landscape in which the act occurred. Long's photography is not photojournalism, then: it seldom depicts something in the act of happening. Any reporter and photographer sent to cover a Richard Long stone walkwork in progress would go for one thing first: a photo of the artist in the act of making the work, picking up, throwing, kicking or skimming stones. Instead, Long's photographs have the disembodied emptiness which Zen Buddhist monks would approve of.

Other photo pieces of Richard Long's include *The Crossing Place of 2 Somerset Walks,* one of my favourite Long photoworks. The location is Long's heartland, the South West of Albion, and the black-and-white picture reveals a crossroads of two metalled country roads. Black and white cows in the background happily munch grass in a meadow, and there's one of those old country signposts, on the left of the frame, one of those signs with the lettering in black, the white sign edged in black. The sign gives the mileage: 'Stawell 1', 'Moorlinch 1' (these are hamlets near the A39, halfway between Street and Bridgwater).

It's a photograph of a typical country scene, but not much else. Indeed, many people would not look at it twice, as there's nothing much 'happening' in it. Further, there is no 'centre' to the photograph, no person or action or event to hold interest. It's not a picture that would maintain the attention of a newspaper audience, unless the caption anchored the photograph to some great event, such as: 'This crossroads is half a mile from the site where Queen Victoria launched the first spacecraft' (unlikely but not impossible), or, even more sensationalist: 'This is the place where mad axeman Jeff Blumenfeld buried his last victim after ritually abusing her assisted by a coven of witches and ten naked A-list celebrities' (slightly less improbable).

Richard Long's photograph in *The Crossing Place of 2 Somerset Walks* (1977), though, has nothing immediately arresting about it. That's why I like it: it has the blankness and ordinariness of Nowhere-In-Particular (yet it so pointedly captures as aspect of rural Britain). It looks like the sort of picture art students take as they wander about aimlessly with a camera. Or perhaps someone has fired off the last couple of frames, to use up the film, after stopping to phone their analyst/ mother/ husband/ lawyer/ trainer in a layby. Long's photograph, however, is firmly anchored in Conceptual art, because the caption says:

THE CROSSING PLACE OF 2 SOMERSET WALKS

A 40 MILE SOUTHWARD WALK FROM THE AVON BORDER TO THE DORSET BORDER
A 76 MILE EASTWARD WALK FROM THE DEVON BORDER TO THE WILTSHIRE BORDER

The photograph, it turns out, is about walking, the experience of a walk. 'A figure walking down his road, making his mark.'[3] The photograph that accompanies the walk *A Hundred Tors In a Hundred Hours* is simpler: it's a photograph of a tor (Combestone Tor); just the rocks themselves, no one else's in the picture. Underneath the photograph is a list of the 100 clumps of Dartmoor rock that Long visited during his walk (Yes Tor, Black Tor, Shelstone Tor, Sourton Tor, and so on [RL, 93]).

Note that almost all of Richard Long's photographs are

taken during the daytime (with twilight and occasional dawn shots too). Nighttime photography doesn't seem to be something Long has ventured into, even though many of his walkworks take place at night (Long will sometimes walk through a day and into the night). Night photography requires different technicalities (a tripod is fairly essential, fast film, additional lighting). While some sculptors have produced pieces which're meant to be viewed at night (Andy Goldsworthy, James Turrell, Nancy Holt), Long tends to consign nighttime art to his textworks. In an early work (1970), conducted on Dartmoor (naturally), Long walked throughout the night, guided by his compass, along the same straight line, over six consecutive nights, documenting the time it took him each night.

The relationship between titles and the documentation and artworks is precarious in land art, because the photography, the documentation and the title and description of the artwork is often all that remains of it. Long's cairns or lines made by flattening grass will soon be lost. Stuart Morris wrote:

> Richard Long's records of travel challenged fundamental availability to perception, showing temporary arrangements of on-site materials as [a] reminder of some transient human presence.[4]

This is how the art of contemporary (postmodern) artists such as Richard Long, Yves Klein, Andy Warhol, Joseph Beuys and Carl Andre differs from traditional Western art. They use the *actual object*, a process begun by Marcel Duchamp with his *Urinal*, *Bicycle Wheel* and *Bottle Rack* and developed by Kurt Schwitters. Instead of using a replica or imitation or image of a rock or piece of wood, Long uses the rock and wood themselves. The confusions of this relationship between reality and illusion, object and image, life and art in Long's art are compounded by his use of photography, which instantly renders everything an image, a mode of representation, a simulation, a copy, subject to all the strictures and structures of art and representation. The photographs in Long's art are plainly *not* the object in itself, but a representation of it, which is very different, and much more complicated.

The land artist has to face up to the fact that most people know about her/ his art from photographs. Most people who know of Richard Long have *not* seen a Richard Long exhibition; have *not* seen his art in its outdoor environment; have *not* seen the sculptor making a work. They have bought the books, or seen photos of his art in magazines and books. For the punter who consumes art in books and printed material (or on TV or radio or the internet) the 'real' art object doesn't need to exist: what counts is the representation of it in digital, electronic and printed media. But this would upset a realist/ sensualist (i.e., a modernist) like Long, who still enshrines the sculpted object. Yet that is how much art is consumed. Punters have bought the books, seen the photos in magazines and that, for them, is Richard Long's art. Thus, the *photographs* of Long's sculptures are *already* 'so real' that they have, for the consumer, replaced the art itself. In an age of simulcra (Jean Baudrillard), the simulcra not the art predominates. The photographs are incomplete on their own, as artworks: they require the spectator to create the rest of the artwork by using their imagination and memory, the cultural response, by remembering what it was like to be on a mountain, or in a forest, or on a walk. To recall what it was like to be a child, touching stones or snow or ice.[5]

The viewer, then, supplies the 'reality', the 'real' experience, the effect, which the photographs suggest but cannot complete. This could be another reason for the continuing popularity of land art: that land art leaves some part of the sculptures incomplete, and the viewer can supply the rest from their many memories of the real world (because the viewer *likes* to do a bit of work of deciphering and interpreting. Also, the viewer is given just enough decoding to do, but not too much – getting the balance right is critical). A kind of art of interactivity, fed by nature photography. It's also a not insignificant fact that by the time the photographs are published or exhibited in a gallery, most of Long's sculptures have already ceased to exist (they've been blown away, collapsed, eroded, dissolved, dismantled, etc).

Of course, art consumers would probably like to know that the stones *really were* placed in a circle on a Nepalese mountainside, or that Richard Long really *did* walk through the Shirakami mountains in Japan in 1997 when he made *A Walk In a Green Forest*. It's probably essential, in fact, for many spectators to think that Long really made those works. But Yves Klein faked his *Leap* (which enhanced it), and invited people to see an empty gallery. In the age of art impresarios and art 'terrorists' (such as Yves Klein, Andy Warhol, Claes Oldenburg, Jeff Koons, Bruce Nauman, Piero Manzoni, Gilbert & George, the KLF), when artworks are only known through radio, TV, the web and the press, Richard Long could have faked everything. (There are numerous techniques to fake still images – not just with computers, digital manipulation and Photoshop, but older methods such as montage, airbrushing and printing separate negatives. Consider masters of photographic superimposition such as Oscar Rejlander, Henry Peach Robinson, Alexander Rodchenko, Max Ernst or John Heartfield).

10

Dartmoor: 'A Place of Regeneration'

For me Dartmoor is a place of regeneration, knowledge, history and continuity.

Richard Long[1]

I can't analyze why it is mysterious, why it is beautiful to walk across Dartmoor in a straight line all day, but it is. And because it is beautiful for me to do that, it is good enough for me to make it into art.

Richard Long[2]

Dartmoor is Richard Long's main 'landscape of the soul' (although the area around Bristol would also contend for that title, with possibly parts of rural Scotland as a runner-up). Dartmoor re-appears in one guise or another in most of Long's exhibitions and books. The names of particular places begin to take on a holy aspect, part of a personal litany: Great Gnat's Head, West Dart River, Longford Tor, River Tavy, Grimspound, Great Miss Tor, and so on. In a textwork such as *A Straight Northward Walk Across Dartmoor* (1979), the inventory of beloved sites (East Dart River, Whitehorse Hill, Naker's Hill) is interspersed with Long's familiar shorthand phrases, listed in a vertical format: 'cairn', 'bracken', 'red lake'.[3] In one show and book, *Mountains and Water*, Dartmoor is the site or a component of many of the artworks: *Dartmoor Riverbed*

Stones, Dart, Tamar, Exe, Two Straight Twelve Mile Walks on Dartmoor, Great Gnat's Head, Tide Walk, Dartmoor Stones and *Muddy Boots Walk*. Any retrospective book or exhibition of Long's is bound to feature a good proportion of Dartmoor works. This is from *Mirage* (1998): *Alternatives and Equivalents* (1996):

A FOUR DAY WALK ON DARTMOOR

EITHER SLOW WALKING
OR MEANDERING WALKING
OR STRAIGHT WALKING
OR FAST WALKING

Richard Long enjoys Dartmoor for its very abstractness: it is a landscape with seemingly few 'human' marks on it (allowing artists plenty of leeway to imagine whatever they like).

> I also like moorland. Dartmoor can be wonderful. It has very flat hills. It is like an abstract landscape, which is very suitable for making a straight walk. I can walk in a straight line in this very beautiful, empty, flat place... (IC, 2, 14)

Long does simple things in his art. He goes for walks. He does the same thing over and over again: following circular or straight lines on maps and as indicated by his compass. Relying on the compass reading or a line on a map prepared beforehand creates a very simple structure (which can be tough to follow), and frees the artist up for an exploration of other aspects of a walk (Long is still mapreading while he's walking pre-planned routes). The flatness and abstraction of the Dartmoor terrain is particularly suited, Long says, to a straight line walk. In mountainous regions, straight line walks are impractical (even for shaman who can fly), so each walk is defined by its location:

> each walk fits the place. I can do straight line on Dartmoor
> and I can do a footpath walk in Nepal. Another thing to say
> about the straight line is, I can do them whatever the
> weather. If the mist comes down I can just look at the
> compass. I cannot see where I am going but I can still make
> a walk. (IC, 2, 14)

Although it seems 'flat', Dartmoor is quite high above sea level – high for Britain, that is. The peaks in the North of Dartmoor are over 2,000 feet; the mean elevation of Dartmoor proper is 1,200 feet. As one stands on the High Moors and look outwards, one sees just how elevated it is, how the lowland in the distance is gently rolling green pastures, while the moors slope upwards by 500 or 600 feet.

The amount of history (or 'heritage', to use that very 1980s word) in, on and around Dartmoor is impressive. It is a landscape, for a start, which has changed little since it was formed some 280 million years ago. It is part of the tract of granite that runs from Devon through Cornwall to the Scilly Isles. Dartmoor has a deep sense of prehistory, and of ancient life (humans have lived here for around 7,000 years – Dartmoor was above the deeply wooded areas which covered much of England. It also had water in abundance, rocks aplenty for building materials, areas to farm and keep animals, and other factors). There are many human artefacts on Dartmoor – hut circles, cairns, stone circles, stone rows (60 plus), old tracks, old settlements, walls, as well as gorges, bogs, clay pits, quarries, cairns and clapper bridges. These centuries of human history and human marks on the landscape form an important element of Richard Long's art. Always he emphasizes the sense of travelling over ground that many people before him have trod upon; in Dartmoor, one is made aware of this 7,000 year historical dimension continually.

There's just enough within the landscape to hold the eye in Dartmoor, yet not too much that the walker can't let their imaginations run wild. It's easy to imagine Dartmoor being used as film location requiring no set dressing at all for a battle between a Roman legion and a band of Celts or Saxons; a group of mediæval knights galloping on horseback; King Lear in the storm on the heath; and the wide expanses of low hills are perfect for a Napoleonic conflict, where every section of the forces is visible from the upper slopes.

Plenty of artists have lived in Dartmoor or visited it to make art: J.M.W. Turner, Thomas Girtin, Edward Lear, Edward Burra, John Skeaping, and Graham Ovenden.[4] Long's contemporary, sculptor Peter Randall-Page, lives on Dartmoor (at Drewsteignton). Alan Lee, the fantasy illustrator who contributed immensely to *The Lord of the Rings* films, lives – like fellow illustrator Brian Froud – at Chagford.

One part of Dartmoor Richard Long keeps returning to: the heads of the rivers Tamar, Exe, East Dart, West Dart, Tavy and others. This is the Northern and wildest part of the moor, the part where soldiers are trained, and where there are a number of Ministry of Defence firing ranges (Okehampton Range, Merrivale Range, Willsworthy Range). This part of Dartmoor has 'DANGER AREA' printed in red over it on the map (visitors are discouraged or forbidden to pass – the military has taken over huge chunks of the British Isles, including some of the loveliest, wildest and most interesting regions, such as Dartmoor, Wales and Dorset).

The landscape of this part of Dartmoor is 'bleak', in the traditional, *Wuthering Heights* sense (i.e., the classic Dartmoorscape). It appears featureless to someone used to a densely-layered cultural space, like a city. Of course, there *are* features: stone walls and fences, which are built all over Dartmoor, including up very steep inclines; observation posts; cairns; streams; pools; Dartmoor letterboxes; paths and tracks; heather; bracken; peat; Dartmoor ponies; tors; sheepfolds; and rocks *everywhere*. The sources of the rivers themselves are simply little pools in among the long grass and bogs (the visitor expecting more will be disappointed by the river sources).

Two Walks was an early Long Dartmoor walkwork (1972), a map-and-photo-work (i.e., the work comprised part of a map of Dartmoor, and a small photograph of a stone cross where two walks met (near the main road, the B3212, one of the most spectacular roads in England, which runs across the centre of Dartmoor).

Long's *A Walk On Dartmoor* (2001) is a photographic work which embodies the appealing absence of Dartmoor's terrain: it consists of a colour plate of the classic Dartmoorscape: bare, grassy hills receding to the horizon, a blue sky, and a couple of birds on the wing. It's the area around the East Dart River, Wistman's Wood and Sittaford Tor (Wistman's Wood is a terrifically atmospheric spot of stunted oaks and mossy boulders North of Two Bridges, perfect for an encounter with fairies out of Grimms' fairy tales). In a way, the picture in *A Walk On Dartmoor* says everything and nothing. The emptiness is precisely the fullness (in the 'less is more' manner of Eastern mysticism).

The text opposite the image in the *Walking the Line* book (2002) is also cryptically spare (with a palindromic quality):

> RIVER TO WOOD
> WOOD TO TOR
> TOR TO RIVER
> RIVER TO TOR
> TOR TO WOOD
> WOOD TO RIVER[5]

Dartmoor has its own very commanding atmosphere, look and feeling. Britain is a very crowded little island, but in parts of Dartmoor it can feel very wild and isolated. With the wind and rain whipping around, it can seem to go on for miles. But it's not that big at all. And in any part of Dartmoor the visitor can't ever be more than a few miles from the nearest human being. There are plenty of regions more remote than Dartmoor in Britain (central Wales or the Scottish highlands or Southern Ireland, for instance), but Dartmoor creates an unforgettable impression.

Dartmoor is all contradiction: although the stereotype

image of Dartmoor is of wild, harsh moorland, it is in fact carefully managed, and human marks are all over it. Even in the most remote spots there are manifestations of humanity. The stone walls, for instance, run everywhere, and must have taken months or years to construct. Although it seems to stretch on forever, it is not that big: Dartmoor National Park is 23 miles East to West and 24 miles North to South. It comprises only 365 square miles. The granite tableland itself is some 300 square miles. For Britain, that's a sizable portion of land; in many another territory, it's a backyard.

Even after a few visits to Dartmoor all of the main villages, roads and landmarks become familiar, so for Richard Long, who's been using Dartmoor as his backdoor studio for decades, they must be intimately known: Ashburton, Dartmeet, Princetown, Two Bridges, Postbridge, Moretonhampstead, Castle Drogo, Merrivale, Grimspound, Widecombe-in-the-Moor. The tors themselves are a wonderful creation of nature for easy navigation. Each one is a sculpture (like Dartmoor itself), as Barbara Hepworth said of the moors in Northern Britain, and each one is individual: Rough Tor, Hound Tor, Vixen Tor, Sheep's Tor... You couldn't plan a series of landmarks for a sculpture trail better than the outcrops of weathered granite atop each hill.

What fascinates Richard Long about this sort of moorland may be its purity: it is a place of the source of the rivers: this chimes with the Conceptual artist's project of going to extremes with a process or idea, reaching the essence or source. Thus, once the artist as walker has found a river, one of her/ his automatic inclinations is to follow it to its source (one sees groups of waterproof-clad walkers doing just that in Dartmoor). It is an ancient desire, made most famous, perhaps, in the quest for the source of the Nile in the early modern era (and it's part of the frontier and exploration spirit, once immortalized in the deeds of explorers, mariners and adventurers, but now dubbed the aggressive expansionist acts of capitalism, exploitation and imperialism).

Though no river in the South West (or in all of Britain) has quite the same sense of grandeur and history of the River Nile (though the Thames is packed with history), these little Dartmoor rivers (Dart, Tamar, Exe, Tavy), have their own atmosphere and poetry (indeed, the Dart becomes a grand river when it reaches Dartmouth and, in its way, I'd say the River Dart's as beautiful and spectacular along its winding route as any of the great rivers of the world. And walking beside Dartmoor's rivers and streams is as enriching as anywhere else. Richard Long has encompassed the River Dart in a classic (and poetic) fashion in 1999's *Continuum Walk*, where he carried water culled from the mouth of the river to its source on Dartmoor).

Thus, in that flat grass and peat moorland (as in the *Dart, Tamar, Exe* walk in *Mountains and Water*), Richard Long takes an idea to its extreme, following the river to its source, in a landscape already hypnotically abstract. Another work in the same 1992 exhibition, *Dartmoor Riverbed Stones*, links together a host of the little rivers and streams of Dartmoor: River Mardle, River Tavy, River Plym, River Okement and River Teign. These are the rivers and brooks which Long has known for decades. Walkers have to love these little streams (or at least deal with them), for they have to be forded one way or another (easy on the high moors in the North, where the rivers are fairly small, but trickier further South as they widen towards the sea). One of the specialities of Dartmoor (which saves leaps and lunges) are the clapper bridges and the stepping stones, which appear in Long's artworks. The heavy granite boulders which do for stepping stones and the great clapper bridges fit in so well with Dartmoor's rugged, stony landscape. The reddened, iron ore rivers are the source, too, of much of the life of the moors themselves, as well as providing washing water and (if careful) drinking water for the walker.

Far from being a quiet place Dartmoor is noisy – there is the wind, for a start, sometimes whipping around the face and body, creating all manner of sounds. There are the birds – exquisite skylarks in late Spring, for instance, and buzzards and kestrels. There are sheep, Dartmoor ponies, horses, cows, rabbits and other animals. And there is the rain (and plenty of it). And water everywhere – the many chattering streams, the bogs and the pools. Walking right next to one of the larger rivers, for example, can be extremely loud – the boulders in the rivers create an insistent white noise.

Water is draining off the granite plateau of Dartmoor all the time – there are many springs and streams. This constant presence of water in Dartmoor becomes a key part of Long's walks, as it does for any walker on the moors. When it rains in Dartmoor, it can really rain. It doesn't matter which way the wind is blowing. Even so-called 'sunny' days in Dartmoor are often a brief moment of sunshine followed by clouds, then rain. If one looks at Long's Dartmoor photographs, they are by no means sunny and bright, but often murky and misty (see the photograph that goes with 'Great Gnat's Head', a 1992 walk, in *Mountains and Waters*).

Every footstep in Dartmoor is (or seems to be) waterlogged, every step is upon water, or mud, or peat, or boggy ground (for a hard granite outcrop, Dartmoor is a very squashy, moist place). The water and rainfall is one thing that's striking about Dartmoor, and appears in most of Richard Long's Dartmoor works. The other thing is its height. One thinks of a plateau as something level and low, but Dartmoor has peaks well over 500 metres, which again makes it comparable with mountainous Wales or Scotland. Indeed, the highest town in Britain is in Dartmoor: the dour prison community of Princetown (where, in the swish Dartmoor National Park Information Centre one can see a Richard Long textwork, in amongst the displays of Dartmoor's history, geology and topography).

11

Walking as Ecstasy

I must go walk the woods so wild
And wander here and there.

Sir Thomas Wyatt[1]

Richard Long does sometimes speak in poetic, religious terms of his art – 'art should be a religious experience' he says,[2] but he also reminds viewers: 'I am not a religious traveller' (SF). Although his sculptures alter the world – no physical *object* can avoid altering the world – he maintains (like a Taoist or Zen follower) that he takes his cue from the landscape, instead of imposing on it 'from outside', as it were: 'I use the world as I find it'.[3] Bill Woodrow, a contemporary of Long's, also 'uses' the world as he finds it.[4]

Richard Long's views have something in common with Zen Buddhism, Taoism, Shinto, American Indian religion, Australian aboriginal 'dreaming', archaic shamanism and Western magic.[5] It's not intentional, the Long-Zen connection, and Long is flattered that people find it in his work (FC VI, 18). However, a piece such as 'Mind Rock', in which, during an 11 day walk, the artist bears 'a rock in mind', is given a Zen connotation: first the walk occurs in Japan; it links notions of 'mind' (contemplation) and reality (the rock) in a Zen meditation or *zazen* fashion; and it is a textwork seen next to a photograph that evokes the Japanese Zen gardens (in *Mountains and Waters*). The sculpture and the place are one, in a mystical relationship, as Long points out in his writings:

> The material and the idea are of the place; sculpture and place are one, the same. The place is as far as the eye can see from the sculpture. The place for a sculpture is found by walking. Some works are a succession of particular places along a walk, e.g. *Milestones*. In this work, the walking, the places and the stones all have equal importance.[6]

When he walks, Richard Long has remarked, as so many walkers have said, '[w]hile I am in the landscape... I am in a very good state of mind' (IC 1, 5). The Cornish poet Peter Redgrove told me in 1994 that 'the ideal state for everyday going about is the first stage of orgasmic arousal'.[7] It's typical of Peter Redgrove to eroticize the artist's state of being aware, of being-in-the-world, to sexualize the artist's creativity (he's really just talking about the heightened state of consciousness necessary for making art, or just good living). A religionist or mystic might talk about being in a slight trance, or prayer, or a mild form of spiritual contemplation. Walking as meditation. Or therapy. Or yoga. Or tantra. Or the aboriginal Dreaming.

'Ecstasy' can seem too strong a word for it, but it is ecstasy. It is 'walking' in the Taoist sense; that is, walking as another name for feeling ecstatic. 'A journey in the wilderness becomes a fantastic focus of concentration. I can get totally absorbed in the place and totally absorbed in my work' Long said (IC 1, 14).

The very activity of walking releases chemicals in the brain and body that promote pleasure.[8] Joggers, sports and physical fitness enthusiasts get hooked on them sometimes. 'I think the sexual energy or the energy of creativity or the adrenalin energy you get from being on a mountain, sometimes they are all very close' Richard Long remarked (IC 2, 22). The physical action of walking is soothing, contemplative, sensual. Hamish Fulton spoke of the meditative benefits of walking, how it reduces the 'constant chatter in the head' and promotes 'meditative moments' (2002). Since time immemorial people have 'walked off' their problems; infants can be calmed by walking; and many artists and philosophers were famous for their walks: Arthur Schopenhauer and Immaneul Kant took twilit walks; Thomas Hardy tramped through Dorset; William Wordsworth and Samuel Taylor Coleridge walked in the Lake District; some writers were known as 'supertramps'; Henry Miller was in ecstasy simply by walking around the backstreets of New York and Paris (as eloquently described in trilogies of the *Tropic of Cancer* and *The Rosy Crucifixion*). 'Walking itself has a cultural history, from Pilgrims to the wandering Japanese poets, the English Romantics and contemporary long-distance walkers' said Long (WL, 68).

John Cowper Powys's walks were a vital part of his life: the daily (morning and afternoon) walks, intricately ritualized, which Powys undertook without fail in all weathers in upstate New York, rural Dorset (in Dorchester and East Chaldon) and finally, for the last thirty years of his life, in grim, mountainous and remote North Wales (in Corwen and Blaenau-Ffestiniog).

Or the incredible restlessness and rebellion of French poet-genius Arthur Rimbaud: always running away from home as a teenager (to Paris and Brussels), and being dragged back home to Charleville, the increasingly desperate drifter existence across Europe (London, Stuttgart, walking to Wütrtenberg, then Switzerland, then Italy, the Cyclades, Marseilles, Scandinavia, Hamburg, Antwerp), the fraught affair with Paul Verlaine, joining the Dutch army then deserting, and winding up in Aden and Abyssinia, a profoundly bored businessman (and possible gun-runner and slave trader). Rimbaud always had to be in movement. A life of disenchantment, disaffection, alienation, wandering, debauchery, and intense self-loathing. Oh – and he composed, between the ages of 16 and 19, perhaps the best poetry ever written.

This's from *A Season In Hell*:

> Je dus voyager, distraire les enchantments assemblés sur mon cerveau. Sur la mer, que j'aimais comme si elle eût dû me laver d'une souillure, je voyais se lever la croix consolatrice. J'avais été damné par l'arc-en-ciel. Le Bonheur était ma fatalité, mon remords, mon ver: ma vie serait toujours trop immense pour être dévouée à la force et à la beauté. ("Delirium II: Alchemy of the Word")[9]

Stephen Bann remarked that an artist who makes art by systematically walking through the countryside will seem archaic and even quaint in a few decades, just as the boy scout movement of the 1930s seems intriguing and slightly sinister.

> Just as a person on foot in a rich American suburb is a focus of immediate suspicion, it is conceivable that a person who walks all over roads, lanes and double tracks may soon appear eccentric, if the public pressure protecting rights of way is not maintained. (1994b)

Of course, in many territories walking will not die out for some time. Hundreds of millions of people don't have cars, or transport, or even access to transport.

> For my part [said Robert Louis Stevenson] I travel not to go anywhere, but *to go*. I travel for travel's sake. The great affair is to *move*.[10]

The Australian aborigines' cult of mythic 'dreamtime' is an affinity often cited here with Richard Long's art: walking plays a central role in both (and Long has walked in some of the landscapes sacred to the Australian aborigines). The dream journeys of the aborigines traverse a spiritualized landscape. As James Cowan put it, the 'sacred journey' was imbued at each stage 'with sacred significance', and in the dreaming, when the aborigine enters the dreamworld, 'the land is transformed into a metaphysical landscape saturated with significance' (1989).

To travel the world so often making walks and works, Richard Long must *really* love walking (*really*, *really* love walking). Did I say he must *really love walking*? There are plenty of easier, sedentary ways of living (or earning money). As well as being somewhat compulsive or obsessive (like many artists), Long must also simply really like to walk. He's the ultimate artist as drifter, as nomad, as wanderer, as traveller, as rolling stone (he's made references to rolling stones in his art).[11]

Having done a little bit of walking in wildernesses myself, I know that one is continually aware when walking of things like the light (direction, intensity, clarity, colour, tone, contrast, etc); the sun; the sky and clouds; the wind (the sound, the direction, the power, the chill factor); the quality of the ground (smooth, rough, stony, soft); difficult terrain ahead (marshes, hills, gulleys, cliffs); the horizon; landmarks; other people (including walkers); animals; sounds (aircraft, animals, traffic, people); the air temperature; what the weather's doing; the time; distance travelled so far; distance to go; time out and time back; the route (including detours); the next halt (where and when); when to break for lunch (and where); finding a place to camp; thirst and hunger; and how much food and water is left. So it's no surprise that Richard Long's art continually refers to many of these elements of a walk – they are the fundamental stuff of his art.

In an interview, Richard Long compared being in the landscape to the notion of Zen Buddhist *satori*, the 'hereness' and 'nowness' of mystical experience:

> A walk can often be the means of stripping away many things; it can be the spectacular embodiment of the Zen idea of the "here and now". To be alone for a few days in a wilderness is the simplest, best way to be in a one-to-one relationship with a place.[12]

Richard Long evokes having the *participation mystique* with the Earth, with places and atmospheres and organic materials, that the archaic peoples of the world had (and have). It is a pre-institutionalized, pre-pagan and pantheistic rapport with the world, deliberately eschewing dogma, doctrine and manifestos. It is also part, as many commentators have noted, of a British Romantic tradition, that feeling for nature found in Blake, Turner, Byron, Shelley and Constable.[13]

The archaic shaman is the ancestor of the artist as ecstatic (the shaman is the progenitor of all these interrelated types: poets, artists, musicians, saints, mystics, ascetics and philosophers). The shaman, Mircea Eliade wrote,

> is above all the specialist in ecstasy. It is owing to his capacity for ecstasies – that is, because he is able, at will, to pass out of his body and undertake mystical journeys through all the cosmic regions – that the shaman is a healer, and a director of souls as well as a mystic and visionary.[14]

Again, it's not being suggested here that Richard Long is a shaman (or a latter-day incarnation of a shaman). He doesn't dance with drums, speak to animals, commune with spirits, master fire, undertake mystic journeys, fly through the air, descend to Hell or ascend to Heaven, heal people and shepherd souls to other worlds (at least, I don't think he does. Maybe he has a secret shamanic practice in Bristol – there are a few such enterprises in the area). Rather, many of the elements of shamanism can be discerned in Long's art: the ecstatic walking (walking as trance, walking as meditation, walking as yoga, walking as healing, walking as shamanic flight), the wilderness landscapes, the utopian project (the nostalgia for paradise), the communing with the natural world, the totemic animals, and the sacred stones and objects.

The stone circles and the cairns that Richard Long builds have obvious links to the World Tree or *axis mundi* or centre of the world of shamanism.[15] And it's maybe no coincidence that Long has walked in many regions which are known for shamanism: such as Lappland, South-West America, Mongolia, Peru and rural Japan. (And Long is part of an increasing interest from the 1960s onwards in shamanism, in

Eliade's writing, Grey Owl, Black Elk, John Neihardt, Carlos Casteneda and Don Juan, etc).

What one sees of Richard Long himself suggests a relatively easy and enjoyable life of wandering about, camping, travelling. 'Behind my work is the idea that I have seized an opportunity, won a fantastic freedom, to make art, to lay down abstract ideas, in some of the great places of the world' (RL, 74). Maybe making artwalks is for Long dull, arduous, uninspiring and deadening work, as making art is for some artists, or as work is for those who hate labour. Maybe artwalking is tough, difficult and tedious for Long, like so many jobs are. Somehow, it doesn't seem that way. Long appears to be having a good time.

The pleasure of travel abounds in Richard Long's art: his walks are always partly about the *jouissance* of walking.

> So even with storms or bogs or blisters or tiredness, the way I can make my work is intensely pleasurable and satisfying. Even in the more modest ambience of a road walk, the labyrinth of country roads, the inns, the Bed & Breakfasts, the fabric of country life is still an enjoyable part of making the work and, although not specifically the subject of it, it is implicit in the idea of the work and the place of it. (RL, 74)

Richard Long's art is not angst-ridden, like Vincent van Gogh's or Mark Rothko's; it is not the product of despair and alienation; Long is not a melancholic, obsessive artist like Leonardo da Vinci. He is, in fact, *happy*, a terrible state of affairs for an artist. Happy! Yes: Long is not an artist whose art springs from the depths of rage or sorrow, like some of Amedeo Modigliani's art or Georges Rouault's art seems to. He's not about to rush out into a field and cut off his ear (van Gogh) or shoot himself in his studio (Rothko).

> ...usually I am happy and relaxed [remarked Long]. I would say that the way I make my work is from the things that give me pleasure and the materials that I like using – my work doesn't come from a kind of *angst* or discontent. (RC, 23)

The result of this balanced, relaxed approach to art is that the artworks are the expressions of a celebration of certain places. Richard Long noted:

> A sculpture in a landscape, when it really happens well in a good way, is like a celebration of place and my feelings of me being there and having the right idea at the right time and everything coming together in a good way.

So important are walks for Richard Long, that he regards them as life-nourishing experiences, an essential part of his life:

> After a good walk, yes. After 8 days of seeing almost no people (no talking), long sleeps, deep dreaming, brilliant campsites, sharpened senses, new experiences, new knowledge, getting fit – I always have the feeling of being a slightly changed person after a walk than I was before it. (SF)

The great Chinese sage, Chuang-tzu, wrote: '[i]t is easy to keep from walking, the hard thing is to walk without touching the ground.'[16] Chuang-tzu's paradoxical sentence is typical of Eastern philosophy, where things are simultaneously this and not-this, as in the Zen *koan* or Hinduism's definition of Atman or Brahma. In Taoism, walking itself is a holy activity. 'To 'wander' is the Taoist code word for becoming ecstatic.'[17]

Richard Long is not wholly a walker-artist in the manner of ancient Chinese sages or Japanese wanderer-poets. There are some aspects of the ascetic philosophy of Lao-tzu or the *I Ching* which Long doesn't take up. For instance, the notion of meditation, of 'travelling without moving', the shamanic journeying (in spirit, not in body): one of the most illuminating passages in the *Tao Te Ching* speaks about the benefits of being stationary:

> Without stirring abroad
> One can know the whole world;
> Without looking out of the window

> One can see the way of heaven.
> The further one goes
> The less one knows. (XLVII)

Hélène Cixous, the French feminist, in *Three Steps On the Ladder of Writing* (1993), discussed the connections between walking and creativity which chime with Richard Long's poetry of walking. Cixous eloquently likened the poetic act (or creation, or writing) to movement, in particular walking, to pleasure and sex – to the body in action:

> Walking, dancing, pleasure: these accompany the poetic act. I wonder what kind of poet doesn't wear out their shoes, writes with their head. The true poet is a traveller. Poetry is about travelling on foot and all its substitutes, all forms of transportation.

The poet, reckoned Cixous, creates in motion, writes as s/he moves, moves as s/he writes. Creation, dreaming, movement and art are entwined. The walks take place during the day (usually), but at night the walker is also travelling – in dreaming (like shamanic flight). Hélène Cixous continues (and again, keep in mind Richard Long traversing the world):

> ...we have to walk, to use our whole body to enable the world to become flesh, exactly as this happens in our dreams. In dreams and writing our body is alive: we either use the whole of it or, depending on the dream, a part. We must embark on a body-to-body journey in order to discover the body.

It's in keeping with Cixous' philosophy of embodiment that she should emphasize the body's part in this *jouissance* of creativity. The world can become flesh (lived) only through the body for Cixous. The body can never finally be erased, and Richard Long's art has always been an art of embodiment, of being in the moment physically as well as mentally or spiritually. An art of doing as well as being. Being as movement. Rhythm. Steps. A walk.

Finally, Cixous writes:

> In order to go to the School of Dreams, something must be displaced, starting with the bed. One has to get going. This is what writing is, starting off. It has to do with activity and passivity. This does not mean one will get there. Writing is not arriving; most of the time it's *not arriving*. One must go on foot, with the body. One has to go away, leave the self. How far must one not arrive in order to write, how far must one wander and wear out and have pleasure? One must walk as far as the night. One's own night. Walking through the self toward the dark.[17]

Richard Long's final act would likely be a walk – a Last Walk into the Dark.

Illustrations

On the following pages:
• Some classic landscape painters.
• Images of prehistoric sites in the U.K.
• Images of places linked to Richard Long's art, including Dartmoor in England.

On the following pages are some landscapes linked
to the art of Richard Long, beginning with Dartmoor, England

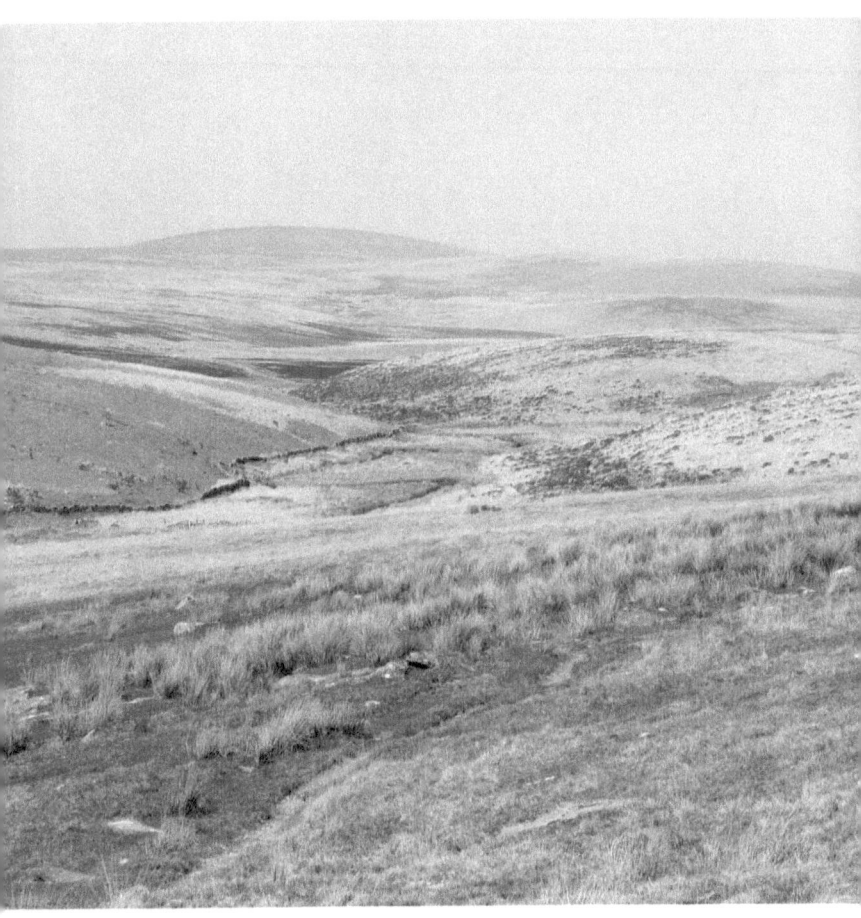

Near Sittaford Tor and Fernworthy Forest, Dartmoor

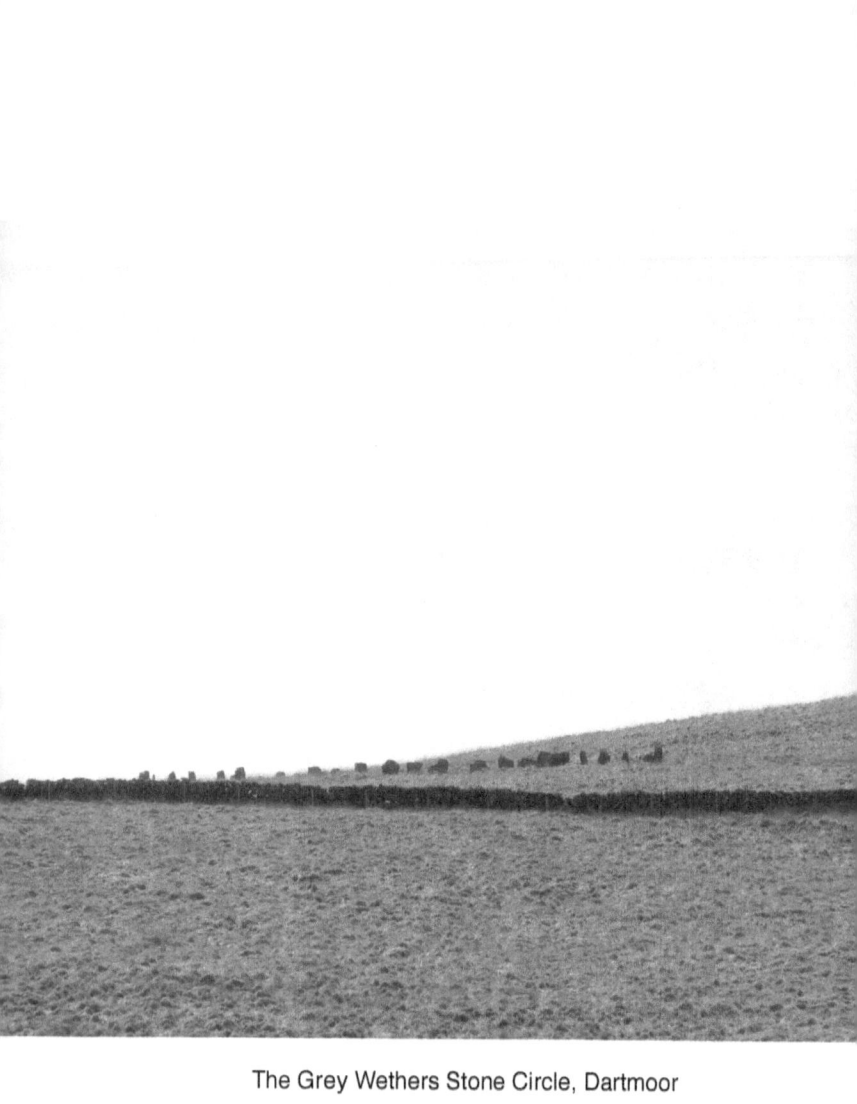

The Grey Wethers Stone Circle, Dartmoor

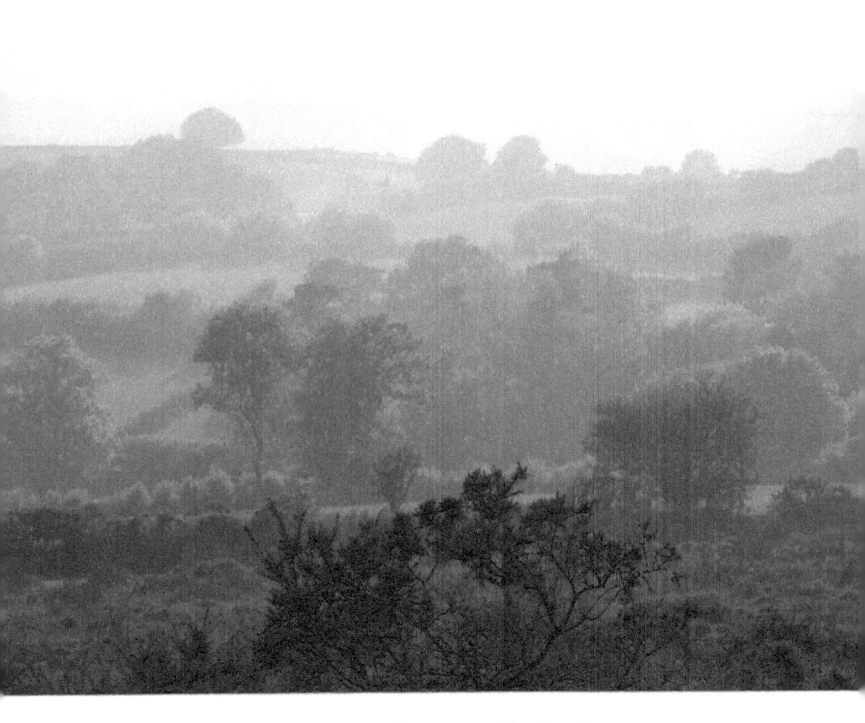

Near Newbridge, Dartmoor, England

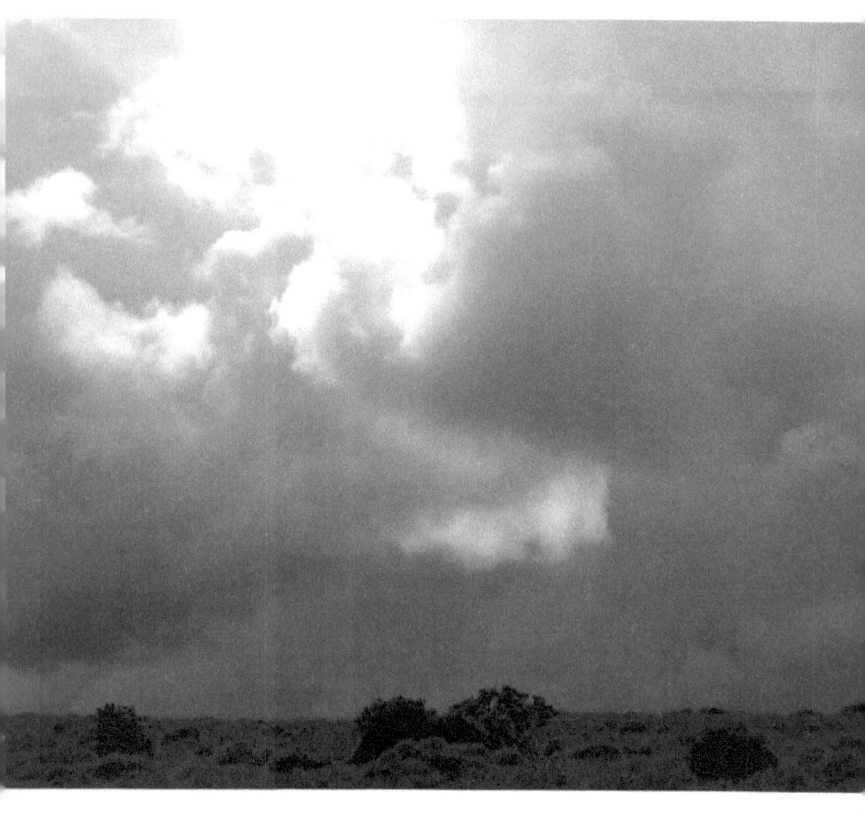

On the high moor in Dartmoor, England

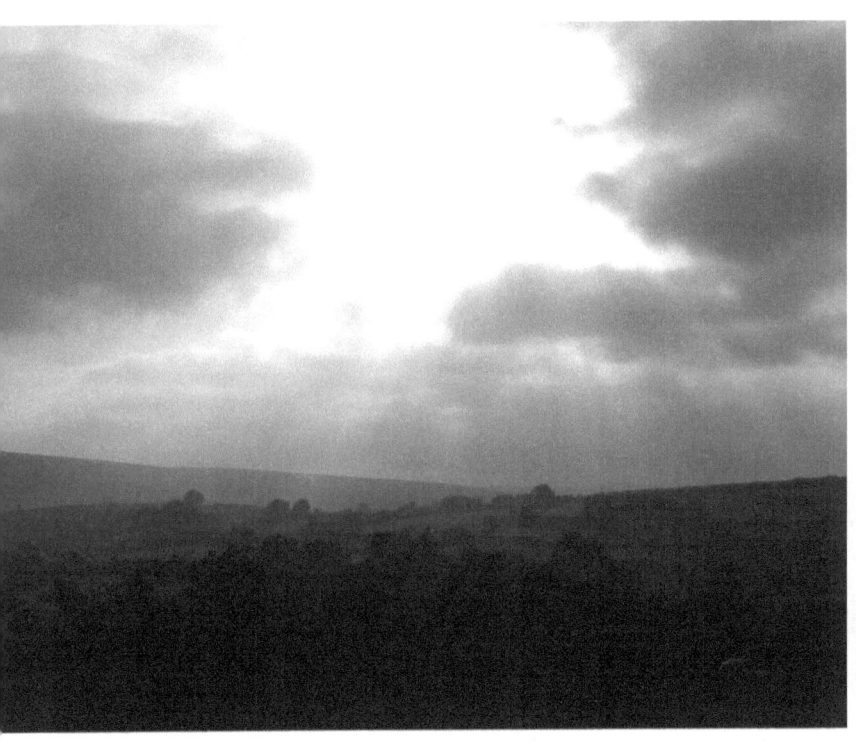

Near Ponsworthy in central Dartmoor, England

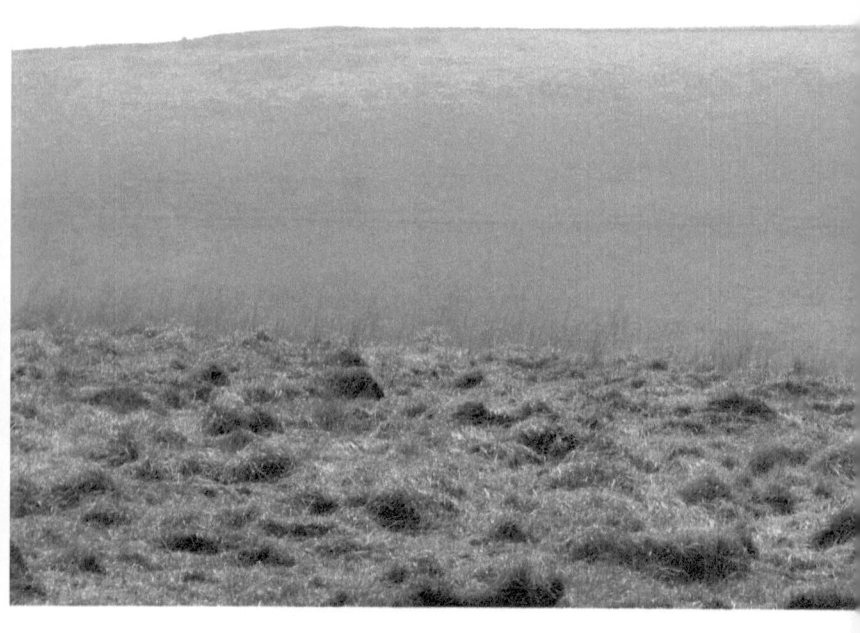

Looking towards Corndon Down in Dartmoor, England

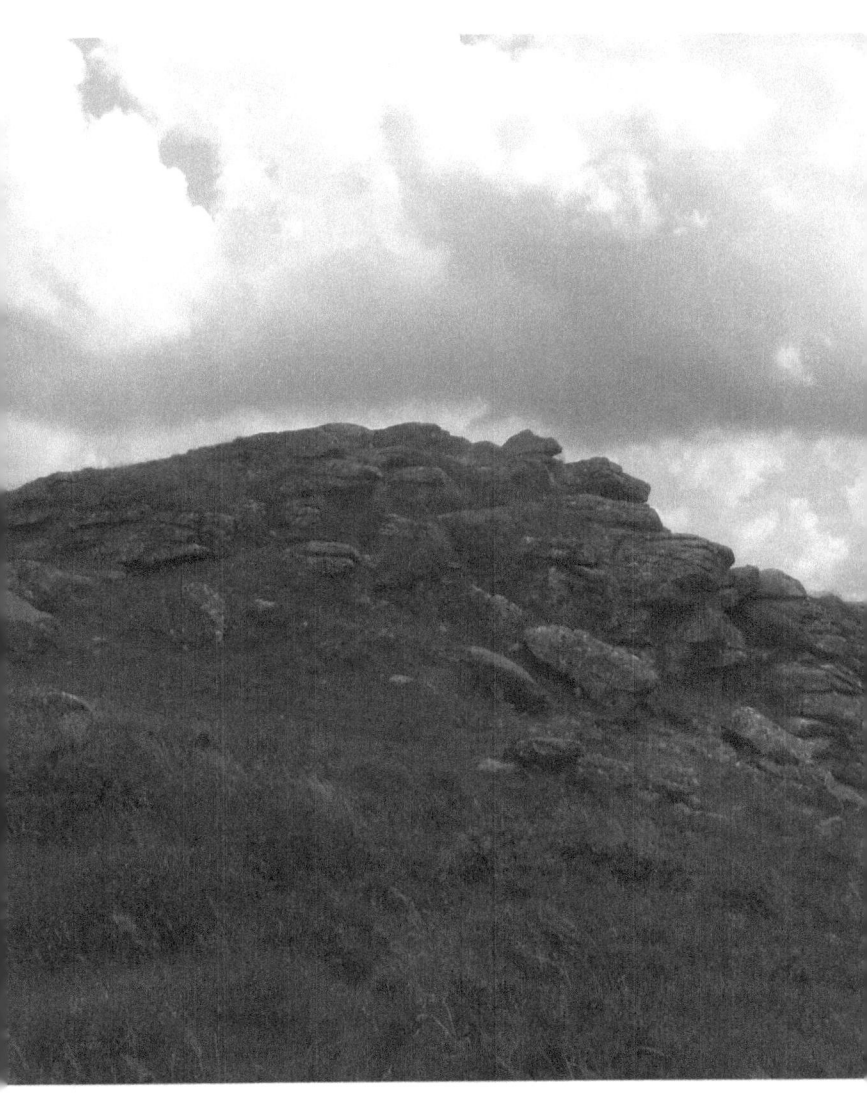

One of Dartmoor's many tors

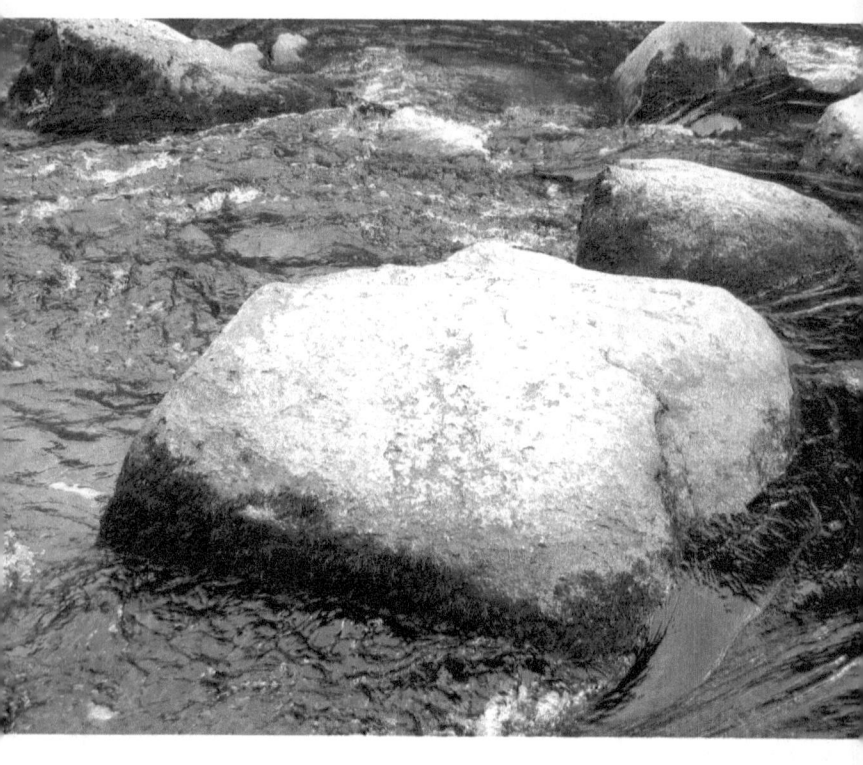

Boulders as stepping stones across the River Dart near Dartmeet, Dartmoor, England

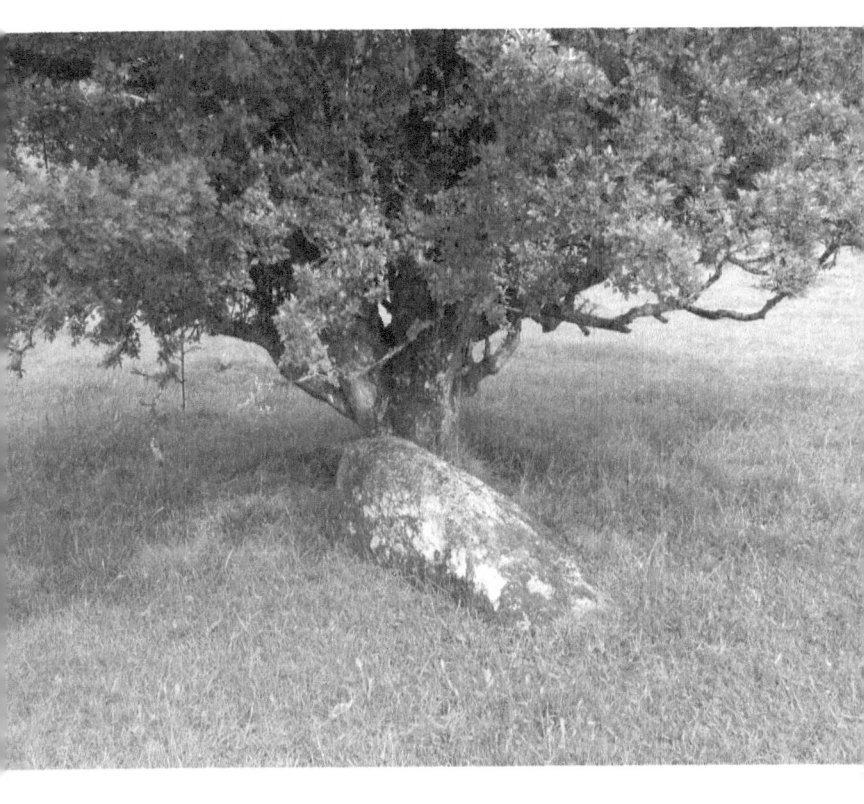
A classic image of England: an oak tree, a granite boulder, and a grassy field. Near Newbridge, Dartmoor

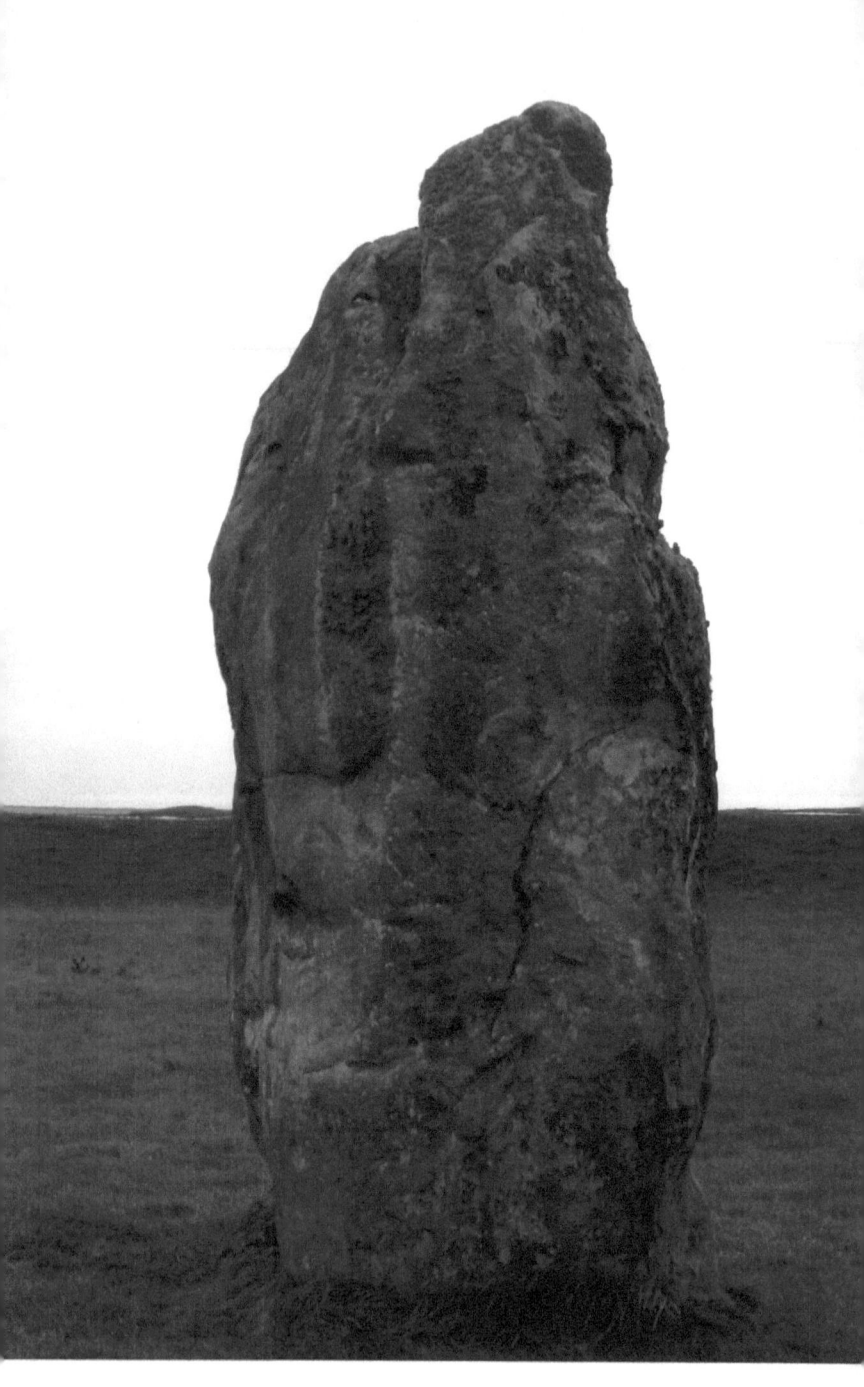

Avebury, Wiltshire, England

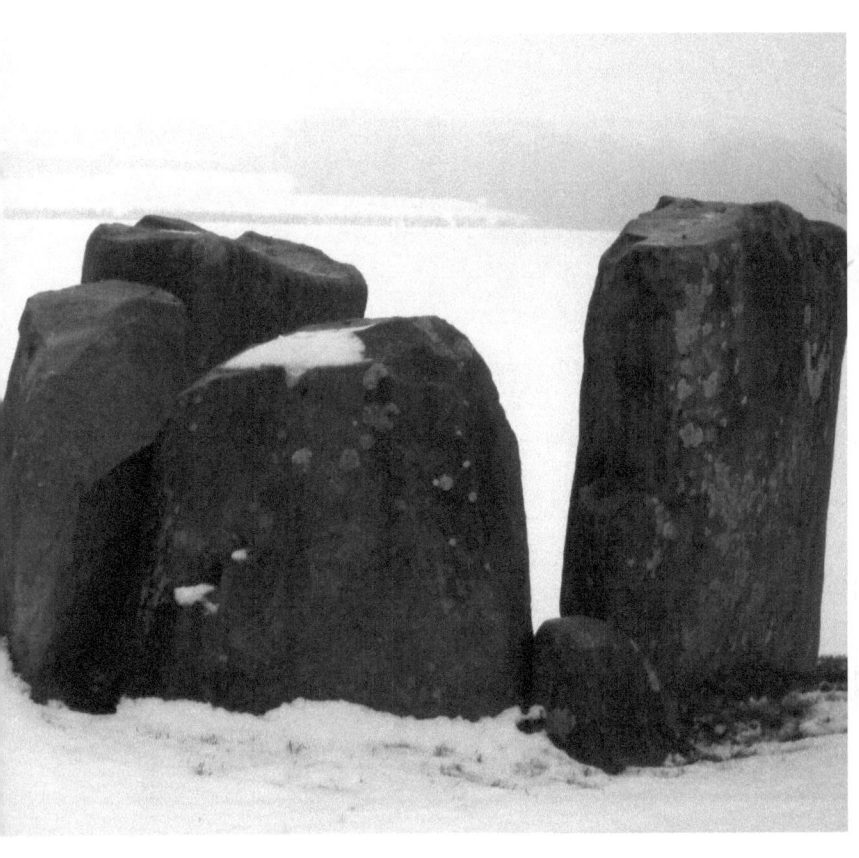

Coldrum Stones, Kent

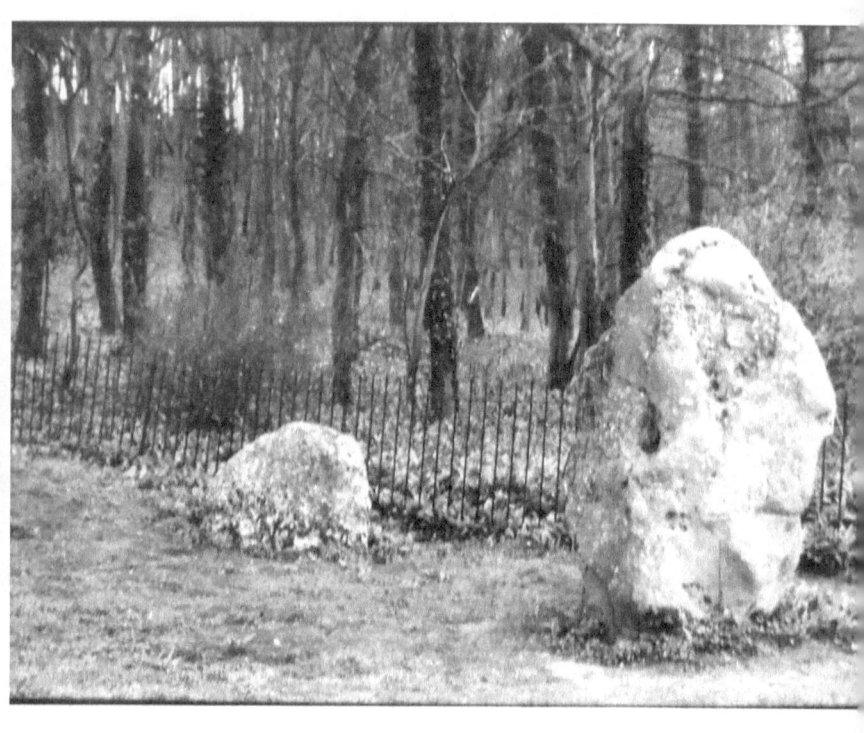

Winterbourne Abbas Stone Circle, Dorset, England

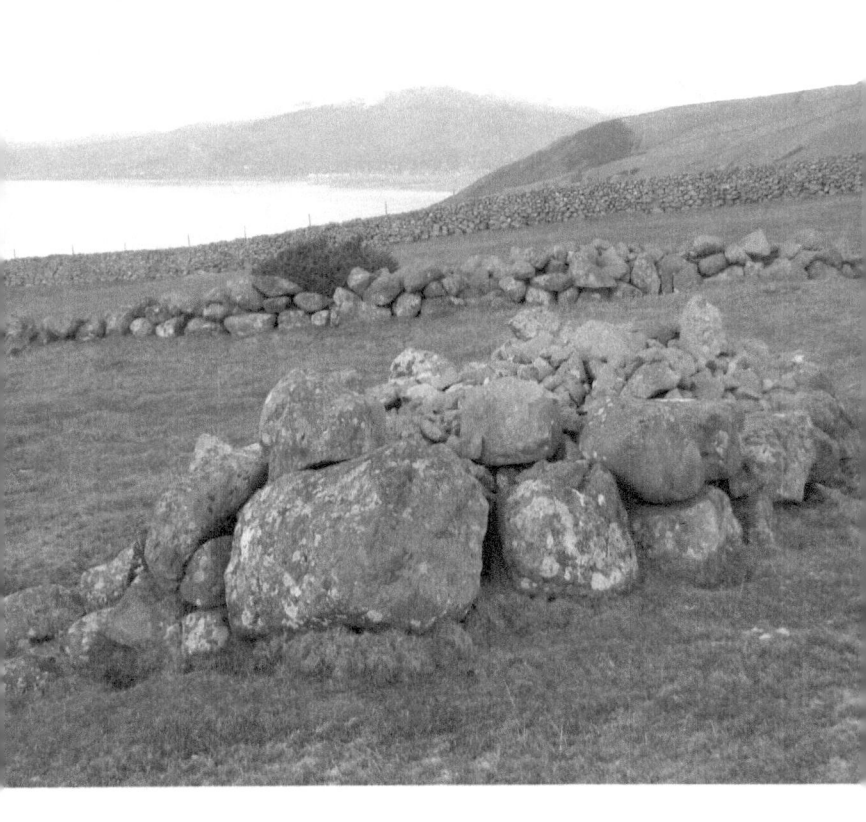

Stone cairn in Snowdonia, North Wales

The Dorset Coast Path, Purbeck, Dorset, England

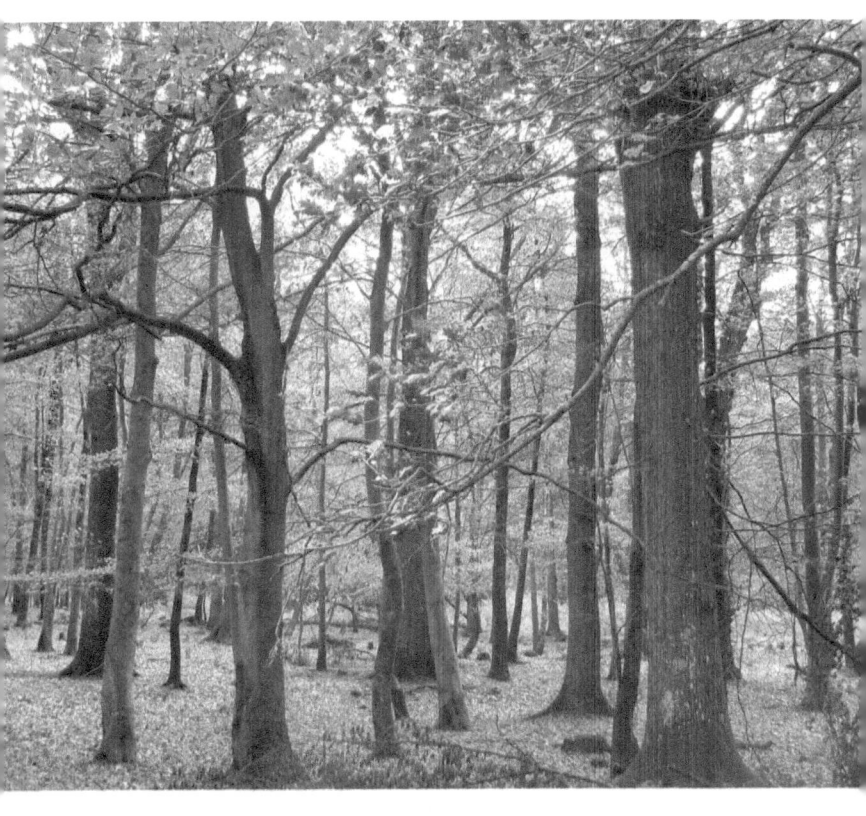

New Forest, Hampshire, England

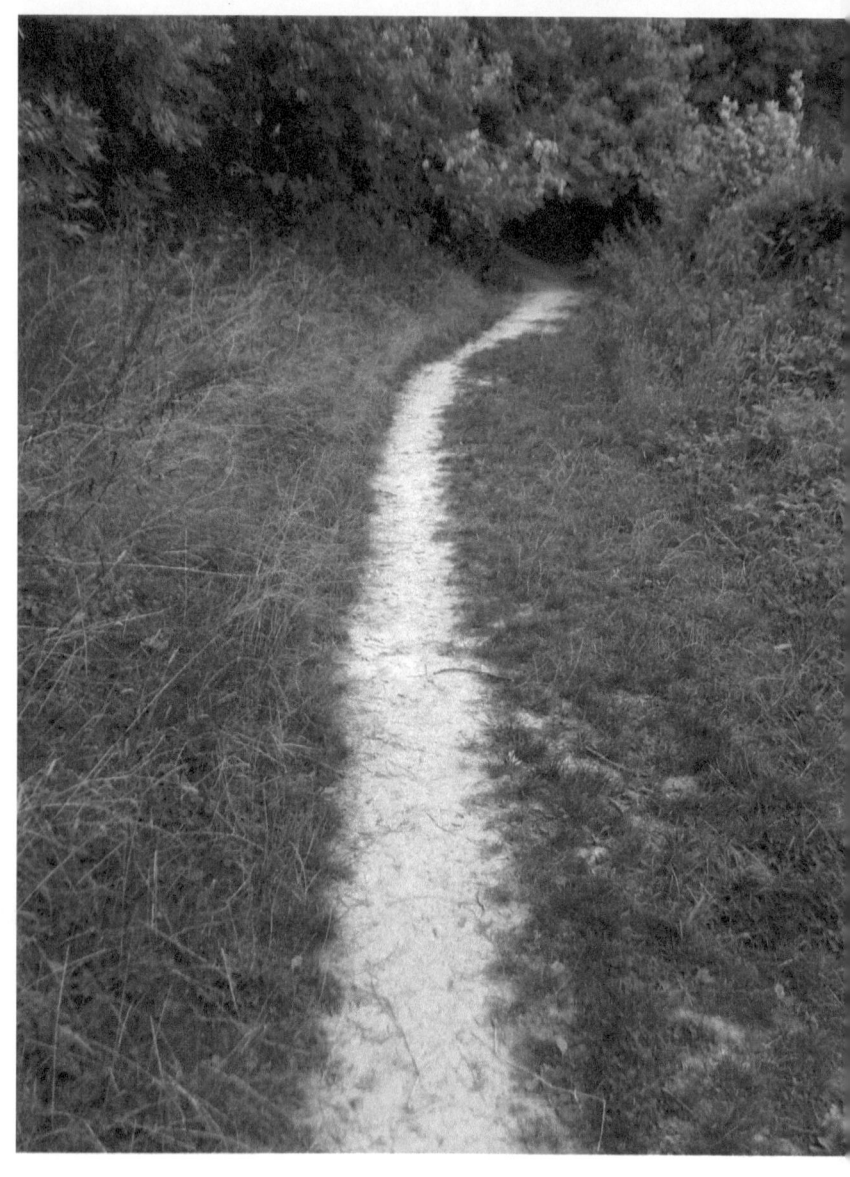

Path at Coldrum Stones, Kent, England.

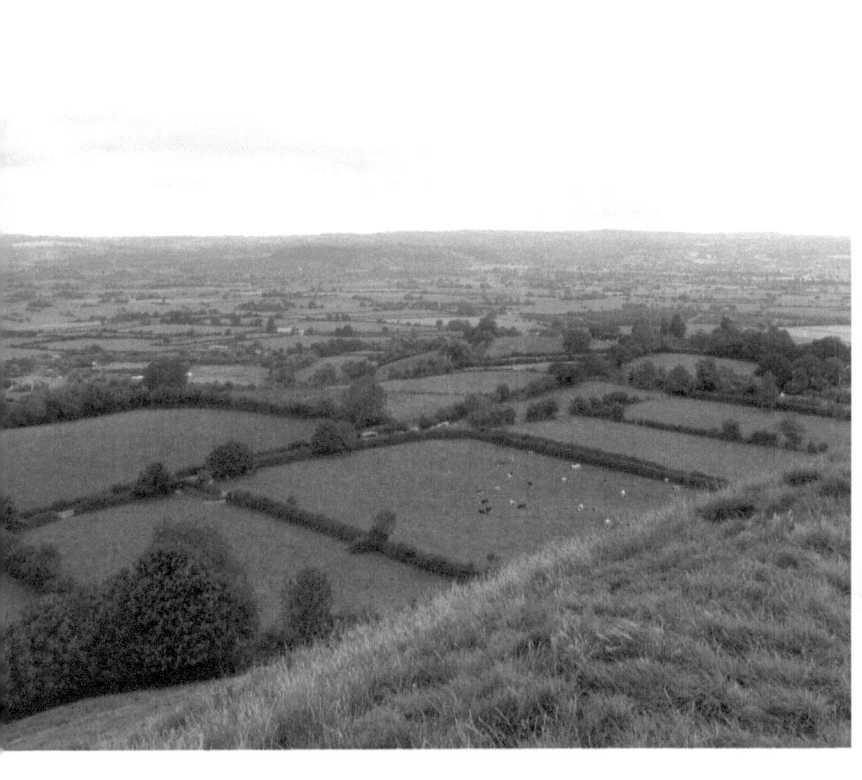

The view from Glastonbury Tor, Somerset, England

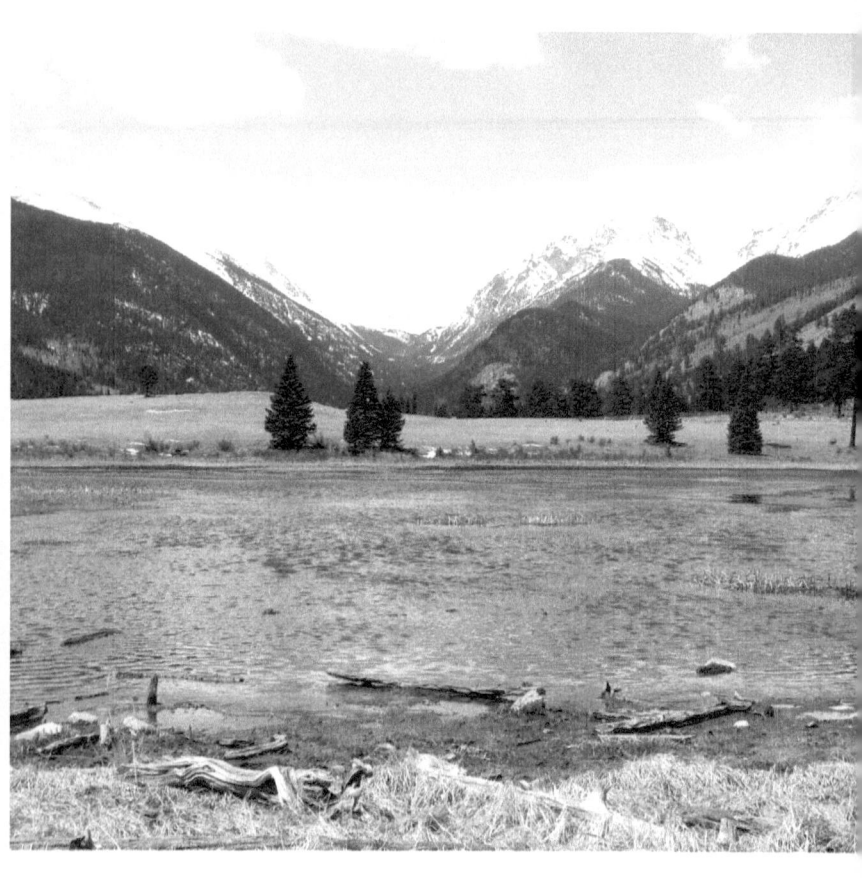

The Rockies, Colorado

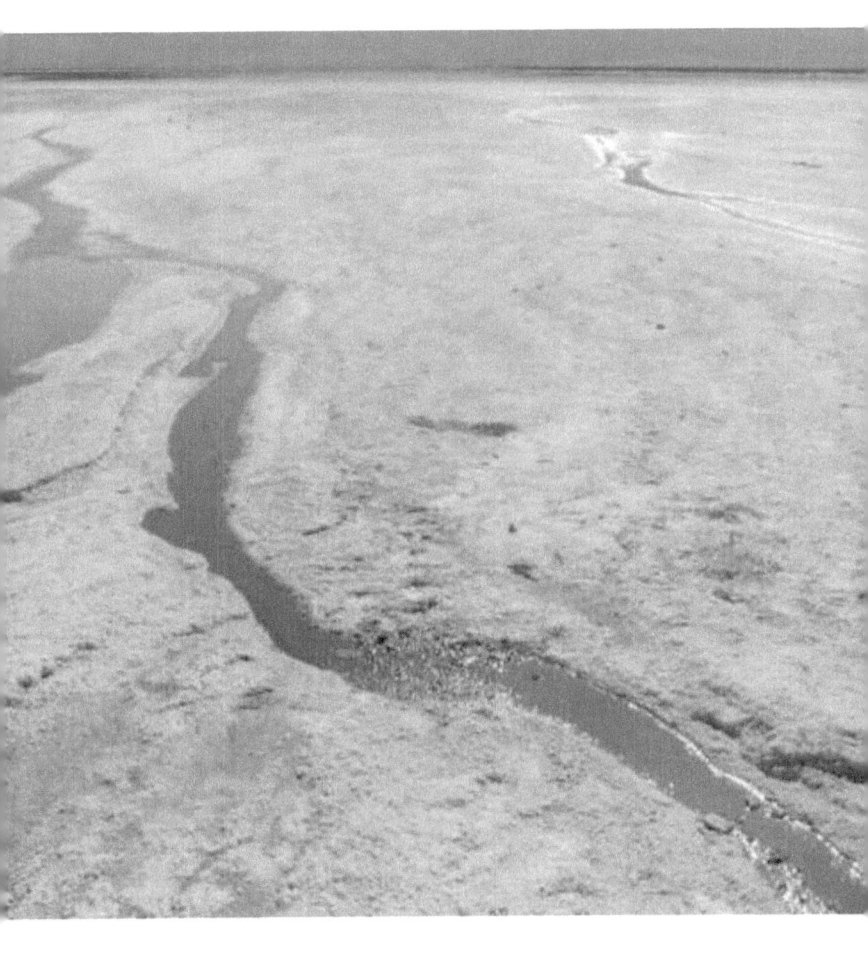

Salt flats in Death Valley, California

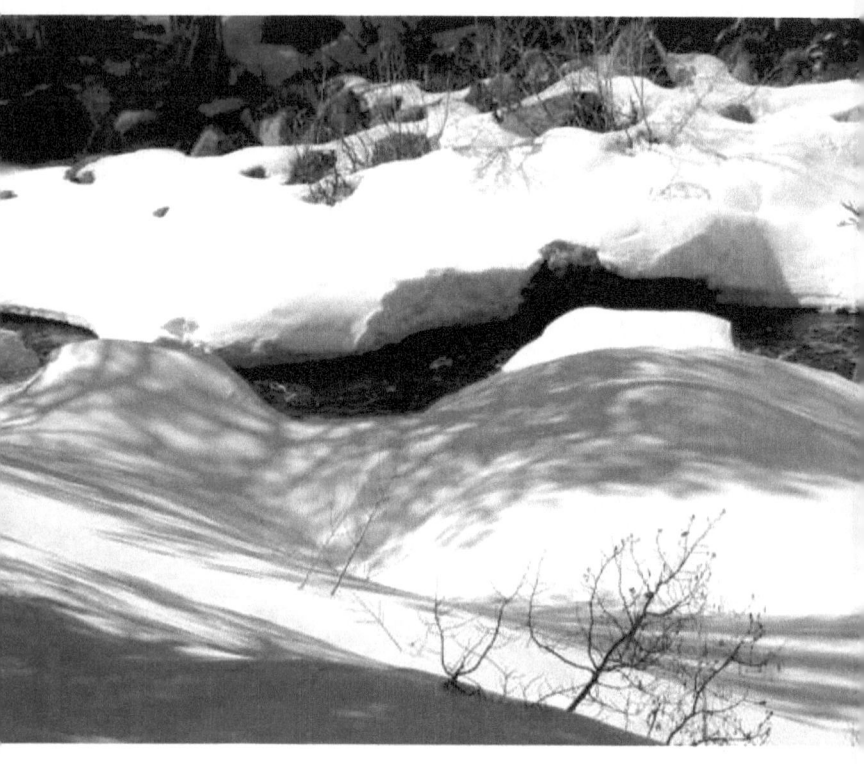

High Sierras, California

Notes

INTRODUCTION

1. W. Malpas, *Andy Goldsworthy: Touching Nature*, Crescent Moon, 1995, 2005; *Richard Long: The Art of Walking*, Crescent Moon, 1995, 1998; *The Art of Andy Goldsworthy*, Crescent Moon, 1998, 2004.

1 • SCULPTURE IN THE CONTEMPORARY ERA

1. R. Krauss, 1979.

LESS IS MORE: ARTE POVERA

1. J. Kounellis, in W. Sharp, 1972.

CONSTANTIN BRANCUSI AND LAND ART

1. H. Moore, in *The Listener*, 1937, quoted in H. Chipp, 595.
2. B. Flanagan, quoted in the catalogue of *Entre el Objeto y la Imagen: Escultura britanica contemporanea*, Palacio de Velasquez, Madrid, 1986, 233.
3. A. Goldsworthy, *Réfuges d'art*, 85.

THE WORLD OF MINIMAL AND POSTMINIMAL ART

1. S. Gablik: "Minimalism", in N. Stangos, ed. *Concepts of Modern Art*, Thames & Hudson, London, 1981, 245.
2. R. Morris, 1966, 20-23. See also: P. Patton, "Robert Morris and the Fire Next Time", *Art News*, 82, 10, Dec, 1983.
3. Quoted in D. Wheeler, 1991, 207.

2 • SCULPTURE AND GENDER

1. B. Hepworth, quoted in A.M. Hammacher, 1968, 99.
2. *Rosarium Philosophorum*, quoted in A.T. Mann, *Sacred Architecture*, Element Books, Shaftesbury, Dorset, 1993, 87.

3 • SPIRIT AND MATTER: LAND ART

ART AND LIFE

1. J. Campbell, *The Power of Myth*, 118.
2. J. Campbell, ib., 230.
3. On the 'pollen path', see J. Campbell, *The Power of Myth*, 230; on Australian 'dreamtime' see P. Devereux: *The Dream-time Earth and Avebury's Open Secrets*, Gothic Image, Glastonbury, 1992, 7-12.
4. Alfred Watkins published *The Old Straight Track* and his theory of 'leys' in 1925.
5. L. Durrell, 1971, 156.

THE ALCHEMY OF MATTER

1. C. Greenberg: "Abstract, Representational, and so forth", in 1961, 133.
2. R. Long, Sante Fe interview.

THE ECONOMICS OF LAND ART

1. A. Henri, *Total Art*, 81-82.
2. Richard Long, quoted in S. Gablik: *Has Modernism Failed?*, Thames & Hudson, London, 1984, 44.
3. 'I make art in the capitalist system which in itself is a political statement (selling art for the next walk)', remarked Hamish Fulton (1995).

THE OBJECT IN LAND ART

1. On Minimalism, see M. Tuchman, 1967; F. Tuten: "American Sculpture of the Sixties", *Arts Magazine*, 41, 7, May, 1967; I. Sandler, *Concrete Expressionism*, Loeb Student Center, New York University, NY, 1965; R. Wollheim: "Minimal Art", *Arts Magazine*, 39, 4, Jan, 1965; D. Mayhall, 1979; R. Krauss, 1973; B. Reise, 1969; P. Tuchman, 1988.
2. See C. Robins, 1966; M. Fried: "Art and Objecthood", 1967.

LAND ART AND CONCEPTUAL ART

1. A noteworthy exhibition of Conceptual art was held at the Kunsthalle in Bern, curated by Harald Szeemann: *When Attitudes Become Form* (1969); some key land artists were involved: Richard Long walked in the mountains and recorded his walk in a gallery statement; Walter de Maria installed a telephone, with a message beside it saying the visitor could talk to him; Jannis Kounellis put bags of grain on a stairway; Michael Heizer created *Berne Depression*, smashing the pavement near the Kunsthalle with a wrecking ball; Joseph Beuys smeared fat along the walls.
2. "Mel Bochner on Malevich", 1974, 62.
3. L. Weiner, in E. Lucie-Smith, 1987, 117.
4. R. Long, 1985, 2, 24.

MAPS

1. R. Long, IC 1, 6.
2. B. Redhead, 54.
3. R. Long, quoted in B. Redhead, 54.
4. Quoted in B. Redhead, 48.
5. F. Colpitt, 60.

LAND ART AND PHOTOGRAPHY

1. S. Mills: "Special Kaye [Tony Kaye]", *Sunday Times Magazine*, June 12, 1994, 55.
2. J. Dibbets, 1970.
3. R. Long, Santa Fe interview.
4. R. Long, in W. Malpas, 1995.
5. R. Long, 1985, 1, 1.
6. R. Smithson, in C. Robins, 1984, 78.

INTERIOR AND EXTERIOR ART

1. Robert Smithson reckoned that a 'work of art when placed in a gallery loses its charge and becomes a portable object or surface disengaged from the outside world' (*Selected Writings*, 132).
2. D. Oppenheim, 1992.
3. D. Nash, in A. McPherson, 30.

LAND ART AND CHANGE

1. R. Long, FC VI, in WC, 16. 'Time passes, a place remains. A walk moves through life, it is physical but afterwards invisible. A sculpture is still, a stopping place, visible' said Long (WF).

LAND ART AS RELIGION

1. M. Basho, *The Narrow Road to the Deep North and Other Travel Sketches*, tr. N. Yuasa, Penguin, London, 1966, 33.
2. M. Ueda: *Matsuo Basho*, Twayne, New York, NY, 1970, 167.
3. R. Long, 1985, part 1, 14.
4. R. Long, 1985, part 2, 22.
5. M. Fried, "Art And Objecthood", 1967, in G. Battock, 1995, 28.

STONE CIRCLES: LAND ART AND PREHISTORIC ART

1. R. Long, letter to the author, in W. Malpas, 1995.
2. The allusions to prehistory would be quite different if Long had stuck a picture of the Cerne Giant next to himself instead of the Wilmington Man. The interpretation might be different, for the Cerne Giant has the biggest phallus in prehistoric (or any) art (at least in the UK).
3. R. Long, 1972, in *Fragments of a Conversation I-VI*, in *Walking in Circles*, 38.

LAND ART AND CONTEMPORARY SCULPTURE IN BRITAIN

1. A. Caro, in L. Alloway, 1961, 1.
2. W. Tucker, 1969, 13.
3. K. Blacker, in P. de Monchaux, 1983, 94.

THE BRITISH LANDSCAPE TRADITION

1. R. Long, interview, April, 1985 (IC 2, 9).
2. C. Andre, quoted in A. Causey, 1977, 126.
3. Long talks about doing things which have a 'deep meaning' for him; he says he has 'the most sublime or profound feelings' when he walks: this is the language of the sublime artist, from the Romantics (Wordsworth, Keats, Turner) to the Abstract Expressionists (Newman, Rothko, Still).

4 • RICHARD LONG AND OTHER LAND ARTISTS

CARL ANDRE

1. C. Andre, quoted in D. Bourdon: "The Razed Sites of Carl Andre", in G. Battock, 1995, 103.
2. In ib., 104.
3. C. Andre, quoted in D. Bourdon, in G. Battock, 1995, 108.
4. T. Smith, quoted in M. Fried, 1967, in G. Battock, 1995, 131.
5. David Lee said that 'Andre repeats one thing in each piece; Smithson repeats one thing but increases its size' (1967, 44).

JAMES TURRELL

1. W. Furlong, in M. Gooding, 2002, 81.

WALTER DE MARIA

1. De Maria proposed another shaft, *Olympic Mountain Project* (1970) – never made – which would have been 400 feet deep and three feet wide.

DAVID NASH

1. See A. McPherson, 1978; H. Adams, 1979; D. Nash, 1980.
2. H. Adams, 1979, 46-47.

ANDY GOLDSWORTHY

1. A. Goldsworthy, in A. Causey, 1980.
2. R. Long, letter to the author, in W. Malpas, 1995.

5 • RICHARD LONG AND HAMISH FULTON

1. H. Fulton, in D. Beal, 2000.
2. H. Fulton, 1995.
3. Michael Archer, comparing the art of Long and Fulton, reckoned that Fulton

'offers possibilities', while Long 'designates'. Long's art was 'intentional in ways which Fulton's is not', and 'Fulton's art is conceptual in ways which Long's is not' (Archer, 1991).

4. H. Fulton, in M. Auping, 1990.

6 • RICHARD LONG: THE ART OF WALKING

1. C. Harrison, in T. Neff, 32.

RICHARD LONG: ARTISTIC BIOGRAPHY

1. H. Thoreau. in *Walking*, 1861, in *The Portable Thoreau*, ed. C. Bode, Viking, New York, NY, 1980, 592.
2. R. Long, FS, in RL, 236.
3. Richard Long's recent one-man shows include Henry Moore Institute, Leeds (1997), Bristol City Museum (1997), Yorkshire Sculpture Park (1998), Guggenheim Museum, Bilbao (2000), Trento (2000), Milwaukee Art Museum (2001), Tate Gallery, St Ives (2002), Stommein Synagoge (2004), Lismore (2006), Stockholm (2007), New York (2007), Edinburgh (2007), Glaurus (2008), Nice (2008) and Tate Britain (2009). Long has often exhibited alongside Carl Andre, an artist he admires a lot (in 1974, 1976, 1979, 1980, 1991), as well as Lawrence Weiner.

Richard Long has had many one-man shows at his UK art dealer, Anthony d'Offay Gallery in London, including 1979, 1980, 1981, 1983, 1984, 1985, 1986, 1988, 1990, 1993, 1995, 1998 and 2000.

There is a *Richard Long Newsletter*, edited by Gerard Vermeulen, in Nijmegen. (This is the best resource for Richard Long material on the internet:
<http://www.therichardlongnewsletter.org>
Richard Long also has his own site, like many artists:
<http://www.richardlong.org>

4. There have been a few TV programmes about Richard Long, including BBC's *Omnibus*, and one or two independent films about the artist, such as Philip Haas's *Stones and Flies: Richard Long in the Sahara*, made in 1988, or Denny Long's *Four Mud Works* (1984), and short films such as *A Round of Desert Flowers* (1987). Audio Arts produced a conversation between Long and William Furlong (1985).
5. A. Seymour: "Walking in Circles", 1.
6. Richard Long, letter to the author, July 11, 1994.
7. Ireland was a very important country for Richard Long, in particular the West of Ireland, County Clare, the stony deserts of the Burren. Long liked the climate, the people, the music: '[i]t is one of the great countries in the world' (1994b). Long discovered Ireland first when he went there, he said (1994b), after being thrown out of Bristol art college in 1964.
8. H. Fulton, in M. Auping, 1982.

RICHARD LONG: HOW TO WALK

1. 'It always amazes me that I can go down to Dartmoor for a walk, and even though it's a relatively small place and in the middle of a crowded island, I can still spend a whole day walking without seeing anyone' said Long (FC VI, 16).
2. See Weston La Barre: *The Ghost Dance*, Allen & Unwin, London, 1972.

3. P. Rodaway, 3.
4. Anne Seymour makes many critical mistakes, too numerous to list. For instance, she says 'there is nothing mystical or religious about Long's work' (Seymour, WC, 12). Then she goes on to note the yogic states of consciousness in his work; the sense of meditation, Zen Buddhism, C.G. Jung, etc.
5. Richard Long: '[e]ven though it is necessary to get a good photograph, the photographs should be as simple as possible... the photographs have got to be fairly simple and straightforward, so that the feeling of the work somehow accurately comes through.' (RC, 24).
6. H. Thoreau, in H. Hugo, 471.
7. R. Rosenblum, in A. Papadakis, 10.
8. 'Working out there in nature, then, Long is a performer in the open-air theatre of the sublime' (David Sylvester).

THE HUMAN TOUCH

1. 'My work is really a self-portrait, in all ways' said Long (GL, 6).
2. R. Long, WAF, in RL, 236.
3. In RL, 196: for the complete work, see illustration.
4. See D. Charles: "Flux de marche avec pietinement", *Traverses*, 14-15, 1979, 81-92.
5. S. Hosokawa: "The Walkman Effect", in R. Middleton & D. Horn, eds. *Popular Music 4: Performers and Audiences*, Cambridge University Press, New York, NY, 1984, 175.
6. M. de Certeau: *L'Invention du quotidien*, Paris, 1980, 180.
7. '[The walk] is never a performance. It is usually a very private, quiet activity. I am happy to make it in solitude' said Long (RC, 20).
8. Jean-Francçois Augoyard: *Pas a Pas. Essai sur le cheminement quotidien en milieu urbain*, Paris, 1979; C. Norberg-Schultz: *Existence, Space and Architecture*, London 1971.
9. In D. Sylvester.
10. R. Long, in WAF in RL, 236.
11. 'Nature is the source of my work' wrote Long (GL, 5).

RICHARD LONG'S EASTERN TURN

1. 5. Chuang-tzu, *Basic Writings*, 44.

CRITICS OF RICHARD LONG ART

1. In M. Gooding, 2002, 70.
2. P. Fuller, 1993, xxxvi-xxxvii.

7 • CIRCLES, LINES, ROWS, SPLASHES AND OTHER FORMS

STONE CIRCLES

1. 'The beauty of Long's work is that it is what you see, and that what you see is all is needed to bring you to a stop and as you look to make you feel that time has stopped, and to fill you with a sense of well-being and completeness'

wrote David Sylvester.
2. In RL, 236.

STONES

1. R. Long, website, 2000.
2. Printed in *Richard Long: Walking the Line*, 45.
3. In *Richard Long: Walking the Line*, 46.

LINES AND ROWS

1. These modern paths were created by (and in association with) organizations such as the Countryside Commission, the Ramblers' Association, local councils and the National Parks.

COLOUR IN RICHARD LONG'S ART

1. Richard Long has spoken of the famous Kyoto garden:

   I have always been impressed by the ancient rock gardens of Kyoto. For me, they are sublime pieces of contemplation, where the world is represented harmoniously by deep thinking, simple materials, space, and peace of mind. And, I like the idea of *ma*. There are some parallels between Japanese art and my work, because nature is our common condition. Also, I think a desire for simplicity and order is a part of human nature (1995a).

TIME AND HISTORY

1. R. Long, quoted in D. Wheeler, 264.
2. M. Eliade, 1984, 186.
3. S. Bann, 1994b.
4. R. Descartes, *Le Discours de la méthode*.

8 • IDEA/ TEXT/ DESIRE: TEXTWORKS

THE IDEA AND THE TEXT

1. D. Reason: "Echo and Reflections", in S. Bann, 1991, 169.
2. Quoted in RL, 201.
3. G. Stein, in J. Rothenberg & P. Joris, eds. *Poems For the Millennium*, University of California Press, Berkeley, CA, 1995
4. R. Long, Orkney, 1994.
5. D. Lee: "Sculpture Outside: The Forest of Dean Sculpture Project", in G. Hughes, 1989, 22.
6. Richard Long, letter to the author, July 11, 1994.
7. R. Long, WAF, 1980, in RL, 236.
8. Long explains:

   I have no idea how many words I write. It is only at the end of the day that I realize that I have got maybe twenty lines. I don't have a fixed number to start with or whatever. I let the work happen. (IC 2, 11)

9. R. Long, in RL, 201.
10. M. Eliade, "Shadows In Archaic Religions", in 1988, 4.
11. R. Long, RC, 23.

WALL DRAWINGS AND HANDPRINTS

1. R. Long, in FS in RL, 236.
2. R. Long, FS in RL, 236.
3. '...the work comes from one person being on his own in nature and the spirit of the work is about that one to one relationship. If many people came to that place it would destroy the spirit of that place' wrote Long (IC 1, 1; also RL, 133-4).
4. If an artwork's made of molecules, it'll still be on the planet, somewhere (this is a sci-fi fantasy wish about the base matter of alchemy, or maybe it's sheer desperation). Thus, works the art lover would yearn to see, such as Michelangelo's lost *Leda,* the half million volumes of the Great Library of Alexandria, Simone Martini's portrait of Francesco Petrarch's beloved Laura, or the Hanging Gardens of Babylon, must still be on Earth somewhere, even if they're just bits of dust.
5. R. Barry, in U. Meyer, 1972, 35.
6. R. Long, quoted in RL, 135.

RICHARD LONG'S BOOKS

1. R. Long, 'Stone Walk', OW, 12.
2. R. Long: *A journey of the same length as the River Avon/ an 84 mile canoe journey down the River Severn,* 1977.
3. Other objects the walker treasures or relies on include boots, maps, the water bottle, and the tent. One would suspect that a seasoned walker like Long would have all sorts of other items he's incorporated over the years: a Walkman or radio, for instance, vitamins or pills, perhaps, or a gas stove.

9 • FROM PHOTOGRAPHY TO INSTALLATIONS

1. 1982, in RL, 193.
2. Wind is 'an elemental part of nature, it's often part of a walk, it's part of the energy of the world' said Long (GL, 8). Ted Hughes says that poets often write their best poems when they deal with elemental forces such as wind.
3. R. Long, in WAF, RL, 236.
4. S. Morris: "A Rhetoric of Silence: Redefinitions of Sculpture in the 1960s and 1970s", in S. Nairne, 198.
5. A. Goldsworthy, *Stone*, 120.

10 • 'A PLACE OF REGENERATION': DARTMOOR

1. R. Long, quoted in G. Greig, 1991.
2. Quoted, in B. Redhead, 48.
3. In RL, 148.
4. See B. Le Messurier, 2002.
5. In *Walking the Line*, 304.

11 • WALKING AS ECSTASY

1. T. Wyatt, in M. Elvy, 6.
2. Quoted in D. Wheeler, 1991, 264.
3. R. Long, in L. Cooke, 1983, 20-21; R. Fuchs, 1974, 172-3.
4. Woodrow trawls the world for materials with which to make sculptures:

   My choice of objects is dictated, I think in the first instance by what is available, what I come across in the streets, on dumps... What I find more interesting about the work, is that these items are material for me that is found in my environments... (B. Woodrow, quoted in *Objects and Sculpture*, Institute of Contemporary Arts, London, 1981, 37.)

5. See A. Seymour: "El Estanque de Basho – una nueva perspectiva", in 1986.
6. R. Long, quoted in E. Lucie-Smith, 1987, 121.
7. P. Redgrove, letter to the author, Apl 20, 1994.
8. R. Long, interview with R. Cork, in D. Sylvester.
9. Arthur Rimbaud, *A Season In Hell*, tr. A. Jary, Crescent Moon, 1998. The translation reads:

   I had to travel, to divert the enchantments that crowded over my brain. On the sea, which I loved as if it were washing away a stain, I saw the consoling cross rise. I had been damned by the rainbow. Happiness was my misfortune, my remorse, my worm: my life would be always too huge to be devoted to strength and beauty. (40-41)

10. R.L. Stevenson, *Travels With a Donkey*. My italics.
11. R. Long, SF. In another interview, though, Long states: '[m]y work is completely independent from all the mystical ideas which were prevalent in the sixties' (1985, 2, 8). 'I wouldn't make any claims to be mystical' (FC VI, 17).
12. See A. Seymour, op.cit.; S. Gablik, op.cit. Lynne Cooke writes that

    by the early 1970s, Long's work had become increasingly interpreted in terms of an atavistic archetypal content, with the artist assuming the mantle of spiritual wanderer. Allusions to a rural, pastoral tradition, often couched in a language of almost Georgian naivete, were gradually replaced by a more universal statement, one in which the concept of the timeless, unchanging order of nature was pre-eminent. (1987, 40).

13. M. Eliade, 1975, 61.
14. M. Eliade, 1975, 64.
15. Chuang-tzu, 54.
16. W. Johnson, *Riding the Ox Home*, 52.
17. Hélène Cixous: *Three Steps on the Ladder of Writing*, Columbia University Press, New York, NY, 1993, 64-65.

Bibliography

RICHARD LONG

Richard Long, Städtisches Musem, Mönchengladbach, 1970
Two Sheepdogs Cross In and Out of the Passing Shadows, Lissom Gallery, London, 1971
From Along a Riverbank, Art & Project, Amsterdam, 1971
John Barleycorn, Stedelijk Museum, Amsterdam, 1973
South America, Konrad Fischer, Düsseldorf, 1973
From Around a Lake, Art & Project, Art & Project, Amsterdam, 1973
Inca Rock Campfire Ash, Scottish National Gallery, Edinburgh, 1974
The North Woods, Whitechapel Art Gallery, London, 1977
A Hundred Stones, Kunsthalle, Bern, 1977
A Straight Hundred Mile Walk In Australia, John Kaldor Project 6, 1977
Rivers and Stones, Newlyn Art Gallery, Cornwall, 1978
Sydamerika, Kalejdoskop, Lund, Sweden, 1978
Aggie Weston's No 16, Coracle Press, London, 1979
River Avon Book, Anthony d'Offay Gallery, London, 1979
Richard Long, Stedelijk Van Abbesmuseum, Eindhoven, 1979
A Walk Past Standing Stones, Coracle Press, London, 1980
Five, Six, Pick Up Sticks, Anthony d'Offay, London, 1980
Twelve Works, London, 1979-1981, Coracle Press, 1981
Richard Long, CAPC Musée d'Art Contemporain, Bordeaux, 1981
Selected Works, National Gallery of Canada, Ottawa, 1982
Mexico, Stedelijk Van Abbesmuseum, Eindhoven, 1982
"Correspondence: Richard Long Replies To a Critic", *Art Monthly*, July, 1983
Touchstones, Arnolfini, Bristol, 1983
Fango, Pietri, Legni, Galleria Tucci Russo, Turin, 1983
Countless Stones, Stedelijk Van Abbemuseum, Eindhoven, 1983
Planes of Vision, Ottenhausen Verlag, Aachen, 1983
River Avon Mud Works, Orchard Gallery, Londonderry, 1984
Postcards, 1968-1982, CAPC Musée d'art Contemporain de Bordeaux, 1984
Sixteen Works, Anthony d'Offay Gallery, London, 1984
Richard Long, Century Cultural Foundation, Tokyo, 1984
Mud Hand Prints, Coracle Press, London, 1984
Richard Long, Fonds Regional d'Art contemporain Aquitaine, 1985
Il Luogo Buono, Padiglione d'Arte Contemporanea, Milan, 1985
Lines of Time, Stichting Edy de Wilde Lezing/ Openbaar Kunst-bezit, Amsterdam, 1985
Richard Long: In Conversation, Parts 1 & 2, MW Press, Noor-dwijk, Holland, 1985-

Muddy Water Falls, MW Press, Noordwijk, Holland, 1986
Richard Long, text by R. Fuchs, Thames & Hudson, London, 1986
Out of the Wind, Donald Young Gallery, Chicago, IL, 1987
Dust Dobros Desert Flowers, Lapis Press, Venice, 1987
Stone Water Miles, Musée Rath, Geneva, 1987
Old World New World, Anthony d'Offay, London, 1988
Angel Flying Too Close To the Ground, Kunstverein St Gallen, 1989
Richard Long, Magasin 3, Stockholm, Sweden, 1990
Kicking Stones, Anthony d'Offay Gallery, London, 1990
Surf Roar, Museum of Contemporary Art, San Diego, CA, 1990
Sur La Route, Musée départmental de Rochechouart, 1990
Nile, Papers of River Muds, Lapis Press, Los Angeles, CA, 1990
Labyrinth, Frankfurt, 1991
Richard Long: Walking in Circles, Hayward Gallery/ Thames & Hudson, London, 1992
An Interview With Richard Long by R. Cork, in *Waking in Circles*
Fragments of a Conversation I-VI, in *Walking in Circles*
Mountains and Water, Anthony d'Offay, London, 1992
River to River, Musée d'Art Moderne de la Ville de Paris, 1993
An Interview with Richard Long, Neery Melkonian, Center for Contemporary Arts, Santa Fe, New Mexico, 1993-94
Interview with G. Lobacheff, 1994a
No Where, interview with C. Kirkpatrick, Piers Arts Centre, Orkney, 1994b
Richard Long, British Council, London, 1994
Richard Long, Kunstsammlung Nordhrhein-Westfalen, Düssel-dorf, 1994
Richard Long, Palazzo delle Esposizione, Rome, 1994
Books, Prints, New York Public Library, New York, NY, 1994
"Question For Richard Long", interview with Yuko Hasegawa, 1995a
Walking, Mud, Stones, Anthony d'Offay, London, 1995b
Dolomite Stones, AR/ Ge Kunst, Bolzano, 1996
Circles, Cycles, Mud, Contemporary Arts Museum, Houston, TX, 1996
Dartmoor Time, Spacex Gallery, Exeter, Devon, 1996
From Time to Time, DAP, 1997
Richard Long, Hatje Cantz, Stuttgart, 1997
A Walk Across England, Thames & Hudson, London, 1997
A Road From the Past To the Future, J. Haldane, Crawford Arts Centre, St Andrews, 1997
Wind Circle, Memory Sticks, Wilhelm Lehmbruck Museum, Duisburg, 1997
Interview with M. Codognato, 1997; in *Mirage*, 1998
Mirage, Phaidon, London, 1998
Every Grain of Sand, Kunstverein Hannover, Hanover, 1999
Being In the Moment, Museum Kurhaus Kleve, Cleves, 1999
Being in the Moment, PARC, Lent, 1999
Spanish Stones, Édiciones Polígrafa, Barcelona, 1999
Selected Walks, 1979-1996, Morning Star Press, 1999
Statement on the Richard Long website, 2000
Richard Long in Leuk, Stiftung Schloss Leuk, 2000
Adamello Walk, Museo d'Arte Moderne, Trento, 2000
Midday, Museum Kurhaus Kleve, Cleves, 2001
Walking and Sleeping, Ivory Press, London

A Moving World, Tate Publishing, London, 2002
Walking the Line, Thames and Hudson, London, 2002
Interview with D. Hooker, *Stepping Stones*, in *Richard Long: Walking the Line*
"I am just passing through the world", *Financial Times*, July 9, 2003a
Dialog, with J. Mashe, Museum kunst palast, Düsseldorf, 2003
Dialog, with J. Mashe, Padiglione d'Arte Contemporanea, Milan, 2003
Here and Now and Then, Haunch of Venison, London, 2003
Floating Time, Akita City, Japan, May, 2004a
"Still walking, after all these years", *The Art Newspaper*, July, 2004b
Richard Long at Kukje Gallery, Kukje Gallery, Seoul, 2004
The Music of Stones, Synagoge Stommeln, Stommeln, 2004
Richard Long: An Encounter, Buson Museum of Modern Art, 2004
Richard Long, Galeria Máno Sequeira, Braga, 2005

OTHERS

H. Adams. "The Woodman", *Art and Artists*, 13, Apl, 1979
W.C. Agee. "Unit, Series, Site: A Judd Lexicon", *Art in America*, May, 1975
L. Alloway. "Interview with Anthony Caro", *Gazette*, 1, 1961
L. Anderson: "Mary Miss", *Artforum*, Nov, 1973
C. Andre. "An Interview with Carl Andre", P. Tuchman, *Artforum*, 8, 10, June, 1970
—. *Carl Andre, Sculpture, 1958-1974*, Kunsthalle, Bern, 1975
—. "Object vs Phenomenon", *Sculpture Today*, The International Sculpture Center, Toronto, 1978
—. *Carl Andre: Sculpture*, State University of New York Press, Albany, NY, 1984
—. *Stichomythia, 12 Dialogues 1962-63*, Whitechapel Art Gallery, London
—. *Carl Andre: works on land*, Exhibitions International, 2001
M. Archer. "A Walk In the Endless Summer From Duncansby Head To the Place of the Camel Dropping", *Art Monthly*, Sept, 1991
M. Auping. *Common Ground*, John & Mable Ringling Museum of Art, Sarasota, 1982
—. "Hamish Fulton", *Art in America*, 71, Feb, 1983
—. "Tracking Fulton", in H. Fulton, 1990
A. Aycock. "Work", "Maze", 1975, in A. Sondheim, 1977
K. Baker. "Andre in Retrospect", *Art in America*, Apl, 1980a
—. "Reckoning with Notation: The Drawings of Pollock, Newman, and Louis", *Artforum*, 18, 10, Summer, 1980b
—. *Minimalism: Art of Circumstance*, Abbeville, New York, NY, 1988
S. Bann & W. Allen, eds. *Interpreting Contemporary Art*, Reaktion Books, London, 1991
—. "Shrines, Gardens, Utopias", *New Literary History*, 24, 4, Autumn, 1994a
—. "The Map As Index of the Real: Land Art and the Authentication of Travel", *Imago Mundi*, 46, British Library, London, 1994b
G. Baro. "Toward Speculation in Pure Form", *Art International*, Summer, 1967
—. "Sculpture made visible: Barry Flanagan in discussion with Gene Baro", *Studio International*, 178, 915, Oct, 1969
G. Battock, ed. *Minimal Art: A Critical Anthology*, University of California Press, Berkeley, CA, 1995

G. Beal. "Richard Long: "the simplicity of walking, the simplicity of stones"", in T. Neff, 1987
—. ed. *Art In the Landscape*, Chinati Foundation, Texas, 2000
J. Beardsley. *Probing the Earth: Contemporary Land Projects,* Smithsonian Press, Washington, 1977
—. *Earthworks and Beyond: Contemporary Art in the Landscape*, Abbeville Press, New York, NY, 1984/ 1998
M.R. Beaumont. "Romantic Sculpture", in A. Papadakis, 1988
A. Benjamin, ed. *Installation Art, Art & Design,* 30, 1993
M. Berger. *Labyrinths: Robert Morris, Minimalism, and the 1960s,* Harper & Row, New York, NY, 1989
L. Biggs. "Richard Long", *Arnolfini Review*, Apl, 1983
—. *Between Object and Image*, British Council, 1986
M. Bochner. "Art in Process – Structures", *Arts Magazine*, 40, 9, 1966
—. "Primary Structures", *Arts*, June, 1966
—. "Systematic", *Arts Magazine*, 41, 1, Nov, 1966
—. "Serial Art Systems: Solipsism", *Arts Magazine*, 41, 8, Summer, 1967
—. "Mel Bochner on Malevich", interview with J. Coplans, *Artforum*, June, 1974
D. Bourdon. "Walter de Maria: The Singular Experience", *Art International*, Dec 20, 1968
—. *Carl Andre: Sculpture, 1959-1977*, Jaap Rietman, New York, NY, 1978
—. *Designing the Earth*, Abrams, New York, NY, 1995
J. Bradley. *Richard Long*, National Gallery of Canada, Ottawa, 1982
D. Brown. "While Out Walking", *Times Literary Supplement*, July 5, 1991
J. Brown *et al. Michael Heizer: Sculpture in Reverse*, see M. Heizer, 1984
J. Burnham. *Beyond Modern Sculpture*, George Braziller, New York, NY, 1968
—. "A Dan Flavin Retrospective in Ottawa", *Artforum*, 8, 4, Dec, 1969
—. "Haacke's Cancelled Show at the Guggenheim", *Artforum*, June, 1971
J. Butterfield. *The Art of Light and Space*, Abbeville Press, New York, NY, 1993
J. Campbell. *The Power of Myth*, with B. Moyers, ed. B.S. Flowers, Doubleday, New York, NY, 1988
—. *An Open Life*, Larson Publications, New York, NY, 1988
T. Castle: "Nancy Holt, Siteseer", *Art in America*, Mch, 1982
A. Causey. "Space and Time in British Land Art", *Studio International*, 193, 98, Feb, 1977
—. *Nature as Material: An Exhibition of Sculpture and Photographs Purchased For the Arts Council Collection*, Arts Council, London, 1980
G. Celant. "Tony Cragg and Industrial Platonism", *Artforum*, 20, 3, Nov, 1981
H.B. Chipp, ed. *Theories of Modern Art*, University Press of California, LA, CA, 1968
Chuang-tzu. *Basic Writings*, tr. B. Watson, Columbia University Press, New York, NY
M. Church. "A shower of stones, a flash in the river", *Sunday Telegraph*, Apl 10, 1994
M. Codognato. Interview with R. Long, 1997; in *Mirage*, 1998
M. Cohen. "Richard Long", review, April 15, 2000
F. Colpitt. *Minimal Art: The Critical Perspective*, University of Washington Press, Seattle, WA, 1990
M. Compton & D. Sylvester. *Robert Morris*, Tate Gallery, London, 1971
—. *Some Notes on the Work of Richard Long*, British Council, London, 1976
L. Cooke. "Richard Long replies to a critic", *Art Monthly*, 68, July, 1983
—. "Between Image and Object: The "New British Sculpture"", in T. Neff, 1987

J. Cowan. *The Mysteries of the Dream-Time*, Prism Press, 1989
P. Curtis. *Modern British Sculpture from the Collection*, Tate Gallery, Liverpool, 1988
A. Davies. "Richard Long and Hamish Fulton", *Art Monthly*, 25, Apl, 1979
R. Davies & T. Knipe, eds. *A Sense of Place. Sculpture in Landscape*, London, 1984
W. de Maria. "The Lightning Field", *Artforum*, 18, 8, Apl, 1980
P. de Monchaux *et al*, eds. *The Sculpture Show*, Arts Council of Great Britain, London, 1983
E. Develing. *Carl Andre*, Gemeentenmeuseum, The Hague, 1969
—. & L. Lippard. *Minimal Art*, Stadtische Kunsthalle, Dusseldorf, 1969
C. Drury. *Silent Spaces*, Thames & Hudson, London, 1998
L. Durrell. *Spirit of Place*, Faber, London, 1971
A. Dyson. *Richard Long: Sao Paulo Biennial 1994*, The British Council, 1994
M. Eliade. *Patterns in Comparative Religion*, Sheed & Ward, London, 1958
—. *Shamanism: Archaic Techniques of Ecstasy*, Princeton University Press, Princeton, NJ, 1972
—. *Myths, Dreams and Mysteries*, Harper & Row, New York, NY, 1975
—. *From Primitives to Zen: A Sourcebook*, Collins, London, 1977
—. *A History of Religious Ideas*, I, Collins, London, 1979
—. *Ordeal by Labyrinth*, University of Chicago Press, Chicago, IL, 1984
—. *Symbolism, the Sacred and the Arts*, Crossroad, New York, NY, 1988
M. Elvy, ed. *The Crescent Moon Book of Nature Poetry*, Crescent Moon, 1994
G. Evans. "Sculpture and Reality", *Studio International*, 177, 908, Feb, 1969
A. Fisher & J. Saward. *The British Maze Guide*, Minotaur Designs, London, 1991
—. & D. Kingham. *Mazes*, Shire Publications, London, 1991
J. Fisher. "Richard Long", *Aspects*, 14, Spring, 1981
N. Foote. "Long Walks", *Artforum*, 18, 10, Summer, 1980
W. Forma. *Five British Sculptors*, New York, NY, 1965
M. Fried. "Shape as Form: Frank Stella's New Paintings", *Artforum*, 5, 3, Nov, 1966
—. "Art and Objecthood", *Artforum*, 5, Summer, 1967
M. Friedman. "Robert Morris: Polemics and Cubes", *Art International*, 10, 10, Dec, 1966
D. Friis-Hansen. *Circles, Cycles, Mud*, Contemporary Arts Museum, 1996
R.H. Fuchs. "Memories of Passing: A Note on Richard Long", *Studio International*, 187, 965, Apl, 1974
—. *Richard Long*, text by R. Fuchs, Thames & Hudson, London, 1986
P. Fuller. Black cloud over the Hayward", *Art Monthly*, 70, Oct, 1983
—. *Peter Fuller's Modern Painters: Reflections on British Art*, ed. J. McDonald, Methuen, London, 1993
H. Fulton. *Hamish Fulton: Selected Walks, 1969-89*, Albright-Knox Art Gallery, Buffalo, New York, NY, 1990
—. *Richard Long*, Thames & Hudson, London, 1991
—. *One Hundred Walks*, Haags Gemeetemuseum, The Hague, 1991
—. "Into a Walk Into Nature", *Thirty One Horrors*, Lenbachhaus, Munich, 1995
—. *Walking Artist*, Annely Juda, London, 1998
—. *Walking Through*, Stour Valley Art Project, Challock, Kent, 1999
—. *Wild Life*, Pocketbooks, Edinburgh, 2000
—. *Walking Artist*, Richter Verlag, Düsseldorf, 2001
—. "Specific Places and Particular Events", in B. Tufnell, 2002
L. Geddes-Brown. "The Long March of Richard Long", *Sunday Times*, March 27, 1983

J. Gibson. *The Senses Considered as a Perceptual System*, Houghton Mifflin, Boston, MA, 1966
T. Godfrey. *Conceptual Art*, Phaidon, London, 1998
A. Goldstein, ed. *Reconsidering the Object of Art: 1965-1975*, Museum of Contemporary Art, L.A., CA, 1995
A. Goldsworthy & J. Fowles. *Andy Goldsworthy*, Viking, London, 1990
—. *Hand to Earth: Andy Goldsworthy, Sculpture, 1976-1990*, Henry Moore Centre for Sculpture, Leeds, Yorkshire, 1990
—. *Stone*, Viking, London, 1994
—. *Wood*, Viking, London, 1996
—. *Hand to Earth: Andy Goldsworthy Sculpture*, T. Friedman, Thames and Hudson, London, 1997 & 2004
—. *Arch*, with D. Craig, Thames & Hudson, London, 1999
—. *Wall*, intr. K. Baker, Thames & Hudson, London, 2000
—. *Time*, Thames & Hudson, London, 2000
—. *Midsummer Snowballs*, intr. J. Collins, Abrams, New York, NY, 2001
—. *Andy Goldsworthy – Réfuges D'Art*, Editions Artha, 2002
—. *Passage*, Thames & Hudson, London, 2004
—. *Enclosure*, Thames & Hudson, London, 2007
M. Golding. "Thoughts on Richard Long", *Modern Painters*, 3, 1, Spring, 1990
—. & W. Furlong. *Song of the Earth*, Thames and Hudson, London, 2002
C. Greenberg. *Art and Culture*, Beacon Press, Boston, MA, 1961
G. Greig. "Circular Tours In the Name of Art", *Sunday Times*, June 16, 1991
A. Haden-Guest. "The King of Wrap", *The Sunday Times Magazine*, Jan, 1994
A.M. Hammacher. *The Sculpture of Barbara Hepworth*, Abrams, New York, NY, 1968
C. Harrison. "Barry Flanagan's sculpture", *Studio International*, 175, 900, May, 1968
—. "Richard Long", *Studio International*, 183, 940, Jan, 1972
B. Haskell. *Donald Judd*, Whitney Museum of American Art, New York, NY, 1988
M. Heizer, D. Oppenheim & R. Smithson. "Discussion", *Avalanche*, 1, Autumn, 1970
—. *Sculpture in Reverse*, Museum of Contemporary Art, Los Angeles, 1984
A. Henri. *Total Art*, Praeger, New York, NY, 1974
Galerie Max Hetzler. *Carl Andre, Gunther Forg, Hubert Kiecol, Richard Long, Meuser, Reinhard Mucha, Bruce Nauman and Ulrich Ruckreim*, Cologne, 1985
R. Hobbs. *Robert Smithson: Sculpture*, Cornell University Press, Ithaca, NY, 1981
—. "Earthworks", *Art Journal*, 42, Fall, 1982
N. Holt. "Amarillo Ramp", *Avalanche*, Fall, 1973
—. "Hydra's Head", *Arts Magazine*, Jan, 1975
—. "Sun Tunnels", *Artforum*, Apl, 1977
R. Hughes. *The Shock of the New*, Thames & Hudson, London, 1991
—. *American Visions: The Epic History of Art In America*, Knopf, New York, NY, 1997
T. Hughes. *Poetry in the Making*, Faber, London, 1969
H.E. Hugo, ed. *The Portable Romantic Reader*, Viking Press, New York, NY, 1957
G. Jeppson. *Richard Long*, Harvard College, Cambridge, MA, 1980
E.H. Johnson, ed. *American Artist on Art*, Harper & Row, New York, NY, 1965
B. Jones. "A New Wave in Sculpture: A survey of recent work by ten younger sculptors", *Artscribe*, 8, Sept, 1977
J. Jones, *The Guardian*, Mch 4, 2000

D. Judd. "In the Galleries", *Arts Magazine*, 37, 10, Sept, 1963
—. "Local History", *Arts Yearbook 7*, 1964
—. "Specific Objects", *Arts Yearbook*, 8, Art Digest, New York, NY, 1965
—. *Complete Writings, 1959-1975*, Nova Scotia College of Art and Design, Halifax, Canada, 1975
—. *Complete Writings, 1975-1986*, Van Abbemuseum, Netherlands, 1987
R.E. Krauss. "Sense and Sensibility: Reflection on Post '60s Sculpture", *Artforum*, 12, Nov, 1973
—. *Passages in Modern Sculpture*, Thames & Hudson, London, 1977
—. "Sculpture in the Expanded Field", *October*, 8, Spring, 1979
D. Kuspitt. "Aycock's Dream Houses", *Art in America*, Sept, 1985
D. Lee. "Opinion: Richard Long and Hamish Fulton", *Arts Review*, July 26, 1991
B. Le Messurier. *Dartmoor Artists*, Halsgrove, Tiverton, Devon, 2002
I. Licht. "Dan Flavin", *Artscanada*, Dec, 1968
L. Lippard. "New York Letter: Apl-June, 1965", *Art International*, 9, 6, 1965
—. "New York Letter: Recent Sculpture as Escape", *Art International*, Feb, 1966a
—. "An Impure Situation", *Art International*, 20 May, 1966b
—. "The Silent Art", *Art in America*, 55, 1, Jan-Feb, 1967a
—. "Rebelliously Romantic?", *New York Times*, June 4, 1967d
—. "Escalataion in Washington", *Art International*, 12, 1, Jan, 1968
—. ed. *Surrealists on Art*, Prentice-Hall, Englewood Cliffs, NJ, 1970
—. *Grids*, Philadelphia Institute of Contemporary Art, PA, 1972b
—. *Six Years: The Dematerialization of the Art Object from 1966 to 1972*, Praeger, New York, NY, 1973
—. *From the Center: feminist essays on women's art*, Dutton, New York, NY, 1976
—. "Complexities: Architectural Sculpture in Nature", *Art in America*, Feb, 1979
—. *Overlay: Contemporary Art and the Art of Prehistory*, Pantheon, New York, NY, 1983
G. Lobacheff. Interview with Richard Long, 1994; in *Mirage*, 1998
E. Lucie-Smith. *Sculpture Since 1945*, Phaidon, London, 1987
W. Malpas. *Andy Goldsworthy: Touching Nature*, Crescent Moon, 1998/ 2004
—. *Land Art*, Crescent Moon, 1996/ 2004
B. Marcelis. "Richard Long: Beaute et ambiguite du Land Art", *Domus*, 601, Dec, 1979
J. van der Marck. *Wrapped Museum*, Museum of Contemporary Art, Chicago, IL, 1969
R. Martin. *The Sculpted Forest: Sculpture in the Forest of Dean*, Redcliff, Bristol, 1990
D. Mayhall: *The Minimal Tradition*, The Aldrich Museum of Contemporary Art, Ridgefield, CT, 1979
A. McPherson. "David Nash: interviewed by Allan McPherson", *Artscribe*, 12, June, 1978
K. McShine. *Primary Structures*, Jewish Museum, New York, NY, 1966
U. Meyer. *Conceptual Art*, Dutton, New York, NY, 1972
M. Miss. *Mary Miss: Interior Works*, Bell Gallery, University of Rhode Island, Autumn, 1981
J.-Y. Mock. *Niki de Sant-Phalle: Exposition Retrospective*, CGP, 1980
R.C. Morgan. "Richard Long's Poststructural Encounters", *Arts*, 61, 6, Feb, 1987
—. *Art Into Ideas*, Cambridge, 1996
R. Morris. "Notes on Sculpture", *Artforum*, Feb, 1966, Oct, 1966, June, 1967, Apl, 1969

—. "Aligned with Nazca", *Artforum*, Oct, 1975
—. *Robert Morris: Mirror Works, 1961-1978*, Leo Castelli Gallery, New York, NY, 1979
—. *et al. Earthworks*, Seattle Art Museum, Seattle, WA, 1979
—. "American Quartet", *Art in America*, Dec, 1981
—. *Selected Works*, Contemporary Arts Museum, Houston, TX, 1981
—. *Continuous Project Altered Daily*, MIT Press, Cambridge, MA, 1993
S. Nairne & N. Serota. *British Sculpture in the Twentieth Century*, Whitechapel Art Gallery, London, 1981
D. Nash. *Fletched Over Ash*, AIR Gallery, 1978
—. "David Nash", *Aspects*, 10, Spring, 1980
—. *Stoves and Hearths*, Duke Street Gallery, London, 1982
T.A. Neff, ed. *A Quiet Revolution: British Sculpture Since 1965*, Thames & Hudson, London, 1987
B. Nemitz. *Trans Plant: Living Vegetation in Contemporary Art*, Hatje Cantz, Stuttgart, 2000
C. Nemser. "An interview with Eva Hesse", *Artforum*, May, 1970
—. "My Memories of Eva Hesse", *Feminist Art Journal*, Winter, 1973
I. Noguchi. *A Sculptor's World*, Harper & Row, New York, NY, 1968
R. Onoratio. *Mary Miss – Perimeters/ Pavilions/ Decoys*, Nassau County Museum, 1979
A.C. Papadakis, ed. *The New Romantics, Art & Design*, 4, 11/12, Academy Group, London, 1988
—. *et al*, eds. *New Art*, Academy Group, London, 1991
R. Parker & G. Pollock. *Old Mistresses: Women, Art an Ideology*, Routledge & Kegan Paul, London, 1981
J.-M. Poinsot. "Richard Long: construire le paysage", *Art Press*, 53, Nov, 1981
G. Pollock: *Vision and Difference: femininity, feminism and histories of art*, Routledge, London, 1988
L. Ponti: "Tony Cragg", *Domus*, 611, Nov, 1980
J.C. Powys. *In Defence of Sensuality*, Gollancz, London, 1930
—. *Maiden Castle*, Cassell, London, 1937
—. *A Glastonbury Romance*, Macdonald, London, 1955
—. *Wolf Solent*, Penguin, London, 1964
—. *Autobiography*, Macdonald, London, 1967
C. Ratcliff. "Robert Ryman Making Distinctions", *Art in America*, June, 1986
S. Rainbird. "Crossing Places: Some Notes on the Works of Richard Long", in *Walking in Circles*
B. Redhead. *The Inspiration of Landscape: Artists in National Parks*, Phaidon, Oxford, 1989
C. Robins. "Object, Structure or Sculpture: Where Are We?", *Arts Magazine*, 40, 9, 1966
—. *The Pluralist Era: American Art, 1968-1981*, Harper & Row, New York, NY, 1984
P. Rodaway. *Sensuous Geographies*, Routledge, London, 1994
W. Romey. "The artist as geographer: Richard Long's Earth Art", *Professional Geographer*, 39, 4, 1987
B. Rose. "New York Letter", *Art International*, Feb 15, 1964
—. "ABC Art", *Art in America*, 53, 5, Nov, 1965
—. Looking at American Sculpture", *Artforum*, 3, Feb, 1965
—. *A New Aesthetic*, Washington Gallery of Modern Art, Washington, DC, 1967

H. Rosenberg. *The De-Definition of Art*, Horizon Press, New York, NY, 1972
—. *Art on the Edge,* Macmillan, London, 1975
R. Rosenblum. "Notes on Sol LeWitt", in Legg, 1978
—. *Modern Painting and the Northern Romantic Tradition*, Thames & Hudson, London, 1978
—. "Romanticism and Retrospective: An Interview with Robert Rosenblum", in A. Papadakis, 1988
S. Ross. "Gardens, earthworks, and environmental art", in S. Kemal, 1993
—. *What Gardens Mean*, University of Chicago Press, Chicago, IL, 1998
I. Sandler. *American Art of the 1960s*, Harper & Row, New York, NY, 1988
—. *Art of the Postmodern Era: From the 1960s to the Early 1990s*, HarperCollins, London, 1997
A. Seymour. *The New Art*, Hayward Gallery, London, 1972
—: "Walking in Circles", in R. Long, *Walking in Circles*
—. "El Estanque de Basho - una nueva perspectiva", in *Piedras Richard Long*, Ministerio de Cultura, Direccion general de Bellas Artes y Archivos and the British Council, 1986
—. "Old World New World", in R. Long, *Old World New World*
W. Sharp *et al. Earth Art*, Andrew Dickson White Museum of Art, Cornell University, Ithaca, NY, 1969
—. "Structure ad Sensibility", *Avalanche*, 5, Summer, 1972
H. J. Smagula. *Currents: Contemporary Directions in the Visual Arts*, Prentice-Hall, Englewood Cliffs, NJ, 1983
D. Smith. *Sculpture and Drawings*, ed. J. Merkert, Prestel-Verlag, Munich, 1986
R. Smithson. "Entropy and the New Monuments", *Artforum*, 4, 10, June, 1966
—. "Incidents of Mirror-Travel in the Yucatan", *Artforum*, Sept, 1967
—. The Monuments of Passaic", *Artforum*, Dec, 1967
—. "Toward the Development of an Air Terminal Site", *Artforum*, Summer, 1967
—. "A Museum of Language in the Vicinity of Art", *Art International*, 12, 3, Mch, 1968
—. *The Writings of Robert Smithson*, ed. N. Holt, New York University Press, New York, NY, 1979
—. *Robert Smithson*, ed. J. Flam, University of California Press, Berkeley, CA, 1996
A. Sondheim, ed. *Post-Movement Art in America*, Dutton, New York, NY, 1977
A. Sonfist, ed. *Art in the Land: A Critical Anthology of Environmental Art*, Dutton, New York, NY, 1983
F. Stella. *Working Space*, Harvard University Press, Cambridge, MA, 1986
N. Stewart. "Richard Long, Lines of Thought: A Conversation with Nick Stewart", *Circa*, Nov, 1984
K. Stiles & P. Selz, eds. *Theories & Documents of Contemporary Art: A Sourcebook of Artists' Writings*, University of California Press, Berkeley, CA, 1996
W.J. Strachan. *Open Air Sculpture in Britain*, Zwemmer, London, 1984
D. Sylvester. *About Modern Art*, Chatto & Windus, London, 1996
Tao Te Ching, Lao-tzu, tr. D.C. Lau, Penguin, London, 1963
M. Tuchman. *American Sculpture of the Sixties*, Los Angeles County Museum of Art, Los Angeles, CA, 1967
P. Tuchman. "Background of a Minimalist: Carl Andre", *Artforum*, Mch, 1978
—. "Minimalism", *Three Decades: The Oliver-Hoffmann Collection*, Museum of Contemporary Art, Chicago, IL, 1988
W. Tucker. "An Essay on Sculpture", *Studio International*, 177, 907, Jan, 1969

—. *The Language of Sculpture*, Thames & Hudson, London, 1974
B. Tufnell & A. Wilson. *Hamish Fulton: Walking Journey,* Tate Publishing, London, 2002
G. de Vries, ed. *On Art: Artists' Writings on the Changed Notion of Art After, 1965*, Cologne, 1974
D. Waldman. "Samaras", *Art News*, Oct, 1966
—. *Carl Andre*, Guggenheim Museum, New York, NY, 1970
—. *Mark Rothko*, Thames & Hudson, London, 1978
J. Wall. "'Marks of Indifference': Aspects of Photography In, Or As, Conceptual Art", in A. Goldstein, 1995
L. Weiner. *Lawrence Weiner, Works,* Anatol AV und Filmproduktion Hamburg, 1977
D. Wheeler. *Art Since Mid-Century: 1945 to the Present*, Thames & Hudson, London, 1991
A. Wildermuth. *Richard Long*, Galerie Buchmann, Basel, 1985
G. Woods *et al*, eds. *Art Without Boundaries*, Thames & Hudson, London, 1972
du Zeitschrift für kultur, *Walking Into Existence*, no. 756, 2005
L. Zelevansky. "Richard Long", *Art News*, 83, 8, Oct, 1984

WEBSITES

Richard Long <www.richardlong.org>
Richard Long Newsletter <therichardlongnewsletter.org>
Earthworks <www.earthworks.org>
The Artists: <www.the-artists.org>
Sculpture at Goodwood, CASS: <www.sculpture.org.uk>
Crescent Moon Publishing: <www.crescentmoon.org.uk>
Robert Smithson <www.robertsmithson.com>
Walter de Maria <www.lightningfield.org>
Christo <www.christojeanneclaude.net>
James Turrell <www.rodencrater.org>
Mary Miss <www.marymiss.com>
Hamish Fulton <www.hamish-fulton.com>
Chris Drury <www.chrisdrury.co.uk>
Donald Judd <www.chinati.org>
Andy Goldsworthy, Sheepfolds site: <www.sheepfolds.org>
Andy Goldsworthy, *Rivers and Tides* DVD <www.skyline.uk.com/riversandtides>

www.ingramcontent.com/pod-product-compliance
Lightning Source LLC
Chambersburg PA
CBHW031616210526
45464CB00004B/1596